Remembering

Speech Day —

June 16, 1945.

POEMS OF SHELLEY

PERCY BYSSHE SHELLEY

From a pen-drawing by
E. Heber Thompson

POEMS OF
SHELLEY

Edited by
Sir Henry Newbolt

THOMAS NELSON & SONS LTD
London Edinburgh Paris Melbourne
Toronto and New York

CONTENTS

—————◆—————

INTRODUCTION

SHELLEY'S star was obscured during his lifetime;
but through the hundred years since his death it has
shone more and more clearly as of the first magnitude.
It will be brighter yet—it still does not rain influence
as it should: and the reason for this is plain. A poet,
with us, is very commonly classed among craftsmen:
he is a singer, a gem-cutter, or a tapestry-weaver; we
concern ourselves, not with the man, but with his work,
and with his work only as it fulfils our purpose and not
as it expresses his intuition. Sometimes we realize
that a poet has had an interesting history, and that
dates or derivations for an account of his poetry may
be supplied from it; but it is seldom admitted or believed that the life and the poetry may be one and
the same. There are cases, we know, in which the two
are not co-extensive; and in others, where the poetry
appears admirable but the life reprobate, it is generally
thought kinder to praise the good and turn away from
the evil.

In this respect Milton and Shelley have suffered a
like fate. Both, in consideration of their poetry, are
forgiven their revolutionary theories and passionate
lives; and in the oblivion of that forgiveness there is
lost a great part of the motive force and the profounder
significance of their work. But there is this difference,

that what we pass over in Milton's case is entirely lamentable—the domestic unkindness and political savagery by which he lost the Paradise of his first happy nature; whereas in Shelley nearly all that is regrettable is also memorable, because however puerile, immoral, or ridiculous it may be, it is part of the real man, and springs from, or is related to, that very ardour for moral and intellectual beauty which was his gift to the world. His life was a strange pattern of tragedy and comedy, a dome of many-coloured glass which stained the white radiance of eternity; but whatever we think of the colours we must accept them for the sake of the light within the lantern.

For those who look at Shelley's career from the outside only, as his contemporaries did and as his detractors would still have us do, it is not difficult to present him as absurd, uncontrolled, even as dangerous to society. The heir to wealth and rank, he was a rebel against all authority and orthodoxy, especially against the authority and orthodoxy of his own father. At Eton he revolted against the fagging system; at Oxford he published in his first year a pamphlet on " The Necessity of Atheism," and for that was not only expelled from the University but forbidden to return home. This was in February 1811, when he was not yet nineteen, and before the autumn he had married Harriet Westbrook, his sister's schoolfellow, a girl who, like himself, had complained of paternal tyranny. In February 1812, the young couple were warned to quit Dublin, where they had printed an " Address to the Irish People ": they settled first in Wales and afterwards at Lynmouth in North Devon. Here Shelley received into his house a second distressed lady, Elizabeth Hitchener, in whom he found at first a " Portia," but afterwards a " Brown Demon."

In 1813 the Shelleys returned to London, and their first child Ianthe was born ; *Queen Mab* was printed, but for private circulation only. In this year Shelley formed a friendship with William Godwin, author of *Political Justice*, and in the summer of 1814, while Harriet was away, he stayed in Godwin's house, fell suddenly in love with his daughter Mary, and in July eloped to France with her accompanied by her step-sister Claire. This act caused great distress to Godwin, though (as Shelley pointed out) it was in accord with the principles which he had himself advocated. Harriet never saw Shelley again, though he invited her to join him and Mary in Switzerland.

In 1815 Shelley's father succeeded Sir Bysshe in the baronetcy, and arranged that his son should receive an income of £1,000 a year. In 1816 Shelley and Byron met and made friends at Geneva ; Shelley and Mary then returned to England and settled at Marlow. *Alastor* was published in this year ; and towards the end of it Harriet's suicide set Shelley free to marry Mary Godwin.

In 1817 he produced *Laon and Cythna*, afterwards called *The Revolt of Islam*. In the winter he fell into ill health, and in the following spring went with his wife and Claire to Italy. At Naples the friendship with Byron was carried further, but did little or nothing to alleviate Shelley's depression, and his physical suffering, by his own account, was " constant and poignant." In June 1819, his son William died in Rome ; in November at Florence another son was born, who afterwards succeeded as Sir Percy Florence Shelley.

During these two years the *Quarterly Review* published a series of violent attacks on Shelley, as a dangerous monster of atheism and revolution. He had achieved public notice at last and was cheerfully humorous over it. " But for them," he said laughing, " I should be utterly unknown."

In January 1820, the Shelleys moved to Pisa, followed by Byron. *Prometheus Unbound*, written in the previous autumn, was published this year. In 1821 yet another distressed damsel attracted Shelley—Emilia Viviani, a novice detained against her will—and he wrote *Epipsychidion* in honour of Platonic love. On February 23, 1821, Keats, to whom Shelley had generously but vainly offered hospitality, died at Rome, and was commemorated in the elegy entitled *Adonais*. This was followed by *Hellas*, a lyrical drama inspired by the struggle of the Greeks for liberty.

In April 1822, the Shelleys, with their friends, Mr. and Mrs. Williams, moved to the Villa Magni on the Gulf of Spezzia, where Shelley bathed, boated, talked to Mrs. Williams, and composed *The Triumph of Life*. On 8th July he set sail from Leghorn with Williams in a new yacht, the *Don Juan*, intending to return to the Villa Magni. A sudden squall or fog came on and the boat was lost—run down probably by a felucca. Shelley's body was washed ashore near Via Reggio, and burnt by Trelawny, Byron, and Leigh Hunt.

The full story, of which this is but a bare outline, would be found, if adequately written, to contain as much pathos, passion, intellectual splendour, and philosophical suggestion as any known to us. But it can only be imagined on a vast scale. Shelley was great in himself and in all his sources and activities ;

the true narrative of his life would contain everything that could illustrate him, including all his poems, letters, and essays in their order among other acts and events. The resulting pattern would be an intricate one, but it would be seen to be a pattern and not a tangle.

For the sake of simplification we may pick out three threads. Shelley began and ended with an instinctive conviction that authority was an unwarrantable hindrance, and convention of any kind a degeneration. Commerce, Law, Government, Religion, devised for the ordering of human life, were used solely by tyrants for selfish and oppressive ends. His doctrine, preached in *Queen Mab*, that all four should be abolished, was naturally held to be merely destructive. Shelley himself, whose creed had nothing negative in it, suppressed the mere denunciations of this piece, and in *Prometheus Unbound* discovered a better way to expound his passionate belief in the spirit of Man. The power of the Oppressor is vaguely typified by Jupiter, whose fall takes place without any charges being implied against the institutions of this or that time or country. Prometheus, or Man, delivered from bondage, unites with Asia, the spirit of love which animates the Universe, and Earth becomes " the calm empire of a happy soul."

As the belief is lofty and the sincerity profound, so the manner of presentation is in this poem masterly. Shelley has ceased to preach : he now sings, as the god sang " when Ilion like a mist rose into towers." And he knew what he was doing, for in his Preface to *Prometheus* he expresses his abhorrence of didactic poetry and his purpose " simply to familiarize the highly refined imagination . . . with beautiful idealisms of moral excellence ; aware that until the mind can love and admire and trust and hope and endure, reasoned principles of moral conduct are seeds cast upon the highway of life which the unconscious passenger tramples into dust, although they would bear the harvest of his happiness." How universal is the truth of this, and how far Shelley had then travelled since the days when he denounced Christianity in *Queen Mab*, may be seen from the concluding lines, in which he sought to raise the heart of a generation still broken by the memories of a great war :—

> " To suffer woes which Hope thinks infinite ;
>   To forgive wrongs darker than death or night ;
>   To defy Power, which seems omnipotent ;
>   To love, and bear ; to hope till Hope creates
>   From its own wreck the thing it contemplates ;
>   Neither to change, nor falter, nor repent ;
>   This, like thy glory, Titan, is to be
>   Good, great and joyous, beautiful and free ;
>   This is alone Life, Joy, Empire, and Victory."

The second thread may be described as " the Pursuit of the Well-Beloved." This, as Mr. Hardy has shown, is a typical and not exceptional motive in human nature, but few men observe and record it of themselves. Shelley considered it " one of the most interesting situations of the human mind," and described it in *Alastor*, a poem which " represents a youth of uncorrupted feelings and adventurous genius led forth by an imagination inflamed and purified through familiarity with all that is excellent and majestic to the contemplation of the universe . . . the magnificence and beauty of the external world. So long as it is possible for his desires to point towards objects thus infinite and unmeasured, he is joyous and tranquil and self-possessed. But the period arrives when these objects cease to suffice. His mind is at

length suddenly awakened, and thirsts for intercourse
with an intelligence similar to itself. He images to
himself the Being whom he loves . . . the vision in
which he embodies his own imaginations unites all of
wonderful, or wise, or beautiful, which the poet, the
philosopher, or the lover, could depicture. The intellectual faculties, the imagination, the functions of sense
have their respective requisitions on the sympathy of
corresponding powers in other human beings. The
poet is represented as uniting these requisitions, and
attaching them to a single image." In this poem the
youth seeks in vain for a prototype of his conception ;
in real life, whether Shelley's or another's, he finds not
only one prototype but others in succession.

In 1813 a sincere little poem to Harriet represents
her as the poet's purer mind and the inspiration of his
song ; " the love that, gleaming through the world,
Wards off the poisonous arrow of its scorn." Eight
years afterwards, in *Epipsychidion,* we find Shelley for
the fourth time in much the same poetical relation,
this time to Emilia, a " Vestal sister," whom he pro-
poses to make the lady of his solitude because she was
the embodiment of his ideal imagination :—

> " There was a Being whom my spirit oft
> Met on its visioned wanderings, far aloft,
> In the clear golden prime of my youth's dawn,
> Upon the fairy isles of sunny lawn,
> Amid the enchanted mountains, and the caves
> Of divine sleep, and on the air-like waves
> Of wonder-level dream, whose tremulous floor
> Paved her light steps,—on an imagined shore,
> Under the grey beak of some promontory
> She met me, robed in such exceeding glory,
> That I beheld her not. In solitudes
> Her voice came to me through the whispering woods . . .

And from the breezes whether low or loud,
And from the rain of every passing cloud,
And from the singing of the summer birds,
And from all sounds, all silence. In the words
Of antique verse and high romance,—in form,
Sound, colour,—in whatever checks that Storm
Which with the shattered present chokes the past ;
And in that best philosophy, whose taste
Makes this cold common hell, our life, a doom
As glorious as a fiery martyrdom ;
Her Spirit was the harmony of truth."

These incidents of a poet's pilgrimage were innocent
enough in intention ; only one of them injured Shelley :
his conduct to Harriet was inexcusable. He could not
see this, and the reason is plain. He was faced with a
not uncommon problem which he thought he fully
understood ; but he had overlooked one element in it :
those " functions of sense " of which he had spoken
in *Alastor*, but whose vital consequences he did not
stay to observe. Imaginative man lives in two worlds,
and so did Shelley, but he persistently undervalued
and put out of mind the one which he shared with his
fellow-mortals. Laws were part of it, and he hated
laws. He did not perceive that there are natural as
well as conventional obligations, and that, if a man
is to have peace, he must at least make and obey his
own rules. The result was not freedom,

" But less of peace in Shelley's mind,
Than calm in waters seem."

The third thread is Shelley's philosophy of human
life. This is based, not upon Science, but upon Faith.
Creation he would, of course, reject, as resting upon the
mere authority of a class of men whom he despised and
detested. No chemical, physical, or biological theory

could interest him, because origin does not explain
result or offer an escape from it. His starting-point
is a passionate, unreasoned belief in man's nature.
This he conceives as springing from the universal spirit
of love and seeking only beauty ; but it is distracted
and distorted by the difficulties and iniquities of mortal
life. These result from a curse laid upon us at birth,
when we enter an existence which conceals reality
from us :—

> " Death is a veil which those who live call life ;
>   They sleep and it is lifted."

The same deliverance, he holds, may be accomplished
by the overthrow of tyranny and convention :—

> " The painted veil, by those who were, called life,
>   Which mimicked, as with colours idly spread,
>   All men believed and hoped, is torn aside ;
>   The loathsome mask has fallen, the man remains
>   Sceptreless, free, uncircumscribed, but man
>   Equal, unclassed, tribeless, and nationless,
>   Exempt from awe, worship, degree, the king
>   Over himself ; just, gentle, wise : but man
>   Passionless ; no, yet free from guilt or pain,
>   Which were, for his will made or suffered them.
>   Nor yet exempt, though ruling them like slaves,
>   From chance, and death, and mutability,
>   The clogs of that which else might oversoar
>   The loftiest star of unascended heaven,
>   Pinnacled dim in the intense inane."

Shelley's belief about death is finally expressed in
a passage of unsurpassed poetical splendour—the last
seventeen stanzas of *Adonais*—and must there be read
entire ; but the passage just quoted from *Prometheus*
is even more suggestive because it seems to contain a
further implication, one found also in the last stanzas
of *The Sensitive Plant* :—

" That garden sweet, that lady fair,
    And all sweet shapes and odours there,
    In truth have never passed away :
    'Tis we, 'tis ours, are changed ; not they.

For love, and beauty, and delight,
    There is no death nor change : their might
    Exceeds our organs, which endure
    No light, being themselves obscure."

In other passages Shelley seems to speak of eternity as an endless time-series ; but the image of the veil lifted by death or by some deliverance in life, even of the whole human race, would appear to be a recognition of the eternal as the equivalent of reality—a state in which we exist or have the power of existing even here, in a world ordinarily perceived under the form of Time. No other poet has come so near to a vision so capable of transforming human life.

                                        HENRY NEWBOLT.

*By kind permission of Messrs. George Bell and Sons,
the text used in this collection is that of the Aldine
Edition, edited by Mr. H. Buxton Forman*

QUEEN MAB

A PHILOSOPHICAL POEM
1813

TO HARRIET ———

WHOSE is the love that, gleaming through the world,
Wards off the poisonous arrow of its scorn ?
  Whose is the warm and partial praise,
  Virtue's most sweet reward ?

Beneath whose looks did my reviving soul
Riper in truth and virtuous daring grow ?
  Whose eyes have I gazed fondly on,
  And loved mankind the more ?

HARRIET ! on thine :—thou wert my purer mind
Thou wert the inspiration of my song ;
  Thine are these early wilding flowers,
  Though garlanded by me.

Then press into thy breast this pledge of love ;
And know, though time may change and years may roll,
  Each floweret gathered in my heart
  It consecrates to thine.

POEMS OF SHELLEY

QUEEN MAB

I

How wonderful is Death,
Death and his brother Sleep !
One, pale as yonder waning moon
With lips of lurid blue ;
The other, rosy as the morn
When throned on ocean's wave
It blushes o'er the world :
Yet both so passing wonderful !

Hath then the gloomy Power
Whose reign is in the tainted sepulchres
Seized on her sinless soul ?
Must then that peerless form
Which love and admiration cannot view
Without a beating heart, those azure veins
Which steal like streams along a field of snow,
That lovely outline, which is fair
As breathing marble, perish ?
Must putrefaction's breath
Leave nothing of this heavenly sight
But loathsomeness and ruin ?

Spare nothing but a gloomy theme,
On which the lightest heart might moralize ?
Or is it only a sweet slumber
Stealing o'er sensation,
Which the breath of roseate morning
Chaseth into darkness ?
Will Ianthe wake again,
Ard give that faithful bosom joy
Whose sleepless spirit waits to catch
Light, life and rapture from her smile ?

Yes ! she will wake again,
Although her glowing limbs are motionless,
And silent those sweet lips,
Once breathing eloquence
That might have soothed a tiger's rage
Or thawed the cold heart of a conqueror.
Her dewy eyes are closed,
And on their lids, whose texture fine
Scarce hides the dark blue orbs beneath,
The baby Sleep is pillowed :
Her golden tresses shade
The bosom's stainless pride,
Curling like tendrils of the parasite
Around a marble column.

Hark ! whence that rushing sound ?
'Tis like the wondrous strain
That round a lonely ruin swells,
Which, wandering on the echoing shore,
The enthusiast hears at evening :
'Tis softer than the west wind's sigh ;
'Tis wilder than the unmeasured notes
Of that strange lyre whose strings
The genii of the breezes sweep ;
Those lines of rainbow light
Are like the moonbeams when they fall

Through some cathedral window, but the teints
    Are such as may not find
    Comparison on earth.

Behold the chariot of the Fairy Queen !
Celestial coursers paw the unyielding air ;
Their filmy pennons at her word they furl,
And stop obedient to the reins of light ;
    These the Queen of spells drew in,
    She spread a charm around the spot,
And, leaning graceful from the ætherial car,
    Long did she gaze, and silently,
      Upon the slumbering maid.

Oh ! not the visioned poet in his dreams,
When silvery clouds float through the wildered brain,
When every sight of lovely, wild and grand
    Astonishes, enraptures, elevates,
      When fancy at a glance combines
      The wondrous, and the beautiful,—
So bright, so fair, so wild a shape
      Hath ever yet beheld,
As that which reined the coursers of the air,
    And poured the magic of her gaze
      Upon the maiden's sleep.

    The broad and yellow moon
      Shone dimly through her form—
That form of faultless symmetry ;
The pearly and pellucid car
    Moved not the moonlight's line :
    'Twas not an earthly pageant :
Those who had looked upon the sight.
    Passing all human glory,
    Saw not the yellow moon,
    Saw not the mortal scene,
    Heard not the night-wind's rush,

Heard not an earthly sound,
Saw but the fairy pageant,
Heard but the heavenly strains
That filled tne lonely dwelling.

The Fairy's frame was slight, yon fibrous cloud,
That catches but the palest tinge of even,
And which the straining eye can hardly seize
When melting into eastern twilight's shadow,
Were scarce so thin, so slight ; but the fair star
That gems the glittering coronet of morn,
Sheds not a light so mild, so powerful,
As that which, bursting from the Fairy's form,
Spread a purpureal halo round the scene,
Yet with an undulating motion,
Swayed to her outline gracefully.

From her celestial car
The Fairy Queen descended,
And thrice she waved her wand
Circled with wreaths of amaranth :
Her thin and misty form
Moved with the moving air,
And the clear si!ver tones,
As thus she spoke, were such
As are unheard by all but gifted ear.

FAIRY

Stars ! your balmiest influence shed !
Elements ! your wrath suspend !
Sleep, Ocean, in the rocky bounds
That circle thy domain !
Let not a breath be seen to stir
Around yon grass-grown ruin's height,
Let even the restless gossamer
Sleep on the moveless air !

Soul of Ianthe ! thou,
Judged alone worthy of the envied boon,
That waits the good and the sincere ; that waits
Those who have struggled, and with resolute will
Vanquished earth's pride and meanness, burst the chains,
The icy chains of custom, and have shone
The day-stars of their age ;—Soul of Ianthe !
  Awake ! arise !

  Sudden arose
 Ianthe's Soul ; it stood
All beautiful in naked purity,
The perfect semblance of its bodily frame.
Instinct with inexpressible beauty and grace,
  Each stain of earthliness
 Had passed away, it reassumed
 Its native dignity, and stood
  Immortal amid ruin.

  Upon the couch the body lay
 Wrapped in the depth of slumber :
Its features were fixed and meaningless,
  Yet animal life was there,
And every organ yet performed
Its natural functions : 'twas a sight
Of wonder to behold the body and soul.
 The self-same lineaments, the same
 Marks of identity were there :
Yet, oh, how different !   One aspires to Heaven,
Pants for its sempiternal heritage,
And ever changing, ever rising still,
  Wantons in endless being.
The other, for a time the unwilling sport
Of circumstance and passion, struggles on ;
Fleets through its sad duration rapidly :
Then, like an useless and worn-out machine,
  Rots, perishes, and passes.

FAIRY

Spirit ! who hast dived so deep ;
Spirit ! who hast soared so high ;
Thou the fearless, thou the mild,
Accept the boon thy worth hath earned,
    Ascend the car with me.

SPIRIT

Do I dream ?   Is this new feeling
But a visioned ghost of slumber ?
    If indeed I am a soul,
A free, a disembodied soul,
    Speak again to me.

FAIRY

I am the fairy MAB : to me 'tis given
The wonders of the human world to keep :
The secrets of the immeasurable past,
In the unfailing consciences of men,
Those stern, unflattering chroniclers, I find :
The future, from the causes which arise
In each event, I gather : not the sting
Which retributive memory implants
In the hard bosom of the selfish man ;
Nor that ecstatic and exulting throb
Which virtue's votary feels when he sums up
The thoughts and actions of a well-spent day
Are unforeseen, unregistered by me :
And it is yet permitted me to rend
The veil of mortal frailty, that the spirit
Clothed in its changeless purity, may know
How soonest to accomplish the great end
For which it hath its being, and may taste
That peace which in the end all life will share.
This is the meed of virtue ; happy Soul,
    Ascend the car with me !

The chains of earth's immurement
   Fell from Ianthe's spirit ;
They shrank and brake like bandages of straw
  Beneath a wakened giant's strength.
    She knew her glorious change,
And felt in apprehension uncontrolled
  New raptures opening round :
Each day-dream of her mortal life,
Each frenzied vision of the slumbers
   That closed each well-spent day,
   Seemed now to meet reality.

The Fairy and the Soul proceeded ;
   The silver clouds disparted ;
And as the car of magic they ascended,
  Again the speechless music swelled,
  Again the coursers of the air
Unfurled their azure pennons, and the Queen,
   Shaking the beamy reins,
   Bade them pursue their way.

   The magic car moved on.
  The night was fair, and countless stars
Studded heaven's dark blue vault,—
   Just o'er the eastern wave
Peeped the first faint smile of morn :—
   The magic car moved on—
   From the celestial hoofs
The atmosphere in flaming sparkles flew,
  And where the burning wheels
Eddied above the mountain's loftiest peak,
   Was traced a line of lightning.
  Now it flew far above a rock,
   The utmost verge of earth,
The rival of the Andes, whose dark brow
   Lowered o'er the silver sea.

Far, far below the chariot's path,
    Calm as a slumbering babe,
    Tremendous Ocean lay.
The mirror of its stillness showed
    The pale and waning stars,
    The chariot's fiery track,
    And the grey light of morn
    Tinging those fleecy clouds
    That canopied the dawn.
Seemed it, that the chariot's way
Lay through the midst of an immense concave,
Radiant with million constellations, tinged
    With shades of infinite colour,
    And semicircled with a belt
    Flashing incessant meteors.

    The magic car moved on.
    As they approached their goal
The coursers seemed to gather speed ;
The sea no longer was distinguished ; earth
    Appeared a vast and shadowy sphere ;
    The sun's unclouded orb
    Rolled through the black concave ;
    Its rays of rapid light
Parted around the chariot's swifter course,
    And fell, like ocean's feathery spray
    Dashed from the boiling surge
    Before a vessel's prow.

    The magic car moved on.
    Earth's distant orb appeared
The smallest light that twinkles in the heaven :
    Whilst round the chariot's way
    Innumerable systems rolled,
    And countless spheres diffused
    An ever-varying glory.
It was a sight of wonder : some

Were hornèd like the crescent moon ;
Some shed a mild and silver beam
Like Hesperus o'er the western sea ;
Some dashed athwart with trains of flame,
Like worlds to death and ruin driven ;
Some shone like suns, and as the chariot passed,
  Eclipsed all other light.

  Spirit of Nature ! here !
In this interminable wilderness
Of worlds, at whose immensity
 Even soaring fancy staggers,
 Here is thy fitting temple.
  Yet not the lightest leaf
That quivers to the passing breeze
 Is less instinct with thee :
 Yet not the meanest worm
That lurks in graves and fattens on the dead
 Less shares thy eternal breath.
  Spirit of Nature ! thou !
Imperishable as this scene,
 Here is thy fitting temple.

II

IF solitude hath ever led thy steps
 To the wild ocean's echoing shore,
  And thou hast lingered there,
  Until the sun's broad orb
Seemed resting on the burnished wave,
 Thou must have marked the lines
Of purple gold, that motionless
 Hung o'er the sinking sphere :
Thou must have marked the billowy clouds
Edged with intolerable radiancy
 Towering like rocks of jet

Crowned with a diamond wreath.
And yet there is a moment,
When the sun's highest point
Peeps like a star o'er ocean's western edge,
When those far clouds of feathery gold,
Shaded with deepest purple, gleam
Like islands on a dark blue sea ;
Then has the fancy soared above the earth,
And furled its wearied wing
Within the Fairy's fane.

Yet not the golden islands
Gleaming in yon flood of light,
Nor the feathery curtains
Stretching o'er the sun's bright couch,
Nor the burnished ocean waves
Paving that gorgeous dome,
So fair, so wonderful a sight
As Mab's ætherial palace could afford.
Yet likest evening's vault, that faery Hall !
As Heaven, low resting on the wave, it spread
Its floors of flashing light,
Its vast and azure dome,
Its fertile golden islands
Floating on a silver sea ;
Whilst suns their mingling beamings darted
Through clouds of circumambient darkness,
And pearly battlements around
Looked o'er the immense of Heaven.

The magic car no longer moved.
The Fairy and the Spirit
Entered the Hall of Spells :
Those golden clouds,
That rolled in glittering billows
Beneath the azure canopy,
With the ætherial footsteps trembled not :

The light and crimson mists,
Floating to strains of thrilling melody
    Through that unearthly dwelling,
Yielded to every movement of the will.
Upon their passive swell the Spirit leaned,
And, for the varied bliss that pressed around,
    Used not the glorious privilege
        Of virtue and of wisdom.

        Spirit ! the Fairy said,
    And pointed to the gorgeous dome,
        This is a wondrous sight
        And mocks all human grandeur ;
But, were it virtue's only meed to dwell
In a celestial palace, all resigned
To pleasurable impulses, inmured
Within the prison of itself, the will
Of changeless nature would be unfulfilled.
Learn to make others happy.   Spirit, come !
This is thine high reward :—the past shall rise ;
Thou shalt behold the present ; I will teach
        The secrets of the future.

        The Fairy and the Spirit
Approached the overhanging battlement.—
    Below lay stretched the universe !
        There, far as the remotest line
        That bounds imagination's flight,
        Countless and unending orbs
        In mazy motion intermingled,
        Yet still fulfilled immutably
            Eternal nature's law.
            Above, below, around
            The circling systems formed
        A wilderness of harmony ;
        Each with undeviating aim,
In eloquent silence, through the depths of space

Pursued its wondrous way.
There was a little light
That twinkled in the misty distance :
None but a spirit's eye
Might ken that rolling orb ;
None but a spirit's eye,
And in no other place
But that celestial dwelling, might behold
Each action of this earth's inhabitants.
But matter, space and time
In those aërial mansions cease to act ;
And all-prevailing wisdom, when it reaps
The harvest of its excellence, o'erbounds
Those obstacles, of which an earthly soul
Fears to attempt the conquest.

The Fairy pointed to the earth.
The Spirit's intellectual eye
Its kindred beings recognized.
The thronging thousands, to a passing view,
Seemed like an anthill's citizens.
How wonderful ! that even
The passions, prejudices, interests,
That sway the meanest being, the weak touch
That moves the finest nerve,
And in one human brain
Causes the faintest thought, becomes a link
In the great chain of nature.

Behold, the Fairy cried,
Palmyra's ruined palaces !—
Behold ! where grandeur frowned ;
Behold ! where pleasure smiled ;
What now remains ?—the memory
Of senselessness and shame—
What is immortal there ?
Nothing—it stands to tell

A melancholy tale, to give
An awful warning : soon
Oblivion will steal silently
The remnant of its fame.
Monarchs and conquerors there
Proud o'er prostrate millions trod—
The earthquakes of the human race ;
Like them, forgotten when the ruin
That marks their shock is past.

Beside the eternal Nile,
The Pyramids have risen.
Nile shall pursue his changeless way :
Those pyramids shall fall ;
Yea ! not a stone shall stand to tell
The spot whereon they stood !
Their very site shall be forgotten
As is their builder's name !

Behold yon sterile spot,
Where now the wandering Arab's tent
Flaps in the desert-blast.
There once old Salem's haughty fane
Reared high to heaven its thousand golden domes,
And in the blushing face of day
Exposed its shameful glory.
Oh ! many a widow, many an orphan cursed
The building of that fane ; and many a father,
Worn out with toil and slavery, implored
The poor man's God to sweep it from the earth,
And spare his children the detested task
Of piling stone on stone, and poisoning
The choicest days of life,
To soothe a dotard's vanity.
There an inhuman and uncultured race
Howled hideous praises to their Dæmon-God ;
They rushed to war, tore from the mother's womb

The unborn child,—old age and infancy
Promiscuous perished ; their victorious arms
Left not a soul to breathe.   Oh ! they were fiends :
But what was he who taught them that the God
Of nature and benevolence hath given
A special sanction to the trade of blood ?
His name and theirs are fading, and the tales
Of this barbarian nation, which imposture
Recites till terror credits, are pursuing
Itself into forgetfulness.

Where Athens, Rome, and Sparta stood,
There is a moral desert now :
The mean and miserable huts,
The yet more wretched palaces,
Contrasted with those ancient fanes,
Now crumbling to oblivion ;
The long and lonely colonnades,
Through which the ghost of Freedom stalks,
      Seem like a well-known tune
Which, in some dear scene we have loved to hear,
      Remembered now in sadness.
      But, oh ! how much more changed,
      How gloomier is the contrast
      Of human nature there !
Where Socrates expired, a tyrant's slave,
A coward and a fool, spreads death around—
      Then, shuddering, meets his own.
Where Cicero and Antoninus lived,
   A cowled and hypocritical monk
      Prays, curses and deceives.

      Spirit ! ten thousand years
      Have scarcely passed away,
Since, in the waste where now the savage drinks
His enemy's blood, and, aping Europe's sons,
   Wakes the unholy song of war,

Arose a stately city,
Metropolis of the western continent :
  There, now, the mossy column-stone,
Indented by time's unrelaxing grasp,
      Which once appeared to brave
      All, save its country's ruin ;
      There the wide forest scene,
Rude in the uncultivated loveliness
      Of gardens long run wild,
Seems, to the unwilling sojourner, whose steps
  Chance in that desert has delayed,
Thus to have stood since earth was what it is.
  Yet once it was the busiest haunt,
Whither, as to a common centre, flocked
  Strangers, and ships, and merchandise :
      Once peace and freedom blessed
      The cultivated plain :
      But wealth, that curse of man,
Blighted the bud of its prosperity :
Virtue and wisdom, truth and liberty,
Fled, to return not, until man shall know
  That they alone can give the bliss
      Worthy a soul that claims
  Its kindred with eternity.

      There's not one atom of yon earth
        But once was living man ;
      Nor the minutest drop of rain,
      That hangeth in its thinnest cloud,
        But flowed in human veins :
        And from the burning plains
      Where Lybian monsters yell,
      From the most gloomy glens
      Of Greenland's sunless clime,
        To where the golden fields
        Of fertile England spread
      Their harvest to the day,

Thou canst not find one spot
Whereon no city stood.

How strange is human pride !
I tell thee that those living things,
To whom the fragile blade of grass,
     That springeth in the morn
     And perisheth ere noon,
     Is an unbounded world ;
I tell thee that those viewless beings,
Whose mansion is the smallest particle
     Of the impassive atmosphere,
     Think, feel and live like man ;
That their affections and antipathies,
     Like his, produce the laws
     Ruling their moral state ;
     And the minutest throb
That through their frame diffuses
     The slightest, faintest motion,
     Is fixed and indispensable
     As the majestic laws
     That rule yon rolling orbs.

The Fairy paused.   The Spirit,
In ecstasy of admiration, felt
All knowledge of the past revived ; the events
     Of old and wondrous times,
Which dim tradition interruptedly
Teaches the credulous vulgar, were unfolded
     In just perspective to the view ;
     Yet dim from their infinitude.
     The Spirit seemed to stand
High on an isolated pinnacle ;
The flood of ages combating below,
The depth of the unbounded universe
     Above, and all around
Nature's unchanging harmony.

III

FAIRY! the Spirit said,
And on the Queen of spells
Fixed her ætherial eyes,
I thank thee. Thou hast given
A boon which I will not resign, and taught
A lesson not to be unlearned. I know
The past, and thence I will essay to glean
A warning for the future, so that man
May profit by his errors, and derive
    Experience from his folly :
For, when the power of imparting joy
Is equal to the will, the human soul
    Requires no other heaven.

MAB

Turn thee, surpassing Spirit!
Much yet remains unscanned.
Thou knowest how great is man,
Thou knowest his imbecility :
Yet learn thou what he is ;
Yet learn the lofty destiny
Which restless time prepares
For every living soul.

Behold a gorgeous palace, that, amid
Yon populous city, rears its thousand towers
And seems itself a city. Gloomy troops
Of sentinels, in stern and silent ranks,
Encompass it around : the dweller there
Cannot be free and happy ; hearest thou not
The curses of the fatherless, the groans
Of those who have no friend ? He passes on :
The King, the wearer of a gilded chain
That binds his soul to abjectness, the fool
Whom courtiers nickname monarch, whilst a slave

Even to the basest appetites—that man
Heeds not the shriek of penury ; he smiles
At the deep curses which the destitute
Mutter in secret, and a sullen joy
Pervades his bloodless heart when thousands groan
But for those morsels which his wantonness
Wastes in unjoyous revelry, to save
All that they love from famine : when he hears
The tale of horror, to some ready-made face
Of hypocritical assent he turns,
Smothering the glow of shame, that, spite of him,
Flushes his bloated cheek.

              Now to the meal
Of silence, grandeur, and excess, he drags
His palled unwilling appetite.   If gold,
Gleaming around, and numerous viands culled
From every clime, could force the loathing sense
To overcome satiety,—if wealth
The spring it draws from poisons not,—or vice,
Unfeeling, stubborn vice, converteth not
Its food to deadliest venom ; then that king
Is happy ; and the peasant who fulfils
His unforced task, when he returns at even,
And by the blazing faggot meets again
Her welcome for whom all his toil is sped,
Tastes not a sweeter meal.

              Behold him now
Stretched on the gorgeous couch ; his fevered brain
Reels dizzily awhile : but ah ! too soon
The slumber of intemperance subsides,
And conscience, that undying serpent, calls
Her venomous brood to their nocturnal task.
Listen ! he speaks ! oh ! mark that frenzied eye—
Oh ! mark that deadly visage.

KING

              No cessation !
Oh ! must this last for ever ! Awful Death,

I wish, yet fear to clasp thee !—Not one moment
Of dreamless sleep ! O dear and blessèd Peace !
Why dost thou shroud thy vestal purity
In penury and dungeons ? wherefore lurkest
With danger, death, and solitude ; yet shun'st
The palace I have built thee ? Sacred Peace !
Oh visit me but once, but pitying shed
One drop of balm upon my withered soul.

Vain man ! that palace is the virtuous heart,
And Peace defileth not her snowy robes
In such a shed as thine. Hark ! yet he mutters ;
His slumbers are but varied agonies,
They prey like scorpions on the springs of life.
There needeth not the hell that bigots frame
To punish those who err : earth in itself
Contains at once the evil and the cure ;
And all-sufficing nature can chastise
Those who transgress her law,—she only knows
How justly to proportion to the fault
The punishment it merits.

                              Is it strange
That this poor wretch should pride him in his woe ?
Take pleasure in his abjectness, and hug
The scorpion that consumes him ? Is it strange
That, placed on a conspicuous throne of thorns,
Grasping an iron sceptre, and immured
Within a splendid prison, whose stern bounds
Shut him from all that's good or dear on earth,
His soul asserts not its humanity ?
That man's mild nature rises not in war
Against a king's employ ? No—'tis not strange.
He, like the vulgar, thinks, feels, acts and lives
Just as his father did ; the unconquered powers
Of precedent and custom interpose
Between a *king* and virtue. Stranger yet,
To those who know not nature, nor deduce
The future from the present, it may seem,

That not one slave, who suffers from the crimes
Of this unnatural being, not one wretch,
Whose children famish, and whose nuptial bed
Is earth's unpitying bosom, rears an arm
To dash him from his throne !

      Those gilded flies
That, basking in the sunshine of a court,
Fatten on its corruption !—what are they ?
—The drones of the community ; they feed
On the mechanic's labour : the starved hind
For them compels the stubborn glebe to yield
Its unshared harvests ; and yon squalid form,
Leaner than fleshless misery, that wastes
A sunless life in the unwholesome mine,
Drags out in labour a protracted death,
To glut their grandeur ; many faint with toil,
That few may know the cares and woe of sloth.

Whence, thinkest thou, kings and parasites arose ?
Whence that unnatural line of drones, who heap
Toil and unvanquishable penury
On those who build their palaces, and bring
Their daily bread ? — From vice, black loathsome
  vice ;
From rapine, madness, treachery, and wrong ;
From all that genders misery, and makes
Of earth this thorny wilderness ; from lust,
Revenge, and murder......And when reason's voice,
Loud as the voice of nature, shall have waked
The nations ; and mankind perceive that vice
Is discord, war, and misery ; that virtue
Is peace, and happiness and harmony ;
When man's maturer nature shall disdain
The playthings of its childhood ;—kingly glare
Will lose its power to dazzle ; its authority
Will silently pass by ; the gorgeous throne
Shall stand unnoticed in the regal hall,
Fast falling to decay ; whilst falsehood's trade

Shall be as hateful and unprofitable
As that of truth is now.

              Where is the fame
Which the vain-glorious mighty of the earth
Seek to eternize ?   Oh ! the faintest sound
From time's light footfall, the minutest wave
That swells the flood of ages, whelms in nothing
The unsubstantial bubble.   Aye ! to-day
Stern is the tyrant's mandate, red the gaze
That flashes desolation, strong the arm
That scatters multitudes.   To-morrow comes :
That mandate is a thunder-peal that died
In ages past ; that gaze, a transient flash
On which the midnight closed, and on that arm
The worm has made his meal.

                  The virtuous man,
Who, great in his humility, as kings
Are little in their grandeur ; he who leads
Invincibly a life of resolute good,
And stands amid the silent dungeon-depths
More free and fearless than the trembling judge,
Who, clothed in venal power, vainly strove
To bind the impassive spirit ;—when he falls,
His mild eye beams benevolence no more :
Withered the hand outstretched but to relieve ;
Sunk reason's simple eloquence, that rolled
But to appal the guilty.   Yes ! the grave
Hath quenched that eye, and death's relentless frost
Withered that arm : but the unfading fame
Which virtue hangs upon its votary's tomb ;
The deathless memory of that man, whom kings
Call to their mind and tremble ; the remembrance
With which the happy spirit contemplates
Its well-spent pilgrimage on earth,
Shall never pass away.

    Nature rejects the monarch, not the man ;
The subject, not the citizen : for kings

And subjects, mutual foes, for ever play
A losing game into each other's hands,
Whose stakes are vice and misery.　The man
Of virtuous soul commands not, nor obeys.
Power, like a desolating pestilence,
Pollutes whate'er it touches ; and obedience,
Bane of all genius, virtue, freedom, truth,
Makes slaves of men, and, of the human frame,
A mechanized automaton.

　　　　　　　　　　　　When Nero,
High over flaming Rome, with savage joy
Lowered like a fiend, drank with enraptured ear
The shrieks of agonizing death, beheld
The frightful desolation spread, and felt
A new created sense within his soul
Thrill to the sight, and vibrate to the sound,
Thinkest thou his grandeur had not overcome
The force of human kindness ? and, when Rome,
With one stern blow, hurled not the tyrant down,
Crushed not the arm red with her dearest blood,
Had not submissive abjectness destroyed
Nature's suggestions ?

　　　　　　　　　　　Look on yonder earth :
The golden harvests spring ; the unfailing sun
Sheds light and life ; the fruits, the flowers, the
　　　trees,
Arise in due succession ; all things speak
Peace, harmony, and love.　The universe,
In nature's silent eloquence, declares
That all fulfil the works of love and joy,—
All but the outcast man.　He fabricates
The sword which stabs his peace ; he cherisheth
The snakes that gnaw his heart ; he raiseth up
The tyrant, whose delight is in his woe,
Whose sport is in his agony.　Yon sun,
Lights it the great alone ?　Yon silver beams,
Sleep they less sweetly on the cottage thatch,
Than on the dome of kings ?　Is Mother Earth

A step-dame to her numerous sons, who earn
Her unshared gifts with unremitting toil ;
A mother only to those puling babes
Who, nursed in ease and luxury, make men
The playthings of their babyhood, and mar
In self-important childishness that peace
Which men alone appreciate ?

Spirit of Nature ! no.
The pure diffusion of thy essence throbs
  Alike in every human heart.
     Thou, aye, erectest there
  Thy throne of power unappealable :
  Thou art the judge beneath whose nod
  Man's brief and frail authority
     Is powerless as the wind
     That passeth idly by.
Thine the tribunal which surpasseth
  The show of human justice,
     As God surpasses man.

Spirit of Nature ! thou
Life of interminable multitudes ;
  Soul of those mighty spheres
Whose changeless paths thro' Heaven's deep silence lie ;
    Soul of that smallest being,
     The dwelling of whose life
    Is one faint April sun-gleam ;—
     Man, like these passive things,
Thy will unconsciously fulfilleth :
  Like theirs, his age of endless peace,
    Which time is fast maturing,
    Will swiftly, surely come ;
And the unbounded frame, which thou pervadest,
    Will be without a flaw
  Marring its perfect symmetry.

IV

How beautiful this night ! the balmiest sigh,
Which vernal zephyrs breathe in evening's ear,
Were discord to the speaking quietude
That wraps this moveless scene.   Heaven's ebon vault
Studded with stars unutterably bright,
Through which the moon's unclouded grandeur rolls,
Seems like a canopy which love had spread
To curtain her sleeping world.   Yon gentle hills,
Robed in a garment of untrodden snow ;
Yon darksome rocks, whence icicles depend,
So stainless, that their white and glittering spires
Tinge not the moon's pure beam ; yon castled steep,
Whose banner hangeth o'er the time-worn tower
So idly, that rapt' fancy deemeth it
A metaphor of peace ; all form a scene
Where musing solitude might love to lift
Her soul above this sphere of earthliness ;
Where silence undisturbed might watch alone,
So cold, so bright, so still.
                              The orb of day,
In southern climes, o'er ocean's waveless field
Sinks sweetly smiling : not the faintest breath
Steals o'er the unruffled deep ; the clouds of eve
Reflect unmoved the lingering beam of day ;
And vesper's image on the western main
Is beautifully still.   To-morrow comes :
Cloud upon cloud, in dark and deepening mass,
Roll o'er the blackened waters ; the deep roar
Of distant thunder mutters awfully ;
Tempest unfolds its pinion o'er the gloom
That shrouds the boiling surge ; the pitiless fiend,
With all his winds and lightnings, tracks his prey ;
The torn deep yawns,—the vessel finds a grave
Beneath its jaggèd gulph.

Ah ! whence yon glare
That fires the arch of heaven ?—that dark red smoke
Blotting the silver moon ? the stars are quenched
In darkness, and the pure and spangling snow
Gleams faintly through the gloom that gathers round !
Hark to that roar, whose swift and deaf'ning peals
In countless echoes through the mountains ring,
Startling pale midnight on her starry throne !
Now swells the intermingling din ; the jar
Frequent and frightful of the bursting bomb ;
The falling beam, the shriek, the groan, the shout,
The ceaseless clangour, and the rush of men
Inebriate with rage :—loud and more loud
The discord grows ; till pale Death shuts the scene,
And o'er the conqueror and the conquered draws
His cold and bloody shroud.—Of all the men
Whom day's departing beam saw blooming there,
In proud and vigorous health ; of all the hearts
That beat with anxious life at sunset there ;
How few survive, how few are beating now !
All is deep silence, like the fearful calm
That slumbers in the storm's portentous pause ;
Save when the frantic wail of widowed love
Comes shuddering on the blast, or the faint moan
With which some soul bursts from the frame of clay
Wrapped round its struggling powers.

　　　　　　　　　The grey morn
Dawns on the mournful scene ; the sulphurous smoke
Before the icy wind slow rolls away,
And the bright beams of frosty morning dance
Along the spangling snow.　There tracks of blood
Even to the forest's depth, and scattered arms,
And lifeless warriors, whose hard lineaments
Death's self could change not, mark the dreadful path
Of the out-sallying victors : far behind,
Black ashes note where their proud city stood.
Within yon forest is a gloomy glen—
Each tree which guards its darkness from the day

Waves o'er a warrior's tomb.

                    I see thee shrink,
Surpassing Spirit !—wert thou human else ?
I see a shade of doubt and horror fleet
Across thy stainless features : yet fear not ;
This is no unconnected misery,
Nor stands uncaused, and irretrievable.
Man's evil nature, that apology
Which kings who rule, and cowards who crouch, set up
For their unnumbered crimes, sheds not the blood
Which desolates the discord-wasted land.
From kings, and priests, and statesmen, war arose,
Whose safety is man's deep unbettered woe,
Whose grandeur his debasement. Let the axe
Strike at the root, the poison-tree will fall ;
And where its venomed exhalations spread
Ruin, and death, and woe, where millions lay
Quenching the serpent's famine, and their bones
Bleaching unburied in the putrid blast,
A garden shall arise, in loveliness
Surpassing fabled Eden.

                    Hath Nature's soul,
That formed this world so beautiful, that spread
Earth's lap with plenty, and life's smallest chord
Strung to unchanging unison, that gave
The happy birds their dwelling in the grove,
That yielded to the wanderers of the deep
The lovely silence of the unfathomed main,
And filled the meanest worm that crawls in dust
With spirit, thought, and love ; on Man alone,
Partial in causeless malice, wantonly
Heaped ruin, vice, and slavery ; his soul
Blasted with withering curses ; placed afar
The meteor happiness, that shuns his grasp,
But serving on the frightful gulph to glare,
Rent wide beneath his footsteps ?

                        Nature !—no !
Kings, priests, and statesmen blast the human flower

Even in its tender bud ; their influence darts
Like subtle poison through the bloodless veins
Of desolate society.   The child,
Ere he can lisp his mother's sacred name,
Swells with the unnatural pride of crime, and lifts
His baby-sword even in a hero's mood.
This infant-arm becomes the bloodiest scourge
Of devastated earth ; whilst specious names,
Learnt in soft childhood's unsuspecting hour,
Serve as the sophisms with which manhood dims
Bright reason's ray, and sanctifies the sword
Upraised to shed a brother's innocent blood.
Let priest-led slaves cease to proclaim that man
Inherits vice and misery, when force
And falsehood hang even o'er the cradled babe,
Stifling with rudest grasp all natural good.

Ah ! to the stranger-soul, when first it peeps
From its new tenement, and looks abroad
For happiness and sympathy, how stern
And desolate a tract is this wide world !
How withered all the buds of natural good !
No shade, no shelter from the sweeping storms
Of pitiless power !   On its wretched frame,
Poisoned, perchance, by the disease and woe
Heaped on the wretched parent whence it sprung
By morals, law, and custom, the pure winds
Of heaven, that renovate the insect tribes,
May breathe not.   The untainting light of day
May visit not its longings.   It is bound
Ere it has life : yea, all the chains are forged
Long ere its being : all liberty and love
And peace is torn from its defencelessness ;
Cursed from its birth, even from its cradle doomed
To abjectness and bondage !

Throughout this varied and eternal world
Soul is the only element, the block

That for uncounted ages has remained.
The moveless pillar of a mountain's weight
Is active, living spirit.   Every grain
Is sentient both in unity and part,
And the minutest atom comprehends
A world of loves and hatreds ; these beget
Evil and good : hence truth and falsehood spring ;
Hence will and thought and action, all the germs
Of pain or pleasure, sympathy or hate,
That variegate the eternal universe.
Soul is not more polluted than the beams
Of heaven's pure orb, ere round their rapid lines
The taint of earth-born atmospheres arise.

Man is of soul and body, formed for deeds
Of high resolve, on fancy's boldest wing
To soar unwearied, fearlessly to turn
The keenest pangs to peacefulness, and taste
The joys which mingled sense and spirit yield.
Or he is formed for abjectness and woe,
To grovel on the dunghill of his fears,
To shrink at every sound, to quench the flame
Of natural love in sensualism, to know
That hour as bless'd when on his worthless days
The frozen hand of Death shall set its seal,
Yet fear the cure, though hating the disease.
The one is man that shall hereafter be ;
The other, man as vice has made him now.

War is the statesman's game, the priest's delight,
The lawyer's jest, the hired assassin's trade,
And, to those royal murderers, whose mean thrones
Are bought by crimes of treachery and gore,
The bread they eat, the staff on which they lean.
Guards, garbed in blood-red livery, surround
Their palaces, participate the crimes
That force defends, and from a nation's rage
Secure the crown, which all the curses reach

That famine, frenzy, woe and penury breathe.
These are the hired bravos who defend
The tyrant's throne—the bullies of his fear :
These are the sinks and channels of worst vice,
The refuse of society, the dregs
Of all that is most vile : their cold hearts blend
Deceit with sternness, ignorance with pride,
All that is mean and villainous, with rage
Which hopelessness of good, and self-contempt,
Alone might kindle ; they are decked in wealth,
Honour and power, then are sent abroad
To do their work.   The pestilence that stalks
In gloomy triumph through some eastern land
Is less destroying.   They cajole with gold,
And promises of fame, the thoughtless youth
Already crushed with servitude : he knows
His wretchedness too late, and cherishes
Repentance for his ruin, when his doom
Is sealed in gold and blood !
Those too the tyrant serve, who, skilled to snare
The feet of justice in the toils of law,
Stand, ready to oppress the weaker still ;
And, right or wrong, will vindicate for gold,
Sneering at public virtue, which beneath
Their pitiless tread lies torn and trampled, where
Honour sits smiling at the sale of truth.

Then grave and hoary-headed hypocrites,
Without a hope, a passion, or a love,
Who, through a life of luxury and lies,
Have crept by flattery to the seats of power,
Support the system whence their honours flow....
They have three words :—well tyrants know their use,
Well pay them for the loan with usury
Torn from a bleeding world !—God, Hell, and Heaven.
A vengeful, pitiless, and almighty fiend,
Whose mercy is a nickname for the rage
Of tameless tigers hungering for blood.

Hell, a red gulph of everlasting fire,
Where poisonous and undying worms prolong
Eternal misery to those hapless slaves
Whose life has been a penance for its crimes.
And Heaven, a meed for those who dare belie
Their human nature, quake, believe, and cringe
Before the mockeries of earthly power.

    These tools the tyrant tempers to his work,
Wields in his wrath, and as he wills destroys,
Omnipotent in wickedness : the while
Youth springs, age moulders, manhood tamely does
His bidding, bribed by short-lived joys to lend
Force to the weakness of his trembling arm.
They rise, they fall ; one generation comes
Yielding its harvest to destruction's scythe.
It fades, another blossoms : yet behold !
Red glows the tyrant's stamp-mark on its bloom,
Withering and cankering deep its passive prime.
He has invented lying words and modes,
Empty and vain as his own coreless heart ;
Evasive meanings, nothings of much sound,
To lure the heedless victim to the toils
Spread round the valley of its paradise.

    Look to thyself, priest, conqueror, or prince !
Whether thy trade is falsehood, and thy lusts
Deep wallow in the earnings of the poor,
With whom thy master was ;—or thou delight'st
In numbering o'er the myriads of thy slain,
All misery weighing nothing in the scale
Against thy short-lived fame : or thou dost load
With cowardice and crime the groaning land,
A pomp-fed king.   Look to thy wretched self !
Aye, art thou not the veriest slave that e'er
Crawled on the loathing earth ?   Are not thy days
Days of unsatisfying listlessness ?
Dost thou not cry, ere night's long rack is o'er,

When will the morning come ?   Is not thy youth
A vain and feverish dream of sensualism ?
Thy manhood blighted with unripe disease ?
Are not thy views of unregretted death
Drear, comfortless, and horrible ?   Thy mind,
Is it not morbid as thy nerveless frame,
Incapable of judgment, hope, or love ?
And dost thou wish the errors to survive
That bar thee from all sympathies of good,
After the miserable interest
Thou hold'st in their protraction ?   When the grave
Has swallowed up thy memory and thyself,
Dost thou desire the bane that poisons earth
To twine its roots around thy coffined clay,
Spring from thy bones, and blossom on thy tomb,
That of its fruit thy babes may eat and die ?

V

   Thus do the generations of the earth
Go to the grave and issue from the womb,
Surviving still the imperishable change
That renovates the world ; even as the leaves
Which the keen frost-wind of the waning year
Has scattered on the forest soil, and heaped
For many seasons there, though long they choke,
Loading with loathsome rottenness the land,
All germs of promise.   Yet when the tall trees
From which they fell, shorn of their lovely shapes,
Lie level with the earth to moulder there,
They fertilize the land they long deformed,
Till from the breathing lawn a forest springs
Of youth, integrity and loveliness,
Like that which gave it life, to spring and die.
Thus suicidal selfishness, that blights
The fairest feelings of the opening heart,
Is destined to decay, whilst from the soil

Shall spring all virtue, all delight, all love,
And judgment cease to wage unnatural war
With passion's unsubduable array.
Twin-sister of religion, selfishness !
Rival in crime and falsehood, aping all
The wanton horrors of her bloody play ;
Yet frozen, unimpassioned, spiritless,
Shunning the light, and owning not its name,
Compelled, by its deformity, to screen
With flimsy veil of justice and of right,
Its unattractive lineaments, that scare
All, save the brood of ignorance : at once
The cause and the effect of tyranny ;
Unblushing, hardened, sensual, and vile ;
Dead to all love but of its abjectness,
With heart impassive by more noble powers
Than unshared pleasure, sordid gain, or fame ;
Despising its own miserable being,
Which still it longs, yet fears, to disenthrall.

Hence commerce springs, the venal interchange
Of all that human art or nature yield ;
Which wealth should purchase not, but want demand,
And natural kindness hasten to supply
From the full fountain of its boundless love,
For ever stifled, drained, and tainted now.
Commerce ! beneath whose poison-breathing shade
No solitary virtue dares to spring,
But poverty and wealth with equal hand
Scatter their withering curses, and unfold
The doors of premature and violent death,
To pining famine and full-fed disease,
To all that shares the lot of human life,
Which poisoned body and soul, scarce drags the chain,
That lengthens as it goes and clanks behind.

Commerce has set the mark of selfishness,
The signet of its all-enslaving power,

Upon a shining ore, and called it gold :
Before whose image bow the vulgar great,
The vainly rich, the miserable proud,
The mob of peasants, nobles, priests, and kings,
And with blind feelings reverence the power
That grinds them to the dust of misery.
But in the temple of their hireling hearts
Gold is a living god, and rules in scorn
All earthly things but virtue.

Since tyrants, by the sale of human life,
Heap luxuries to their sensualism, and fame
To their wide-wasting and insatiate pride,
Success has sanctioned to a credulous world
The ruin, the disgrace, the woe of war.
His hosts of blind and unresisting dupes
The despot numbers ; from his cabinet
These puppets of his schemes he moves at will,
Even as the slaves by force or famine driven,
Beneath a vulgar master, to perform
A task of cold and brutal drudgery ;—
Hardened to hope, insensible to fear,
Scarce living pullies of a dead machine,
Mere wheels of work and articles of trade,
That grace the proud and noisy pomp of wealth !

The harmony and happiness of man
Yields to the wealth of nations ; that which lifts
His nature to the heaven of its pride,
Is bartered for the poison of his soul ;
The weight that drags to earth his towering hopes,
Blighting all prospect but of selfish gain,
Withering all passion but of slavish fear,
Extinguishing all free and generous love
Of enterprise and daring, even the pulse
That fancy kindles in the beating heart
To mingle with sensation, it destroys,—
Leaves nothing but the sordid lust of self,

The grovelling hope of interest and gold,
Unqualified, unmingled, unredeemed
Even by hypocrisy.
                                    And statesmen boast
Of wealth ! The wordy eloquence that lives
After the ruin of their hearts, can gild
The bitter poison of a nation's woe,
Can turn the worship of the servile mob
To their corrupt and glaring idol fame,
From virtue, trampled by its iron tread,
Although its dazzling pedestal be raised
Amid the horrors of a limb-strewn field,
With desolated dwellings smoking round.
The man of ease, who, by his warm fire-side,
To deeds of charitable intercourse
And bare fulfilment of the common laws
Of decency and prejudice, confines
The struggling nature of his human heart,
Is duped by their cold sophistry ; he sheds
A passing tear perchance upon the wreck
Of earthly peace, when near his dwelling's door
The frightful waves are driven,—when his son
Is murdered by the tyrant, or religion
Drives his wife raving mad.   But the poor man,
Whose life is misery, and fear, and care ;
Whom the morn wakens but to fruitless toil ;
Who ever hears his famished offspring's scream,
Whom their pale mother's uncomplaining gaze
For ever meets, and the proud rich man's eye
Flashing command, and the heart-breaking scene
Of thousands like himself ;—he little heeds
The rhetoric of tyranny ; his hate
Is quenchless as his wrongs ; he laughs to scorn
The vain and bitter mockery of words,
Feeling the horror of the tyrant's deeds,
And unrestrained but by the arm of power,
That knows and dreads his enmity.

  The iron rod of penury still compels
Her wretched slave to bow the knee to wealth,
And poison, with unprofitable toil,
A life too void of solace to confirm
The very chains that bind him to his doom.
Nature, impartial in munificence,
Has gifted man with all-subduing will.
Matter, with all its transitory shapes,
Lies subjected and plastic at his feet,
That, weak from bondage, tremble as they tread.
How many a rustic Milton has passed by,
Stifling the speechless longings of his heart,
In unremitting drudgery and care!
How many a vulgar Cato has compelled
His energies, no longer tameless then,
To mould a pin, or fabricate a nail!
How many a Newton, to whose passive ken
Those mighty spheres that gem infinity
Were only specks of tinsel, fixed in heaven
To light the midnights of his native town!

  Yet every heart contains perfection's germ:
The wisest of the sages of the earth,
That ever from the stores of reason drew
Science and truth, and virtue's dreadless tone,
Were but a weak and inexperienced boy,
Proud, sensual, unimpassioned, unimbued
With pure desire and universal love,
Compared to that high being, of cloudless brain,
Untainted passion, elevated will,
Which death (who even would linger long in awe
Within his noble presence, and beneath
His changeless eyebeam) might alone subdue.
Him, every slave now dragging through the filth
Of some corrupted city his sad life,
Pining with famine, swol'n with luxury,
Blunting the keenness of his spiritual sense
With narrow schemings and unworthy cares,

Or madly rushing through all violent crime,
To move the deep stagnation of his soul,—
Might imitate and equal.
　　　　　　　　　But mean lust
Has bound its chains so tight around the earth,
That all within it but the virtuous man
Is venal : gold or fame will surely reach
The price prefixed by selfishness, to all
But him of resolute and unchanging will ;
Whom, nor the plaudits of a servile crowd,
Nor the vile joys of tainting luxury,
Can bribe to yield his elevated soul
To tyranny or falsehood, though they wield
With blood-red hand the sceptre of the world.

All things are sold : the very light of heaven
Is venal ; earth's unsparing gifts of love,
The smallest and most despicable things
That lurk in the abysses of the deep,
All objects of our life, even life itself,
And the poor pittance which the laws allow
Of liberty, the fellowship of man,
Those duties which his heart of human love
Should urge him to perform instinctively,
Are bought and sold as in a public mart
Of undisguising selfishness, that sets
On each its price, the stamp-mark of her reign.
Even love is sold ; the solace of all woe
Is turned to deadliest agony ; old age
Shivers in selfish beauty's loathing arms ;
And youth's corrupted impulses prepare
A life of horror from the blighting bane
Of commerce ; whilst the pestilence that springs
From unenjoying sensualism has filled
All human life with hydra-headed woes.
Falsehood demands but gold to pay the pangs
Of outraged conscience ; for the slavish priest
Sets no great value on his hireling faith :

A little passing pomp, some servile souls,
Whom cowardice itself might safely chain,
Or the spare mite of avarice could bribe
To deck the triumph of their languid zeal,
Can make him minister to tyranny.
More daring crime requires a loftier meed :
Without a shudder, the slave-soldier lends
His arm to murderous deeds, and steels his heart,
When the dread eloquence of dying men,
Low mingling on the lonely field of fame,
Assails that nature, whose applause he sells
For the gross blessings of a patriot mob,
For the vile gratitude of heartless kings,
And for a cold world's good word,—viler still !

There is a nobler glory, which survives
Until our being fades, and, solacing
All human care, accompanies its change ;
Deserts not virtue in the dungeon's gloom,
And, in the precincts of the palace, guides
Its footsteps through that labyrinth of crime ;
Imbues his lineaments with dauntlessness,
Even when, from power's avenging hand, he takes
Its sweetest, last and noblest title—death ;
—The consciousness of good, which neither gold,
Nor sordid fame, nor hope of heavenly bliss,
Can purchase ; but a life of resolute good,
Unalterable will, quenchless desire
Of universal happiness, the heart
That beats with it in unison, the brain,
Whose ever wakeful wisdom toils to change
Reason's rich stores for its eternal weal.

This commerce of sincerest virtue needs
No mediative signs of selfishness,
No jealous intercourse of wretched gain,
No balancings of prudence, cold and long ;
In just and equal measure all is weighed,

One scale contains the sum of human weal,
And one, the good man's heart.

                    How vainly seek
The selfish for that happiness denied
To aught but virtue ! Blind and hardened, they,
Who hope for peace amid the storms of care,
Who covet power they know not how to use,
And sigh for pleasure they refuse to give,—
Madly they frustrate still their own designs ;
And, where they hope that quiet to enjoy
Which virtue pictures, bitterness of soul,
Pining regrets, and vain repentances,
Disease, disgust, and lassitude, pervade
Their valueless and miserable lives.

But hoary-headed selfishness has felt
Its death-blow, and is tottering to the grave :
A brighter morn awaits the human day,
When every transfer of earth's natural gifts
Shall be a commerce of good words and works ;
When poverty and wealth, the thirst of fame,
The fear of infamy, disease and woe,
War with its million horrors, and fierce hell
Shall live but in the memory of Time,
Who, like a penitent libertine, shall start,
Look back, and shudder at his younger years.

VI

    ALL touch, all eye, all ear,
The Spirit felt the Fairy's burning speech.
    O'er the thin texture of its frame,
The varying periods painted changing glows,
      As on a summer even,
When soul-enfolding music floats around,
    The stainless mirror of the lake
    Re-images the eastern gloom,

Mingling convulsively its purple hues
    With sunset's burnished gold.

    Then thus the Spirit spoke :
It is a wild and miserable world !
    Thorny, and full of care,
Which every fiend can make his prey at will.
  O Fairy ! in the lapse of years,
    Is there no hope in store ?
    Will yon vast suns roll on
  Interminably, still illuming
The night of so many wretched souls,
    And see no hope for them ?
Will not the universal Spirit e'er
Revivify this withered limb of Heaven ?

    The Fairy calmly smiled
In comfort, and a kindling gleam of hope
Suffused the Spirit's lineaments.
Oh ! rest thee tranquil ; chase those fearful doubts,
Which ne'er could rack an everlasting soul,
That sees the chains which bind it to its doom.
Yes ! crime and misery are in yonder earth,
    Falsehood, mistake, and lust ;
    But the eternal world
Contains at once the evil and the cure.
Some eminent in virtue shall start up,
    Even in perversest time :
The truths of their pure lips, that never die,
Shall bind the scorpion falsehood with a wreath
    Of ever-living flame,
Until the monster sting itself to death.

  How sweet a scene will earth become !
Of purest spirits, a pure dwelling-place,
Symphonious with the planetary spheres ;
When man, with changeless nature coalescing,
Will undertake regeneration's work,

When its ungenial poles no longer point
  To the red and baleful sun
  That faintly twinkles there.

  Spirit ! on yonder earth,
 Falsehood now triumphs ; deadly power
Has fixed its seal upon the lip of truth !
  Madness and misery are there !
The happiest is most wretched !   Yet confide,
Until pure health-drops, from the cup of joy,
Fall like a dew of balm upon the world.
Now, to the scene I show, in silence turn,
And read the blood-stained charter of all woe,
Which nature soon, with recreating hand,
Will blot in mercy from the book of earth.
How bold the flight of passion's wandering wing,
How swift the step of reason's firmer tread,
How calm and sweet the victories of life,
How terrorless the triumph of the grave !
How powerless were the mightiest monarch's arm,
Vain his loud threat, and impotent his frown !
How ludicrous the priest's dogmatic roar !
The weight of his exterminating curse,
How light ! and his affected charity,
To suit the pressure of the changing times,
What palpable deceit !—but for thy aid,
Religion ! but for thee, prolific fiend,
Who peoplest earth with dæmons, hell with men,
And heaven with slaves !

 Thou taintest all thou lookest upon !—the stars,
Which on thy cradle beamed so brightly sweet,
Were gods to the distempered playfulness
Of thy untutored infancy : the trees,
The grass, the clouds, the mountains, and the sea,
All living things that walk, swim, creep, or fly,
Were gods : the sun had homage, and the moon
Her worshipper.   Then thou becamest, a boy,

More daring in thy frenzies : every shape,
Monstrous or vast, or beautifully wild,
Which, from sensation's relics, fancy culls ;
The spirit of the air, the shuddering ghost,
The genii of the elements, the powers
That give a shape to nature's varied works,
Had life and place in the corrupt belief
Of thy blind heart : yet still thy youthful hands
Were pure of human blood. Then manhood gave
Its strength and ardour to thy frenzied brain ;
Thine eager gaze scanned the stupendous scene,
Whose wonders mocked the knowledge of thy pride :
Their everlasting and unchanging laws
Reproached thine ignorance. Awhile thou stood'st
Baffled and gloomy ; then thou didst sum up
The elements of all that thou didst know ;
The changing seasons, winter's leafless reign,
The budding of the heaven-breathing trees,
The eternal orbs that beautify the night,
The sunrise, and the setting of the moon,
Earthquakes and wars, and poisons and disease,
And all their causes, to an abstract point,
Converging, thou didst bend and called it God !
The self-sufficing, the omnipotent,
The merciful, and the avenging God !
Who, prototype of human misrule, sits
High in heaven's realm, upon a golden throne,
Even like an earthly king ; and whose dread work,
Hell, gapes for ever for the unhappy slaves
Of fate, whom he created, in his sport,
To triumph in their torments when they fell !
Earth heard the name ; earth trembled, as the smoke
Of his revenge ascended up to heaven,
Blotting the constellations ; and the cries
Of millions, butchered in sweet confidence
And unsuspecting peace, even when the bonds
Of safety were confirmed by wordy oaths
Sworn in his dreadful name, rung through the land ;

Whilst innocent babes writhed on thy stubborn spear,
And thou didst laugh to hear the mother's shriek
Of maniac gladness, as the sacred steel
Felt cold in her torn entrails!

Religion! thou wert then in manhood's prime:
But age crept on: one God would not suffice
For senile puerility; thou framedst
A tale to suit thy dotage, and to glut
Thy misery-thirsting soul, that the mad fiend
Thy wickedness had pictured might afford
A plea for sating the unnatural thirst
For murder, rapine, violence, and crime,
That still consumed thy being, even when
Thou heard'st the step of fate;—that flames might light
Thy funeral scene, and the shrill horrent shrieks
Of parents dying on the pile that burned
To light their children to thy paths, the roar
Of the encircling flames, the exulting cries
Of thine apostles, loud commingling there,
        Might sate thine hungry ear
        Even on the bed of death!

But now contempt is mocking thy grey hairs;
Thou art descending to the darksome grave,
Unhonoured and unpitied, but by those
Whose pride is passing by like thine, and sheds
Like thine a glare that fades before the sun
Of truth, and shines but in the dreadful night
That long has lowered above the ruined world.

Throughout these infinite orbs of mingling light,
Of which yon earth is one, is wide diffused
A spirit of activity and life,
That knows no term, cessation, or decay;
That fades not when the lamp of earthly life,
Extinguished in the dampness of the grave,
Awhile there slumbers, more than when the babe

In the dim newness of its being feels
The impulses of sublunary things,
And all is wonder to unpractised sense:
But, active, steadfast, and eternal, still
Guides the fierce whirlwind, in the tempest roars,
Cheers in the day, breathes in the balmy groves,
Strengthens in health, and poisons in disease;
And in the storm of change, that ceaselessly
Rolls round the eternal universe, and shakes
Its undecaying battlement, presides,
Apportioning with irresistible law
The place each spring of its machine shall fill;
So that, when waves on waves tumultuous heap
Confusion to the clouds, and fiercely driven
Heaven's lightnings scorch the uprooted ocean-fords,
Whilst, to the eye of shipwrecked mariner,
Lone sitting on the bare and shuddering rock,
All seems unlinked contingency and chance,—
No atom of this turbulence fulfils
A vague and unnecessitated task,
Or acts but as it must and ought to act.
Even the minutest molecule of light,
That in an April sunbeam's fleeting glow
Fulfils its destined though invisible work,
The universal Spirit guides; nor less,
When merciless ambition, or mad zeal,
Has led two hosts of dupes to battle-field,
That, blind, they there may dig each other's graves,
And call the sad work glory, does it rule
All passions: not a thought, a will, an act,
No working of the tyrant's moody mind,
Nor one misgiving of the slaves who boast
Their servitude, to hide the shame they feel,
Nor the events enchaining every will,
That from the depths of unrecorded time
Have drawn all-influencing virtue, pass
Unrecognized, or unforeseen by thee,
Soul of the Universe! eternal spring

Of life and death, of happiness and woe,
Of all that chequers the phantasmal scene
That floats before our eyes in wavering light,
Which gleams but on the darkness of our prison,
  Whose chains and massy walls
  We feel, but cannot see.

 Spirit of Nature ! all-sufficing Power,
Necessity ! thou mother of the world !
Unlike the God of human error, thou
Requir'st no prayers or praises ; the caprice
Of man's weak will belongs no more to thee
Than do the changeful passions of his breast
To thy unvarying harmony : the slave,
Whose horrible lusts spread misery o'er the world,
And the good man, who lifts, with virtuous pride,
His being, in the sight of happiness
That springs from his own works ; the poison-tree,
Beneath whose shade all life is withered up,
And the fair oak, whose leafy dome affords
A temple where the vows of happy love
Are registered, are equal in thy sight :
No love, no hate thou cherishest ; revenge
And favouritism, and worst desire of fame
Thou know'st not : all that the wide world contains
Are but thy passive instruments, and thou
Regard'st them all with an impartial eye,
Whose joy or pain thy nature cannot feel,
  Because thou hast not human sense,
  Because thou art not human mind.

 Yes ! when the sweeping storm of time
Has sung its death-dirge o'er the ruined fanes
And broken altars of the almighty fiend,
Whose name usurps thy honours, and the blood
Through centuries clotted there has floated down
The tainted flood of ages, shalt thou live
Unchangeable ! A shrine is raised to thee,

Which, nor the tempest breath of time,
Nor the interminable flood,
Over earth's slight pageant rolling,
      Availeth to destroy,—
The sensitive extension of the world.
   That wondrous and eternal fane,
Where pain and pleasure, good and evil join,
To do the will of strong necessity,
   And life, in multitudinous shapes,
Still pressing forward where no term can be,
   Like hungry and unresting flame
Curls round the eternal columns of its strength.

VII

SPIRIT

I WAS an infant when my mother went
To see an atheist burned.   She took me there :
The dark-robed priests were met around the pile ;
The multitude was gazing silently ;
And, as the culprit passed with dauntless mien,
Tempered disdain in his unaltering eye,
Mixed with a quiet smile, shone calmly forth :
The thirsty fire crept round his manly limbs ;
His resolute eyes were scorched to blindness soon ;
His death-pang rent my heart ! the insensate mob
Uttered a cry of triumph, and I wept.
Weep not, child ! cried my mother, for that man
Has said, There is no God.

FAIRY

                  There is no God !
Nature confirms the faith his death-groan sealed :
Let heaven and earth, let man's revolving race,
His ceaseless generations tell their tale ;
Let every part depending on the chain
That links it to the whole, point to the hand

That grasps its term ! let every seed that falls
In silent eloquence unfold its store
Of argument : infinity within,
Infinity without, belie creation ;
The exterminable spirit it contains
Is nature's only God ; but human pride
Is skilful to invent most serious names
To hide its ignorance.

　　　　　　　　The name of God
Has fenced about all crime with holiness,
Himself the creature of his worshippers,
Whose names and attributes and passions change,
Seeva, Buddh, Foh, Jehovah, God, or Lord,
Even with the human dupes who build his shrines,
Still serving o'er the war-polluted world
For desolation's watch-word ; whether hosts
Stain his death-blushing chariot-wheels, as on
Triumphantly they roll, whilst Brahmins raise
A sacred hymn to mingle with the groans ;
Or countless partners of his power divide
His tyranny to weakness ; or the smoke
Of burning towns, the cries of female helplessness,
Unarmed old age, and youth, and infancy,
Horribly massacred, ascend to heaven
In honour of his name ; or, last and worst,
Earth groans beneath religion's iron age,
And priests dare babble of a God of peace,
Even whilst their hands are red with guiltless blood,
Murdering the while, uprooting every germ
Of truth, exterminating, spoiling all,
Making the earth a slaughter-house !

　　　　　O Spirit ! through the sense
By which thy inner nature was apprised
　　Of outward shows, vague dreams have rolled.
　　And varied reminiscences have waked
　　　　Tablets that never fade ;
　　All things have been imprinted there,

The stars, the sea, the earth, the sky,
Even the unshapeliest lineaments
  Of wild and fleeting visions
    Have left a record there
    To testify of earth.

These are my empire, for to me is given
The wonders of the human world to keep,
And fancy's thin creations to endow
With manner, being, and reality ;
Therefore a wondrous phantom from the dreams
Of human error's dense and purblind faith,
I will evoke, to meet thy questioning.
    Ahasuerus, rise !

    A strange and woe-worn wight
  Arose beside the battlement,
    And stood unmoving there.
His inessential figure cast no shade
    Upon the golden floor ;
His port and mien bore mark of many years,
And chronicles of untold ancientness
Were legible within his beamless eye :
  Yet his cheek bore the mark of youth ;
Freshness and vigour knit his manly frame ;
The wisdom of old age was mingled there
  With youth's primeval dauntlessness ;
    And inexpressible woe,
Chastened by fearless resignation, gave
An awful grace to his all-speaking brow.

SPIRIT

Is there a God ?

AHASUERUS

Is there a God !—aye, an almighty God,
And vengeful as almighty !   Once his voice

Was heard on earth : earth shuddered at the sound ;
The fiery-visaged firmament expressed
Abhorrence, and the grave of nature yawned
To swallow all the dauntless and the good
That dared to hurl defiance at his throne,
Girt as it was with power. None but slaves
Survived,—cold-blooded slaves who did the work
Of tyrannous omnipotence ; whose souls
No honest indignation ever urged
To elevated daring, to one deed
Which gross and sensual self did not pollute.
These slaves built temples for the omnipotent fiend,
Gorgeous and vast : the costly altars smoked
With human blood, and hideous pæans rung
Through all the long-drawn aisles. A murderer heard
His voice in Egypt, one whose gifts and arts
Had raised him to his eminence in power,
Accomplice of omnipotence in crime,
And confidant of the all-knowing one.
　　　These were Jehovah's words.

　From an eternity of idleness
I, God, awoke ; in seven days' toil made earth
From nothing ; rested, and created man :
I placed him in a paradise, and there
Planted the tree of evil, so that he
Might eat and perish, and my soul procure
Wherewith to sate its malice, and to turn,
Even like a heartless conqueror of the earth,
All misery to my fame. The race of men
Chosen to my honour, with impunity
May sate the lusts I planted in their heart.
Here I command thee hence to lead them on,
Until, with hardened feet, their conquering troops
Wade on the promised soil through woman's blood,
And make my name be dreaded through the land.
Yet ever burning flame and ceaseless woe
Shall be the doom of their eternal souls,

With every soul on this ungrateful earth,
Virtuous or vicious, weak or strong,—even all
Shall perish, to fulfil the blind revenge
(Which you, to men, call justice) of their God.

                    The murderer's brow
Quivered with horror.
                God omnipotent,
Is there no mercy ? must our punishment
Be endless ? will long ages roll away,
And see no term ?   Oh ! wherefore hast thou made
In mockery and wrath this evil earth ?
Mercy becomes the powerful—be but just :
O God ! repent and save.
                 One way remains :
I will beget a son, and he shall bear
The sins of all the world ; he shall arise
In an unnoticed corner of the earth,
And there shall die upon a cross, and purge
The universal crime ; so that the few
On whom my grace descends, those who are marked
As vessels to the honour of their God,
May credit this strange sacrifice, and save
Their souls alive : millions shall live and die,
Who ne'er shall call upon their Saviour's name,
But, unredeemed, go to the gaping grave.
Thousands shall deem it an old woman's tale,
Such as the nurses frighten babes withal :
These in a gulph of anguish and of flame
Shall curse their reprobation endlessly,
Yet tenfold pangs shall force them to avow,
Even on their beds of torment, where they howl,
My honour and the justice of their doom.
What then avail their virtuous deeds, their thoughts
Of purity, with radiant genius bright,
Or lit with human reason's earthly ray ?
Many are called, but few will I elect.
Do thou my bidding, Moses !

                  Even the murderer's cheek
Was blanched with horror, and his quivering lips
Scarce faintly uttered—O almighty one,
I tremble and obey !

    O Spirit ! centuries have set their seal
On this heart of many wounds, and loaded brain,
Since the Incarnate came : humbly he came,
Veiling his horrible Godhead in the shape
Of man, scorned by the world, his name unheard,
Save by the rabble of his native town,
Even as a parish demagogue.   He led
The crowd ; he taught them justice, truth and peace,
In semblance ; but he lit within their souls
The quenchless flames of zeal, and bless'd the sword
He brought on earth to satiate with the blood
Of truth and freedom his malignant soul.
At length his mortal frame was led to death.
I stood beside him : on the torturing cross
No pain assailed his unterrestrial sense ;
And yet he groaned.   Indignantly I summed
The massacres and misery which his name
Had sanctioned in my country, and I cried,
Go ! go ! in mockery.
A smile of godlike malice reillumined
His fading lineaments.—I go, he cried,
But thou shalt wander o'er the unquiet earth
Eternally.——The dampness of the grave
Bathed my imperishable front.   I fell,
And long lay tranced upon the charmèd soil.
When I awoke hell burned within my brain,
Which staggered on its seat ; for all around
The mouldering relics of my kindred lay,
Even as the Almighty's ire arrested them,
And in their various attitudes of death
My murdered children's mute and eyeless skulls
Glared ghastily upon me.
                  But my soul,

From sight and sense of the polluting woe
Of tyranny, had long learned to prefer
Hell's freedom to the servitude of heaven.
Therefore I rose, and dauntlessly began
My lonely and unending pilgrimage,
Resolved to wage unweariable war
With my almighty tyrant, and to hurl
Defiance at his impotence to harm
Beyond the curse I bore. The very hand
That barred my passage to the peaceful grave
Has crushed the earth to misery, and given
Its empire to the chosen of his slaves.
These have I seen, even from the earliest dawn
Of weak, unstable and precarious power ;
Then preaching peace, as now they practise war,
So, when they turned but from the massacre
Of unoffending infidels, to quench
Their thirst for ruin in the very blood
That flowed in their own veins, and pitiless zeal
Froze every human feeling, as the wife
Sheathed in her husband's heart the sacred steel,
Even whilst its hopes were dreaming of her love ;
And friends to friends, brothers to brothers stood
Opposed in bloodiest battle-field, and war,
Scarce satiable by fate's last death-draught waged,
Drunk from the winepress of the Almighty's wrath ;
Whilst the red cross, in mockery of peace,
Pointed to victory ! When the fray was done,
No remnant of the exterminated faith
Survived to tell its ruin, but the flesh,
With putrid smoke poisoning the atmosphere,
That rotted on the half-extinguished pile.

Yes ! I have seen God's worshippers unsheathe
The sword of his revenge, when grace descended,
Confirming all unnatural impulses,
To sanctify their desolating deeds ;
And frantic priests waved the ill-omened cross

O'er the unhappy earth ; then shone the sun
On showers of gore from the upflashing steel
Of safe assassination, and all crime
Made stingless by the spirits of the Lord,
And blood-red rainbows canopied the land.

Spirit ! no year of my eventful being
Has passed unstained by crime and misery,
Which flows from God's own faith. I've marked his
    slaves,
With tongues whose lies are venomous, beguile
The insensate mob, and, whilst one hand was red
With murder, feign to stretch the other out
For brotherhood and peace ; and that they now
Babble of love and mercy, whilst their deeds
Are marked with all the narrowness and crime
That freedom's young arm dare not yet chastise,
Reason may claim our gratitude, who now
Establishing the imperishable throne
Of truth, and stubborn virtue, maketh vain
The unprevailing malice of my foe,
Whose bootless rage heaps torments for the brave,
Adds impotent eternities to pain,
Whilst keenest disappointment racks his breast
To see the smiles of peace around them play,
To frustrate or to sanctify their doom.

Thus have I stood,—through a wild waste of years
Struggling with whirlwinds of mad agony,
Yet peaceful, and serene, and self-enshrined,
Mocking my powerless tyrant's horrible curse
With stubborn and unalterable will,
Even as a giant oak, which heaven's fierce flame
Had scathèd in the wilderness, to stand
A monument of fadeless ruin there ;
Yet peacefully and movelessly it braves
The midnight conflict of the wintry storm,
    As in the sunlight's calm it spreads

Its worn and withered arms on high
To meet the quiet of a summer's noon.

The Fairy waved her wand :
    Ahasuerus fled
Fast as the shapes of mingled shade and mist,
That lurk in the glens of a twilight grove,
    Flee from the morning beam :
  The matter of which dreams are made
  Not more endowed with actual life
  Than this phantasmal portraiture
  Of wandering human thought.

VIII

THE present and the past thou hast beheld :
It was a desolate sight. Now, Spirit, learn
    The secrets of the future.—Time !
Unfold the brooding pinion of thy gloom,
Render thou up thy half-devoured babes,
And from the cradles of eternity,
Where millions lie lulled to their portioned sleep
By the deep murmuring stream of passing things,
Tear thou that gloomy shroud.—Spirit, behold
    Thy glorious destiny !

    Joy to the Spirit came.
Through the wide rent in Time's eternal veil,
Hope was seen beaming through the mists of fear :
    Earth was no longer hell ;
    Love, freedom, health, had given
Their ripeness to the manhood of its prime,
    And all its pulses beat
Symphonious to the planetary spheres :
    Then dulcet music swelled
Concordant with the life-strings of the soul ;
It throbbed in sweet and languid beatings there,

Catching new life from transitory death :
Like the vague sighings of a wind at even,
That wakes the wavelets of the slumbering sea
And dies on the creation of its breath,
And sinks and rises, fails and swells by fits,—
　　Was the pure stream of feeling
　　　That sprung from these sweet notes,
And o'er the Spirit's human sympathies
With mild and gentle motion calmly flowed.

　　　Joy to the Spirit came,—
　　Such joy as when a lover sees
The chosen of his soul in happiness,
　　　And witnesses her peace
Whose woe to him were bitterer than death,
　　　Sees her unfaded cheek
Glow mantling in first luxury of health,
　　　Thrills with her lovely eyes,
Which like two stars amid the heaving main
　　　Sparkle through liquid bliss.

Then in her triumph spoke the Fairy Queen :
I will not call the ghost of ages gone
To unfold the frightful secrets of its lore ;
　　　The present now is past,
And those events that desolate the earth
Have faded from the memory of Time,
Who dares not give reality to that
Whose being I annul.　To me is given
The wonders of the human world to keep,
Space, matter, time, and mind.　Futurity
Exposes now its treasure ; let the sight
Renew and strengthen all thy failing hope.
O human Spirit ! spur thee to the goal
Where virtue fixes universal peace,
And midst the ebb and flow of human things,
Show somewhat stable, somewhat certain still,
A lighthouse o'er the wild of dreary waves.

The habitable earth is full of bliss ;
Those wastes of frozen billows that were hurled
By everlasting snow-storms round the poles,
Where matter dared not vegetate or live,
But ceaseless frost round the vast solitude
Bound its broad zone of stillness, are unloosed ;
And fragrant zephyrs there from spicy isles
Ruffle the placid ocean-deep, that rolls
Its broad, bright surges to the sloping sand,
Whose roar is wakened into echoings sweet
To murmur through the heaven-breathing groves
And melodize with man's blessed nature there.

Those deserts of immeasurable sand,
Whose age-collected fervours scarce allowed
A bird to live, a blade of grass to spring,
Where the shrill chirp of the green lizard's love
Broke on the sultry silentness alone,
Now teem with countless rills and shady woods,
Corn-fields and pastures and white cottages ;
And where the startled wilderness beheld
A savage conqueror stained in kindred blood,
A tigress sating with the flesh of lambs
The unnatural famine of her toothless cubs,
Whilst shouts and howlings through the desert rang,
Sloping and smooth the daisy-spangled lawn,
Offering sweet incense to the sun-rise, smiles
To see a babe before his mother's door,
    Sharing his morning's meal
  With the green and golden basilisk
    That comes to lick his feet.

Those trackless deeps, where many a weary sail
Has seen, above the illimitable plain,
Morning on night, and night on morning rise,
Whilst still no land to greet the wanderer spread
Its shadowy mountains on the sun-bright sea,
Where the loud roarings of the tempest-waves

So long have mingled with the gusty wind
In melancholy loneliness, and swept
The desert of those ocean solitudes,
But vocal to the sea-bird's harrowing shriek,
The bellowing monster, and the rushing storm,
Now to the sweet and many-mingling sounds
Of kindliest human impulses respond.
Those lonely realms bright garden-isles begem,
With lightsome clouds and shining seas between
And fertile valleys resonant with bliss,
Whilst green woods overcanopy the wave,
Which like a toil-worn labourer leaps to shore
To meet the kisses of the flowrets there.

All things are recreated, and the flame
Of consentaneous love inspires all life :
The fertile bosom of the earth gives suck
To myriads, who still grow beneath her care,
Rewarding her with their pure perfectness :
The balmy breathings of the wind inhale
Her virtues, and diffuse them all abroad :
Health floats amid the gentle atmosphere,
Glows in the fruits, and mantles on the stream :
No storms deform the beaming brow of heaven,
Nor scatter in the freshness of its pride
The foliage of the ever verdant trees ;
But fruits are ever ripe, flowers ever fair,
And autumn proudly bears her matron grace,
Kindling a flush on the fair cheek of spring,
Whose virgin bloom beneath the ruddy fruit
Reflects its tint and blushes into love.

The lion now forgets to thirst for blood :
There might you see him sporting in the sun
Beside the dreadless kid ; his claws are sheathed,
His teeth are harmless, custom's force has made
His nature as the nature of a lamb.
Like passion's fruit, the nightshade's tempting bane

Poisons no more the pleasure it bestows :
All bitterness is past ; the cup of joy
Unmingled mantles to the goblet's brim,
And courts the thirsty lips it fled before.

But chief, ambiguous man, he that can know
More misery, and dream more joy than all ;
Whose keen sensations thrill within his breast
To mingle with a loftier instinct there,
Lending their power to pleasure and to pain,
Yet raising, sharpening, and refining each ;
Who stands amid the ever-varying world,
The burthen or the glory of the earth ;
He chief perceives the change, his being notes
The gradual renovation, and defines
Each movement of its progress on his mind.

Man, where the gloom of the long polar night
Lowers o'er the snow-clad rocks and frozen soil,
Where scarce the hardiest herb that braves the frost
Basks in the moonlight's ineffectual glow,
Shrank with the plants, and darkened with the night ;
His chilled and narrow energies, his heart,
Insensible to courage, truth, or love,
His stunted stature and imbecile frame,
Marked him for some abortion of the earth,
Fit compeer of the bears that roam around,
Whose habits and enjoyments were his own :
His life a feverish dream of stagnant woe,
Whose meagre wants but scantily fulfilled
Apprised him ever of the joyless length
Which his short being's wretchedness had reached ;
His death a pang which famine, cold and toil
Long on the mind, whilst yet the vital spark
Clung to the body stubbornly, had brought :
All was inflicted here that earth's revenge
Could wreak on the infringers of her law ;
One curse alone was spared—the name of God.

Nor where the tropics bound the realms of day
With a broad belt of mingling cloud and flame,
Where blue mists through the unmoving atmosphere
Scattered the seeds of pestilence, and fed
Unnatural vegetation, where the land
Teemed with all earthquake, tempest and disease,
Was man a nobler being; slavery
Had crushed him to his country's bloodstained dust;
Or he was bartered for the fame of power,
Which all internal impulses destroying,
Makes human will an article of trade;
Or he was changed with Christians for their gold,
And dragged to distant isles, where to the sound
Of the flesh-mangling scourge, he does the work
Of all-polluting luxury and wealth,
Which doubly visits on the tyrants' heads
The long-protracted fulness of their woe;
Or he was led to legal butchery,
To turn to worms beneath that burning sun,
Where kings first leagued against the rights of men,
And priests first traded with the name of God.

Even where the milder zone afforded man
A seeming shelter, yet contagion there,
Blighting his being with unnumbered ills,
Spread like a quenchless fire; nor truth till late
Availed to arrest its progress, or create
That peace which first in bloodless victory waved
Her snowy standard o'er this favoured clime:
There man was long the train-bearer of slaves,
The mimic of surrounding misery,
The jackal of ambition's lion-rage,
The bloodhound of religion's hungry zeal.

Here now the human being stands adorning
This loveliest earth with taintless body and mind;
Bless'd from his birth with all bland impulses,
Which gently in his noble bosom wake

All kindly passions and all pure desires.
Him, still from hope to hope the bliss pursuing,
Which from the exhaustless lore of human weal
Draws on the virtuous mind, the thoughts that rise
In time-destroying infiniteness, gift
With self-enshrined eternity, that mocks
The unprevailing hoariness of age ;
And man, once fleeting o'er the transient scene
Swift as an unremembered vision, stands
Immortal upon earth : no longer now
He slays the lamb that looks him in the face,
And horribly devours his mangled flesh,
Which still avenging nature's broken law
Kindled all putrid humours in his frame,
All evil passions, and all vain belief,
Hatred, despair, and loathing in his mind,
The germs of misery, death, disease, and crime.
No longer now the wingèd habitants,
That in the woods their sweet lives sing away,
Flee from the form of man ; but gather round,
And prune their sunny feathers on the hands
Which little children stretch in friendly sport
Towards these dreadless partners of their play.
All things are void of terror : man has lost
His terrible prerogative, and stands
An equal amidst equals : happiness
And science dawn though late upon the earth ;
Peace cheers the mind, health renovates the frame ;
Disease and pleasure cease to mingle here,
Reason and passion cease to combat there ;
Whilst each unfettered o'er the earth extend
Their all-subduing energies, and wield
The sceptre of a vast dominion there ;
Whilst every shape and mode of matter lends
Its force to the omnipotence of mind,
Which from its dark mine drags the gem of truth
To decorate its paradise of peace.

IX

O HAPPY Earth ! reality of Heaven !
To which those restless souls that ceaselessly
Throng through the human universe aspire ;
Thou consummation of all mortal hope !
Thou glorious prize of blindly-working will !
Whose rays, diffused throughout all space and time,
Verge to one point and blend for ever there :
Of purest spirits thou pure dwelling-place !
Where care and sorrow, impotence and crime,
Languor, disease, and ignorance dare not come :
O happy Earth, reality of Heaven !

Genius has seen thee in thy passionate dreams ;
And dim forebodings of thy loveliness,
Haunting the human heart, have there entwined
Those rooted hopes of some sweet place of bliss
Where friends and lovers meet to part no more.
Thou art the end of all desire and will,
The product of all action ; and the souls
That by the paths of an aspiring change
Have reached thy haven of perpetual peace,
There rest from the eternity of toil
That framed the fabric of thy perfectness.

Even Time, the conqueror, fled thee in his fear ;
That hoary giant, who, in lonely pride,
So long had ruled the world, that nations fell
Beneath his silent footstep.   Pyramids,
That for millenniums had withstood the tide
Of human things, his storm-breath drove in sand
Across that desert where their stones survived
The name of him whose pride had heaped them there.
Yon monarch, in his solitary pomp,
Was but the mushroom of a summer day,
That his light-wingèd footstep pressed to dust :

Time was the king of earth : all things gave way
Before him, but the fixed and virtuous will,
The sacred sympathies of soul and sense,
That mocked his fury and prepared his fall.

Yet slow and gradual dawned the morn of love ;
Long lay the clouds of darkness o'er the scene,
Till from its native heaven they rolled away :
First, Crime triumphant o'er all hope careered
Unblushing, undisguising, bold and strong ;
Whilst Falsehood, tricked in Virtue's attributes,
Long sanctified all deeds of vice and woe,
Till done by her own venomous sting to death,
She left the moral world without a law,
No longer fettering passion's fearless wing,
Nor searing reason with the brand of God.
Then steadily the happy ferment worked ;
Reason was free ; and wild though passion went
Through tangled glens and wood-embosomed meads,
Gathering a garland of the strangest flowers,
Yet like the bee returning to her queen,
She bound the sweetest on her sister's brow,
Who meek and sober kissed the sportive child,
No longer trembling at the broken rod.

Mild was the slow necessity of death :
The tranquil spirit failed beneath its grasp,
Without a groan, almost without a fear,
Calm as a voyager to some distant land,
And full of wonder, full of hope as he.
The deadly germs of languor and disease
Died in the human frame, and purity
Bless'd with all gifts her earthly worshippers.
How vigorous then the athletic form of age !
How clear its open and unwrinkled brow !
Where neither avarice, cunning, pride, or care,
Had stamped the seal of grey deformity
On all the mingling lineaments of time.

How lovely the intrepid front of youth !
Which meek-eyed courage decked with freshest grace ;
Courage of soul that dreaded not a name,
And elevated will, that journeyed on
Through life's phantasmal scene in fearlessness,
With virtue, love, and pleasure, hand in hand.

Then, that sweet bondage which is freedom's self,
And rivets with sensation's softest tie
The kindred sympathies of human souls,
Needed no fetters of tyrannic law :
Those delicate and timid impulses
In nature's primal modesty arose,
And with undoubted confidence disclosed
The growing longings of its dawning love,
Unchecked by dull and selfish chastity,
That virtue of the cheaply virtuous,
Who pride themselves in senselessness and frost.
No longer prostitution's venomed bane
Poisoned the springs of happiness and life ;
Woman and man, in confidence and love,
Equal and free and pure together trod
The mountain-paths of virtue, which no more
Were stained with blood from many a pilgrim's feet.

Then, where, through distant ages, long in pride
The palace of the monarch-slave had mocked
Famine's faint groan and penury's silent tear,
A heap of crumbling ruins stood, and threw
Year after year their stones upon the field,
Wakening a lonely echo ; and the leaves
Of the old thorn, that on the topmost tower
Usurped the royal ensign's grandeur, shook
In the stern storm that swayed the topmost tower
And whispered strange tales in the whirlwind's ear.

Low through the lone cathedral's roofless aisles
The melancholy winds a death-dirge sung :

It were a sight of awfulness to see
The works of faith and slavery, so vast,
So sumptuous, yet so perishing withal !
Even as the corpse that rests beneath its wall.
A thousand mourners deck the pomp of death
To-day, the breathing marble glows above
To decorate its memory, and tongues
Are busy of its life : to-morrow, worms
In silence and in darkness seize their prey.

Within the massy prison's mouldering courts,
Fearless and free the ruddy children played,
Weaving gay chaplets for their innocent brows
With the green ivy and the red wall-flower,
That mock the dungeon's unavailing gloom ;
The ponderous chains, and gratings of strong iron,
There rusted amid heaps of broken stone
That mingled slowly with their native earth :
There the broad beam of day, which feebly once
Lighted the cheek of lean captivity
With a pale and sickly glare, then freely shone
On the pure smiles of infant playfulness :
No more the shuddering voice of hoarse despair
Pealed through the echoing vaults, but soothing notes
Of ivy-fingered winds and gladsome birds
And merriment were resonant around.

These ruins soon left not a wreck behind :
Their elements, wide scattered o'er the globe,
To happier shapes were moulded, and became
Ministrant to all blissful impulses :
Thus human things were perfected, and earth,
Even as a child beneath its mother's love,
Was strengthened in all excellence, and grew
Fairer and nobler with each passing year.

Now Time his dusky pennons o'er the scene
Closes in steadfast darkness, and the past

Fades from our charmèd sight.   My task is done :
Thy lore is learned.   Earth's wonders are thine own,
With all the fear and all the hope they bring.
My spells are past : the present now recurs.
Ah me ! a pathless wilderness remains
Yet unsubdued by man's reclaiming hand.
Yet, human Spirit, bravely hold thy course,
Let virtue teach thee firmly to pursue
The gradual paths of an aspiring change :
For birth and life and death, and that strange state
Before the naked soul has found its home,
All tend to perfect happiness, and urge
The restless wheels of being on their way,
Whose flashing spokes, instinct with infinite life,
Bicker and burn to gain their destined goal :
For birth but wakes the spirit to the sense
Of outward shows, whose unexperienced shape
New modes of passion to its frame may lend ;
Life is its state of action, and the store
Of all events is aggregated there
That variegate the eternal universe ;
Death is a gate of dreariness and gloom,
That leads to azure isles and beaming skies
And happy regions of eternal hope.
Therefore, O Spirit ! fearlessly bear on :
Though storms may break the primrose on its stalk,
Though frosts may blight the freshness of its bloom,
Yet spring's awakening breath will woo the earth,
To feed with kindliest dews its favourite flower,
That blooms in mossy banks and darksome glens,
Lighting the green wood with its sunny smile.

Fear not then, Spirit, death's disrobing hand,
So welcome when the tyrant is awake,
So welcome when the bigot's hell-torch burns ;
'Tis but the voyage of a darksome hour,
The transient gulph-dream of a startling sleep.
Death is no foe to virtue : earth has seen

Love's brightest roses on the scaffold bloom,
Mingling with freedom's fadeless laurels there,
And presaging the truth of visioned bliss.
Are there not hopes within thee, which this scene
Of linked and gradual being has confirmed?
Whose stingings bade thy heart look further still,
When to the moonlight walk by Henry led,
Sweetly and sadly thou didst talk of death?
And wilt thou rudely tear them from thy breast,
Listening supinely to a bigot's creed,
Or tamely crouching to the tyrant's rod,
Whose iron thongs are red with human gore?
Never: but bravely bearing on, thy will
Is destined an eternal war to wage
With tyranny and falsehood, and uproot
The germs of misery from the human heart.
Thine is the hand whose piety would soothe
The thorny pillow of unhappy crime,
Whose impotence an easy pardon gains,
Watching its wanderings as a friend's disease:
Thine is the brow whose mildness would defy
Its fiercest rage, and brave its sternest will,
When fenced by power and master of the world.
Thou art sincere and good; of resolute mind,
Free from heart-withering custom's cold control,
Of passion lofty, pure and unsubdued.
Earth's pride and meanness could not vanquish thee,
And therefore art thou worthy of the boon
Which thou hast now received: virtue shall keep
Thy footsteps in the path that thou hast trod,
And many days of beaming hope shall bless
Thy spotless life of sweet and sacred love.
Go, happy one, and give that bosom joy
  Whose sleepless spirit waits to catch
  Light, life and rapture from thy smile.

The Fairy waves her wand of charm.
Speechless with bliss the Spirit mounts the car,

That rolled beside the battlement,
Bending her beamy eyes in thankfulness.
　Again the enchanted steeds were yoked,
　Again the burning wheels inflame
The steep descent of heaven's untrodden way.
　Fast and far the chariot flew :
　The vast and fiery globes that rolled
　Around the Fairy's palace-gate
Lessened by slow degrees and soon appeared
Such tiny twinklers as the planet orbs
That there attendant on the solar power
With borrowed light pursued their narrower way.
　　Earth floated then below :
　　The chariot paused a moment there ;
　　The Spirit then descended :
The restless coursers pawed the ungenial soil,
Snuffed the gross air, and then, their errand done,
Unfurled their pinions to the winds of heaven.
　　The Body and the Soul united then,
A gentle start convulsed Ianthe's frame :
Her veiny eyelids quietly unclosed ;
Moveless awhile the dark blue orbs remained :
She looked around in wonder and beheld
Henry, who kneeled in silence by her couch,
Watching her sleep with looks of speechless love,
　　And the bright beaming stars
　　That through the casement shone.

ALASTOR

OR

THE SPIRIT OF SOLITUDE

SHELLEY'S PREFACE

THE poem entitled "ALASTOR," may be considered as allegorical of one of the most interesting situations of the human mind. It represents a youth of uncorrupted feelings and adventurous genius led forth by an imagination inflamed and purified through familiarity with all that is excellent and majestic, to the contemplation of the universe. He drinks deep of the fountains of knowledge, and is still insatiate. The magnificence and beauty of the external world sinks profoundly into the frame of his conceptions, and affords to their modifications a variety not to be exhausted. So long as it is possible for his desires to point towards objects thus infinite and unmeasured, he is joyous, and tranquil, and self-possessed. But the period arrives when these objects cease to suffice. His mind is at length suddenly awakened and thirsts for intercourse with an intelligence similar to itself. He images to himself the Being whom he loves. Conversant with speculations of the sublimest and most perfect natures, the vision in which he embodies his own imaginations unites all of wonderful, or wise, or beautiful, which the poet, the philosopher, or the lover could depicture. The intellectual faculties, the imagination, the functions of sense, have their respective requisitions on the sympathy of corresponding powers in other human beings. The Poet is represented as uniting these requisitions, and attaching them to a single image. He seeks in vain for a prototype of his conception. Blasted by his disappointment, he descends to an untimely grave.

The picture is not barren of instruction to actual men. The Poet's self-centred seclusion was avenged by the furies of an irresistible passion pursuing him to speedy ruin. But that Power which strikes the luminaries of the world with sudden darkness and extinction, by awakening them to too exquisite a perception of its influences, dooms to a slow and poisonous decay those meaner spirits that dare to abjure its dominion. Their destiny is more abject and inglorious as their delinquency is more contemptible and pernicious. They who, deluded by no generous error, instigated by no sacred thirst of doubtful knowledge, duped by no illustrious superstition, loving nothing on this earth, and cherishing no hopes beyond, yet keep aloof from sympathies with their kind, rejoicing neither in human joy nor mourning with human grief; these, and such as they, have their apportioned curse. They languish, because none feel with them their common nature. They are morally dead. They are neither friends, nor lovers, nor fathers, nor citizens of the world, nor benefactors of their country. Among those who attempt to exist without human sympathy, the pure and tender-hearted perish through the intensity and passion of their search after its communities, when the vacancy of their spirit suddenly makes itself felt. All else, selfish, blind, and torpid, are those unforeseeing multitudes who constitute, together with their own, the lasting misery and loneliness of the world. Those who love not their fellow-beings, live unfruitful lives, and prepare for their old age a miserable grave.

> The good die first,
> And those whose hearts are dry as summer dust,
> Burn to the socket!

December 14, 1815.

ALASTOR

OR

THE SPIRIT OF SOLITUDE

Nondum amabam, et amare amabam, quærebam quid amarem,
amans amare.—*Confess. St. August.*

EARTH, ocean, air, belovèd brotherhood!
If our great Mother has imbued my soul
With aught of natural piety to feel
Your love, and recompense the boon with mine;
If dewy morn, and odorous noon, and even,
With sunset and its gorgeous ministers,
And solemn midnight's tingling silentness;
If autumn's hollow sighs in the sere wood,
And winter robing with pure snow and crowns
Of starry ice the grey grass and bare boughs;
If spring's voluptuous pantings when she breathes
Her first sweet kisses, have been dear to me;
If no bright bird, insect, or gentle beast
I consciously have injured, but still loved
And cherished these my kindred; then forgive
This boast, belovèd brethren, and withdraw
No portion of your wonted favour now!

Mother of this unfathomable world!
Favour my solemn song, for I have loved
Thee ever, and thee only; I have watched
Thy shadow, and the darkness of thy steps,
And my heart ever gazes on the depth
Of thy deep mysteries. I have made my bed

In charnels and on coffins, where black death
Keeps record of the trophies won from thee,
Hoping to still these obstinate questionings
Of thee and thine, by forcing some lone ghost,
Thy messenger, to render up the tale
Of what we are.   In lone and silent hours,
When night makes a weird sound of its own stillness,
Like an inspired and desperate alchymist
Staking his very life on some dark hope,
Have I mixed awful talk and asking looks
With my most innocent love, until strange tears
Uniting with those breathless kisses, made
Such magic as compels the charmèd night
To render up thy charge : . . . and, though ne'er yet
Thou hast unveiled thy inmost sanctuary,
Enough from incommunicable dream,
And twilight phantasms, and deep noonday thought,
Has shone within me, that serenely now
And moveless, as a long-forgotten lyre
Suspended in the solitary dome
Of some mysterious and deserted fane,
I wait thy breath, Great Parent, that my strain
May modulate with murmurs of the air,
And motions of the forests and the sea,
And voice of living beings, and woven hymns
Of night and day, and the deep heart of man.

There was a Poet whose untimely tomb
No human hands with pious reverence reared,
But the charmed eddies of autumnal winds
Built o'er his mouldering bones a pyramid
Of mouldering leaves in the waste wilderness :—
A lovely youth,—no mourning maiden decked
With weeping flowers, or votive cypress wreath,
The lone couch of his everlasting sleep :—
Gentle, and brave, and generous,—no lorn bard
Breathed o'er his dark fate one melodious sigh :
He lived, he died, he sung, in solitude.

Strangers have wept to hear his passionate notes,
And virgins, as unknown he passed, have pined
And wasted for fond love of his wild eyes.
The fire of those soft orbs has ceased to burn,
And Silence, too enamoured of that voice,
Locks its mute music in her rugged cell.

By solemn vision, and bright silver dream,
His infancy was nurtured.   Every sight
And sound from the vast earth and ambient air,
Sent to his heart its choicest impulses.
The fountains of divine philosophy
Fled not his thirsting lips, and all of great,
Or good, or lovely, which the sacred past
In truth or fable consecrates, he felt
And knew.   When early youth had passed, he left
His cold fireside and alienated home
To seek strange truths in undiscovered lands.
Many a wide waste and tangled wilderness
Has lured his fearless steps ; and he has bought
With his sweet voice and eyes, from savage men,
His rest and food.   Nature's most secret steps
He like her shadow has pursued, where'er
The red volcano overcanopies
Its fields of snow and pinnacles of ice
With burning smoke, or where bitumen lakes
On black bare pointed islets ever beat
With sluggish surge, or where the secret caves
Rugged and dark, winding among the springs
Of fire and poison, inaccessible
To avarice or pride, their starry domes
Of diamond and of gold expand above
Numberless and immeasurable halls,
Frequent with crystal column, and clear shrines
Of pearl, and thrones radiant with chrysolite.
Nor had that scene of ampler majesty
Than gems or gold, the varying roof of heaven
And the green earth, lost in his heart its claims

To love and wonder ; he would linger long
In lonesome vales, making the wild his home,
Until the doves and squirrels would partake
From his innocuous hand his bloodless food,
Lured by the gentle meaning of his looks,
And the wild antelope, that starts whene'er
The dry leaf rustles in the brake, suspend
Her timid steps to gaze upon a form
More graceful than her own.

                                    His wandering step,
Obedient to high thoughts, has visited
The awful ruins of the days of old :
Athens, and Tyre, and Balbec, and the waste
Where stood Jerusalem, the fallen towers
Of Babylon, the eternal pyramids,
Memphis and Thebes, and whatsoe'er of strange
Sculptured on alabaster obelisk
Or jasper tomb, or mutilated sphynx,
Dark Æthiopia in her desert hills
Conceals.   Among the ruined temples there,
Stupendous columns, and wild images
Of more than man, where marble dæmons watch
The Zodiac's brazen mystery, and dead men
Hang their mute thoughts on the mute walls around,
He lingered, poring on memorials
Of the world's youth, through the long burning day
Gazed on those speechless shapes, nor, when the moon
Filled the mysterious halls with floating shades,
Suspended he that task, but ever gazed
And gazed, till meaning on his vacant mind
Flashed like strong inspiration, and he saw
The thrilling secrets of the birth of time.

Meanwhile an Arab maiden brought his food,
Her daily portion, from her father's tent,
And spread her matting for his couch, and stole
From duties and repose to tend his steps :—
Enamoured, yet not daring for deep awe

To speak her love :—and watched his nightly sleep,
Sleepless herself, to gaze upon his lips
Parted in slumber, whence the regular breath
Of innocent dreams arose : then, when red morn
Made paler the pale moon, to her cold home
Wildered, and wan, and panting, she returned.

The Poet wandering on, through Arabie
And Persia, and the wild Carmanian waste,
And o'er the aërial mountains which pour down
Indus and Oxus from their icy caves,
In joy and exultation held his way ;
Till in the vale of Cashmire, far within
Its loneliest dell, where odorous plants entwine
Beneath the hollow rocks a natural bower,
Beside a sparkling rivulet he stretched
His languid limbs. A vision on his sleep
There came, a dream of hopes that never yet
Had flushed his cheek. He dreamed a veilèd maid
Sate near him, talking in low solemn tones.
Her voice was like the voice of his own soul
Heard in the calm of thought ; its music long,
Like woven sounds of streams and breezes, held
His inmost sense suspended in its web
Of many-coloured woof and shifting hues.
Knowledge and truth and virtue were her theme,
And lofty hopes of divine liberty,
Thoughts the most dear to him, and poesy,
Herself a poet. Soon the solemn mood
Of her pure mind kindled through all her frame
A permeating fire : wild numbers then
She raised, with voice stifled in tremulous sobs
Subdued by its own pathos : her fair hands
Were bare alone, sweeping from some strange harp
Strange symphony, and in their branching veins
The eloquent blood told an ineffable tale.
The beating of her heart was heard to fill
The pauses of her music, and her breath

Tumultuously accorded with those fits
Of intermitted song.   Sudden she rose,
As if her heart impatiently endured
Its bursting burthen : at the sound he turned,
And saw by the warm light of their own life
Her glowing limbs beneath the sinuous veil
Of woven wind, her outspread arms now bare,
Her dark locks floating in the breath of night,
Her beamy bending eyes, her parted lips
Outstretched, and pale, and quivering eagerly.
His strong heart sunk and sickened with excess
Of love.   He reared his shuddering limbs and quelled
His gasping breath, and spread his arms to meet
Her panting bosom : . . . she drew back a while,
Then, yielding to the irresistible joy,
With frantic gesture and short breathless cry
Folded his frame in her dissolving arms.
Now blackness veiled his dizzy eyes, and night
Involved and swallowed up the vision ; sleep,
Like a dark flood suspended in its course,
Rolled back its impulse on his vacant brain.

　　Roused by the shock he started from his trance—
The cold white light of morning, the blue moon
Low in the west, the clear and garish hills,
The distinct valley and the vacant woods,
Spread round him where he stood.   Whither have fled
The hues of heaven that canopied his bower
Of yesternight ?   The sounds that soothed his sleep,
The mystery and the majesty of Earth,
The joy, the exultation ?   His wan eyes
Gaze on the empty scene as vacantly
As ocean's moon looks on the moon in heaven.
The spirit of sweet human love has sent
A vision to the sleep of him who spurned
Her choicest gifts.   He eagerly pursues
Beyond the realms of dream that fleeting shade ;
He overleaps the bounds.   Alas ! alas !

Were limbs, and breath, and being intertwined
Thus treacherously ?   Lost, lost, for ever lost,
In the wide pathless desert of dim sleep,
That beautiful shape !   Does the dark gate of death
Conduct to thy mysterious paradise,
O Sleep ?   Does the bright arch of rainbow clouds,
And pendent mountains seen in the calm lake,
Lead only to a black and watery depth,
While death's blue vault, with loathliest vapours hung,
Where every shade which the foul grave exhales
Hides its dead eye from the detested day,
Conduct, O Sleep, to thy delightful realms ?
This doubt with sudden tide flowed on his heart,
The insatiate hope which it awakened stung
His brain even like despair.

                While daylight held
The sky, the Poet kept mute conference
With his still soul.   At night the passion came,
Like the fierce fiend of a distempered dream,
And shook him from his rest, and led him forth
Into the darkness.—As an eagle grasped
In folds of the green serpent, feels her breast
Burn with the poison, and precipitates
Through night and day, tempest, and calm, and
      cloud,
Frantic with dizzying anguish, her blind flight
O'er the wide aëry wilderness : thus driven
By the bright shadow of that lovely dream,
Beneath the cold glare of the desolate night,
Through tangled swamps and deep precipitous dells,
Startling with careless step the moon-light snake,
He fled.   Red morning dawned upon his flight,
Shedding the mockery of its vital hues
Upon his cheek of death.   He wandered on
Till vast Aornos seen from Petra's steep
Hung o'er the low horizon like a cloud ;
Through Balk, and where the desolated tombs
Of Parthian kings scatter to every wind

4

Their wasting dust, wildly he wandered on,
Day after day, a weary waste of hours,
Bearing within his life the brooding care
That ever fed on its decaying flame.
And now his limbs were lean ; his scattered hair
Sered by the autumn of strange suffering
Sung dirges in the wind ; his listless hand
Hung like dead bone within its withered skin ;
Life, and the lustre that consumed it, shone
As in a furnace burning secretly
From his dark eyes alone.   The cottagers,
Who ministered with human charity
His human wants, beheld with wondering awe
Their fleeting visitant.   The mountaineer,
Encountering on some dizzy precipice
That spectral form, deemed that the Spirit of wind
With lightning eyes, and eager breath, and feet
Disturbing not the drifted snow, had paused
In its career : the infant would conceal
His troubled visage in his mother's robe
In terror at the glare of those wild eyes,
To remember their strange light in many a dream
Of after-times ; but youthful maidens, taught
By nature, would interpret half the woe
That wasted him, would call him with false names
Brother, and friend, would press his pallid hand
At parting, and watch, dim through tears, the path
Of his departure from their father's door.

  At length upon the lone Chorasmian shore
He paused, a wide and melancholy waste
Of putrid marshes.   A strong impulse urged
His steps to the sea-shore.   A swan was there,
Beside a sluggish stream among the reeds.
It rose as he approached, and with strong wings
Scaling the upward sky, bent its bright course
High over the immeasurable main.
His eyes pursued its flight.—" Thou hast a home,

Beautiful bird ; thou voyagest to thine home,
Where thy sweet mate will twine her downy neck
With thine, and welcome thy return with eyes
Bright in the lustre of their own fond joy.
And what am I that I should linger here,
With voice far sweeter than thy dying notes,
Spirit more vast than thine, frame more attuned
To beauty, wasting these surpassing powers
In the deaf air, to the blind earth, and heaven
That echoes not my thoughts ? '' A gloomy smile
Of desperate hope wrinkled his quivering lips.
For sleep, he knew, kept most relentlessly
Its precious charge, and silent death exposed,
Faithless perhaps as sleep, a shadowy lure,
With doubtful smile mocking its own strange charms.

Startled by his own thoughts he looked around.
There was no fair fiend near him, not a sight
Or sound of awe but in his own deep mind.
A little shallop floating near the shore
Caught the impatient wandering of his gaze.
It had been long abandoned, for its sides
Gaped wide with many a rift, and its frail joints
Swayed with the undulations of the tide.
A restless impulse urged him to embark
And meet lone Death on the drear ocean's waste ;
For well he knew that mighty Shadow loves
The slimy caverns of the populous deep.

The day was fair and sunny, sea and sky
Drank its inspiring radiance, and the wind
Swept strongly from the shore, blackening the waves.
Following his eager soul, the wanderer
Leaped in the boat, he spread his cloak aloft
On the bare mast, and took his lonely seat,
And felt the boat speed o'er the tranquil sea
Like a torn cloud before the hurricane.

As one that in a silver vision floats
Obedient to the sweep of odorous winds
Upon resplendent clouds, so rapidly
Along the dark and ruffled waters fled
The straining boat.—A whirlwind swept it on,
With fierce gusts and precipitating force,
Through the white ridges of the chafèd sea.
The waves arose.   Higher and higher still
Their fierce necks writhed beneath the tempest's scourge
Like serpents struggling in a vulture's grasp.
Calm and rejoicing in the fearful war
Of wave ruining on wave, and blast on blast
Descending, and black flood on whirlpool driven
With dark obliterating course, he sate :
As if their genii were the ministers
Appointed to conduct him to the light
Of those belovèd eyes, the Poet sate
Holding the steady helm.   Evening came on,
The beams of sunset hung their rainbow hues
High 'mid the shifting domes of sheeted spray
That canopied his path o'er the waste deep ;
Twilight, ascending slowly from the east,
Entwined in duskier wreaths her braided locks
O'er the fair front and radiant eyes of day ;
Night followed, clad with stars.   On every side
More horribly the multitudinous streams
Of ocean's mountainous waste to mutual war
Rushed in dark tumult thundering, as to mock
The calm and spangled sky.   The little boat
Still fled before the storm ; still fled, like foam
Down the steep cataract of a wintry river ;
Now pausing on the edge of the riven wave :
Now leaving far behind the bursting mass
That fell, convulsing ocean.   Safely fled—
As if that frail and wasted human form,
Had been an elemental god.

                              At midnight
The moon arose : and lo ! the ætherial cliffs

Of Caucasus, whose icy summits shone
Among the stars like sunlight, and around
Whose caverned base the whirlpools and the waves
Bursting and eddying irresistibly
Rage and resound for ever.—Who shall save ?—
The boat fled on,—the boiling torrent drove,—
The crags closed round with black and jaggèd arms,
The shattered mountain overhung the sea,
And faster still, beyond all human speed,
Suspended on the sweep of the smooth wave,
The little boat was driven.   A cavern there
Yawned, and amid its slant and winding depths
Ingulphed the rushing sea.   The boat fled on
With unrelaxing speed.—" Vision and Love ! "
The Poet cried aloud, " I have beheld
The path of thy departure.   Sleep and death
Shall not divide us long ! "

               The boat pursued
The windings of the cavern.   Daylight shone
At length upon that gloomy river's flow ;
Now, where the fiercest war among the waves
Is calm, on the unfathomable stream
The boat moved slowly.   Where the mountain, riven,
Exposed those black depths to the azure sky,
Ere yet the flood's enormous volume fell
Even to the base of Caucasus, with sound
That shook the everlasting rocks, the mass
Filled with one whirlpool all that ample chasm ;
Stair above stair the eddying waters rose
Circling immeasurably fast, and laved
With alternating dash the gnarled roots
Of mighty trees, that stretched their giant arms
In darkness over it.   I' the midst was left,
Reflecting, yet distorting every cloud,
A pool of treacherous and tremendous calm.
Seized by the sway of the ascending stream,
With dizzy swiftness, round, and round, and round,
Ridge after ridge the straining boat arose,

Till on the verge of the extremest curve,
Where through an opening of the rocky bank,
The waters overflow, and a smooth spot
Of glassy quiet 'mid those battling tides
Is left, the boat paused shuddering.—Shall it sink
Down the abyss ? Shall the reverting stress
Of that resistless gulph embosom it ?
Now shall it fall ?—A wandering stream of wind,
Breathed from the west, has caught the expanded sail,
And, lo ! with gentle motion, between banks
Of mossy slope, and on a placid stream,
Beneath a woven grove it sails, and, hark !
The ghastly torrent mingles its far roar,
With the breeze murmuring in the musical woods.
Where the embowering trees recede, and leave
A little space of green expanse, the cove
Is closed by meeting banks, whose yellow flowers
For ever gaze on their own drooping eyes,
Reflected in the crystal calm. The wave
Of the boat's motion marred their pensive task,
Which nought but vagrant bird, or wanton wind,
Or falling spear-grass, or their own decay
Had e'er disturbed before. The Poet longed
To deck with their bright hues his withered hair,
But on his heart its solitude returned,
And he forbore. Not the strong impulse hid
In those flushed cheeks, bent eyes, and shadowy frame
Had yet performed its ministry : it hung
Upon his life, as lightning in a cloud
Gleams, hovering ere it vanish, ere the floods
Of night close over it.
                              The noonday sun
Now shone upon the forest, one vast mass
Of mingling shade, whose brown magnificence
A narrow vale embosoms. There, huge caves,
Scooped in the dark base of their aëry rocks
Mocking its moans, respond and roar for ever.
The meeting boughs and implicated leaves

Wove twilight o'er the Poet's path, as led
By love, or dream, or god, or mightier Death,
He sought in Nature's dearest haunt, some bank,
Her cradle, and his sepulchre.   More dark
And dark the shades accumulate.   The oak,
Expanding its immense and knotty arms,
Embraces the light beech.   The pyramids
Of the tall cedar overarching, frame
Most solemn domes within, and far below,
Like clouds suspended in an emerald sky,
The ash and the acacia floating hang
Tremulous and pale.   Like restless serpents, clothed
In rainbow and in fire, the parasites,
Starred with ten thousand blossoms, flow around
The grey trunks, and, as gamesome infants' eyes,
With gentle meanings, and most innocent wiles,
Fold their beams round the hearts of those that love,
These twine their tendrils with the wedded boughs
Uniting their close union ; the woven leaves
Make net-work of the dark blue light of day,
And the night's noontide clearness, mutable
As shapes in the weird clouds.   Soft mossy lawns
Beneath these canopies extend their swells,
Fragrant with perfumed herbs, and eyed with blooms
Minute yet beautiful.   One darkest glen
Sends from its woods of musk-rose, twined with jasmine,
A soul-dissolving odour, to invite
To some more lovely mystery.   Through the dell,
Silence and Twilight here, twin-sisters, keep
Their noonday watch, and sail among the shades,
Like vaporous shapes half seen ; beyond, a well,
Dark, gleaming, and of most translucent wave,
Images all the woven boughs above,
And each depending leaf, and every speck
Of azure sky, darting between their chasms ;
Nor aught else in the liquid mirror laves
Its portraiture, but some inconstant star
Between one foliaged lattice twinkling fair,

Or, painted bird, sleeping beneath the moon,
Or gorgeous insect floating motionless,
Unconscious of the day, ere yet his wings,
Have spread their glories to the gaze of noon.

Hither the Poet came.   His eyes beheld
Their own wan light through the reflected lines
Of his thin hair, distinct in the dark depth
Of that still fountain ; as the human heart,
Gazing in dreams over the gloomy grave,
Sees its own treacherous likeness there.   He heard
The motion of the leaves, the grass that sprung
Startled and glanced and trembled even to feel
An unaccustomed presence, and the sound
Of the sweet brook that from the secret springs
Of that dark fountain rose.   A Spirit seemed
To stand beside him—clothed in no bright robes
Of shadowy silver or enshrining light,
Borrowed from aught the visible world affords
Of grace, or majesty, or mystery ;—
But, undulating woods, and silent well,
And leaping rivulet, and evening gloom
Now deepening the dark shades, for speech assuming,
Held commune with him, as if he and it
Were all that was,—only . . . when his regard
Was raised by intense pensiveness, . . . two eyes,
Two starry eyes, hung in the gloom of thought,
And seemed with their serene and azure smiles
To beckon him.

Obedient to the light
That shone within his soul, he went, pursuing
The windings of the dell.—The rivulet
Wanton and wild, through many a green ravine
Beneath the forest flowed.   Sometimes it fell
Among the moss with hollow harmony
Dark and profound.   Now on the polished stones
It danced ; like childhood laughing as it went :

Then, through the plain in tranquil wanderings crept,
Reflecting every herb and drooping bud
That overhung its quietness.—" O stream !
Whose source is inaccessibly profound,
Whither do thy mysterious waters tend ?
Thou imagest my life. Thy darksome stillness,
Thy dazzling waves, thy loud and hollow gulphs,
Thy searchless fountain, and invisible course
Have each their type in me : and the wide sky,
And measureless ocean may declare as soon
What oozy cavern or what wandering cloud
Contains thy waters, as the universe
Tell where these living thoughts reside, when stretched
Upon thy flowers my bloodless limbs shall waste
I' the passing wind ! "

                 Beside the grassy shore
Of the small stream he went ; he did impress
On the green moss his tremulous step, that caught
Strong shuddering from his burning limbs. As one
Roused by some joyous madness from the couch
Of fever, he did move ; yet, not like him,
Forgetful of the grave, where, when the flame
Of his frail exultation shall be spent,
He must descend. With rapid steps he went
Beneath the shade of trees, beside the flow
Of the wild babbling rivulet ; and now
The forest's solemn canopies were changed
For the uniform and lightsome evening sky.
Grey rocks did peep from the spare moss, and stemmed
The struggling brook : tall spires of windlestrae
Threw their thin shadows down the rugged slope,
And naught but gnarled roots of ancient pines,
Branchless and blasted, clenched with grasping roots
The unwilling soil. A gradual change was here,
Yet ghastly. For, as fast years flow away,
The smooth brow gathers, and the hair grows thin
And white, and where irradiate dewy eyes

Had shone, gleam stony orbs :—so from his steps
Bright flowers departed, and the beautiful shade
Of the green groves, with all their odorous winds
And musical motions.   Calm, he still pursued
The stream, that with a larger volume now
Rolled through the labyrinthine dell ; and there
Fretted a path through its descending curves
With its wintry speed.   On every side now rose
Rocks, which, in unimaginable forms,
Lifted their black and barren pinnacles
In the light of evening, and its precipice
Obscuring the ravine, disclosed above,
'Mid toppling stones, black gulphs and yawning caves,
Whose windings gave ten thousand various tongues
To the loud stream.   Lo ! where the pass expands
Its stony jaws, the abrupt mountain breaks,
And seems, with its accumulated crags,
To overhang the world : for wide expand
Beneath the wan stars and descending moon
Islanded seas, blue mountains, mighty streams,
Dim tracts and vast, robed in the lustrous gloom
Of leaden-coloured even, and fiery hills
Mingling their flames with twilight, on the verge
Of the remote horizon.   The near scene,
In naked and severe simplicity,
Made contrast with the universe.   A pine,
Rock-rooted, stretched athwart the vacancy
Its swinging boughs, to each inconstant blast
Yielding one only response, at each pause
In most familiar cadence, with the howl,
The thunder and the hiss of homeless streams
Mingling its solemn song, whilst the broad river,
Foaming and hurrying o'er its rugged path,
Fell into that immeasurable void
Scattering its waters to the passing winds.

Yet the grey precipice and solemn pine,
And torrent, were not all ;—one silent nook

Was there.   Even on the edge of that vast mountain,
Upheld by knotty roots and fallen rocks,
It overlooked in its serenity
The dark earth, and the bending vault of stars.
It was a tranquil spot, that seemed to smile
Even in the lap of horror.   Ivy clasped
The fissured stones with its entwining arms,
And did embower with leaves for ever green,
And berries dark, the smooth and even space
Of its inviolated floor, and here
The children of the autumnal whirlwind bore,
In wanton sport, those bright leaves, whose decay,
Red, yellow, or ætherially pale,
Rivals the pride of summer.   'Tis the haunt
Of every gentle wind, whose breath can teach
The wilds to love tranquility.   One step,
One human step alone, has ever broken
The stillness of its solitude :—one voice
Alone inspired its echoes ;—even that voice
Which hither came, floating among the winds,
And led the loveliest among human forms
To make their wild haunts the depository
Of all the grace and beauty that endued
Its motions, render up its majesty,
Scatter its music on the unfeeling storm,
And to the damp leaves and blue cavern mould,
Nurses of rainbow flowers and branching moss,
Commit the colours of that varying cheek,
That snowy breast, those dark and drooping eyes.

The dim and hornèd moon hung low, and poured
A sea of lustre on the horizon's verge
That overflowed its mountains.   Yellow mist
Filled the unbounded atmosphere, and drank
Wan moonlight even to fulness : not a star
Shone, not a sound was heard ; the very winds,
Danger's grim playmates, on that precipice
Slept, clasped in his embrace.—O, storm of death !

Whose sightless speed divides this sullen night :
And thou, colossal Skeleton, that, still
Guiding its irresistible career
In thy devastating omnipotence,
Art king of this frail world, from the red field
Of slaughter, from the reeking hospital,
The patriot's sacred couch, the snowy bed
Of innocence, the scaffold and the throne,
A mighty voice invokes thee.   Ruin calls
His brother Death.   A rare and regal prey
He hath prepared, prowling around the world ;
Glutted with which thou mayst repose, and men
Go to their graves like flowers or creeping worms,
Nor ever more offer at thy dark shrine
The unheeded tribute of a broken heart.

When on the threshold of the green recess
The wanderer's footsteps fell, he knew that death
Was on him.   Yet a little, ere it fled,
Did he resign his high and holy soul
To images of the majestic past,
That paused within his passive being now,
Like winds that bear sweet music, when they breathe
Through some dim latticed chamber.   He did place
His pale lean hand upon the rugged trunk
Of the old pine.   Upon an ivied stone
Reclined his languid head, his limbs did rest,
Diffused and motionless, on the smooth brink
Of that obscurest chasm ;—and thus he lay,
Surrendering to their final impulses
The hovering powers of life.   Hope and despair,
The torturers, slept ; no mortal pain or fear
Marred his repose, the influxes of sense,
And his own being unalloyed by pain,
Yet feebler and more feeble, calmly fed
The stream of thought, till he lay breathing there
At peace, and faintly smiling :—his last sight
Was the great moon, which o'er the western line

Of the wide world her mighty horn suspended,
With whose dun beams inwoven darkness seemed
To mingle.   Now upon the jaggèd hills
It rests, and still as the divided frame
Of the vast meteor sunk, the Poet's blood,
That ever beat in mystic sympathy
With nature's ebb and flow, grew feebler still:
And when two lessening points of light alone
Gleamed through the darkness, the alternate gasp
Of his faint respiration scarce did stir
The stagnate night:—till the minutest ray
Was quenched, the pulse yet lingered in his heart.
It paused—it fluttered.   But when heaven remained
Utterly black, the murky shades involved
An image, silent, cold, and motionless,
As their own voiceless earth and vacant air.
Even as a vapour fed with golden beams
That ministered on sunlight, ere the west
Eclipses it, was now that wondrous frame—
No sense, no motion, no divinity—
A fragile lute, on whose harmonious strings
The breath of heaven did wander—a bright stream
Once fed with many-voicèd waves—a dream
Of youth, which night and time have quenched for ever,
Still, dark, and dry, and unremembered now.

O, for Medea's wondrous alchemy,
Which wheresoe'er it fell made the earth gleam
With bright flowers, and the wintry boughs exhale
From vernal blooms fresh fragrance!   O, that God,
Profuse of poisons, would concede the chalice
Which but one living man has drained, who now,
Vessel of deathless wrath, a slave that feels
No proud exemption in the blighting curse
He bears, over the world wanders for ever,
Lone as incarnate death!   O, that the dream
Of dark magician in his visioned cave,
Raking the cinders of a crucible

For life and power, even when his feeble hand
Shakes in its last decay, were the true law
Of this so lovely world ! But thou art fled
Like some frail exhalation ; which the dawn
Robes in its golden beams,—ah ! thou hast fled !
The brave, the gentle, and the beautiful,
The child of grace and genius. Heartless things
Are done and said i' the world, and many worms
And beasts and men live on, and mighty Earth
From sea and mountain, city and wilderness,
In vesper low or joyous orison,
Lifts still its solemn voice :—but thou art fled—
Thou canst no longer know or love the shapes
Of this phantasmal scene, who have to thee
Been purest ministers, who are, alas !
Now thou art not. Upon those pallid lips
So sweet even in their silence, on those eyes
That image sleep in death, upon that form
Yet safe from the worm's outrage, let no tear
Be shed—not even in thought. Nor, when those hues
Are gone, and those divinest lineaments,
Worn by the senseless wind, shall live alone
In the frail pauses of this simple strain,
Let not high verse, mourning the memory
Of that which is no more, or painting's woe
Or sculpture, speak in feeble imagery
Their own cold powers. Art and eloquence,
And all the shows o' the world are frail and vain
To weep a loss that turns their lights to shade.
It is a woe too " deep for tears," when all
Is reft at once, when some surpassing Spirit,
Whose light adorned the world around it, leaves
Those who remain behind, not sobs or groans,
The passionate tumult of a clinging hope ;
But pale despair and cold tranquillity,
Nature's vast frame, the web of human things,
Birth and the grave, that are not as they were.

THE CENCI

A TRAGEDY IN FIVE ACTS

1819

DEDICATION

TO

LEIGH HUNT, Esq.

MY DEAR FRIEND,

I inscribe with your name, from a distant country, and after an absence whose months have seemed years, this the latest of my literary efforts.

Those writings which I have hitherto published have been little else than visions which impersonate my own apprehensions of the beautiful and the just. I can also perceive in them the literary defects incidental to youth and impatience ; they are dreams of what ought to be, or may be. The drama which I now present to you is a sad reality. I lay aside the presumptuous attitude of an instructor, and am content to paint, with such colours as my own heart furnishes, that which has been.

Had I known a person more highly endowed than yourself with all that it becomes a man to possess, I had solicited for this work the ornament of his name. One more gentle, honourable, innocent and brave ; one of more exalted toleration for all who do and think evil, and yet himself more free from evil ; one who knows better how to receive, and how to confer a benefit though he must ever confer far more than he can receive ; one of simpler, and, in the highest sense of the word, of purer life and manners I never knew : and I had already been fortunate in friendships when your name was added to the list.

In that patient and irreconcilable enmity with domestic and political tyranny and imposture which the tenour of your life has illustrated, and which, had I health and talents, should illustrate mine, let us, comforting each other in our task, live and die.

All happiness attend you!

Your affectionate friend,

PERCY B. SHELLEY.

ROME, *May* 29, 1819.

PREFACE

A MANUSCRIPT was communicated to me during my travels in Italy, which was copied from the archives of the Cenci Palace at Rome, and contains a detailed account of the horrors which ended in the extinction of one of the noblest and richest families of that city during the Pontificate of Clement VIII., in the year 1599. The story is that an old man, having spent his life in debauchery and wickedness, conceived at length an implacable hatred towards his children ; which showed itself towards one daughter under the form of an incestuous passion, aggravated by every circumstance of cruelty and violence. This daughter, after long and vain attempts to escape from what she considered a perpetual contamination both of body and mind, at length plotted with her mother-in-law and brother to murder their common tyrant. The young maiden who was urged to this tremendous deed by an impulse which overpowered its horror was evidently a most gentle and amiable being, a creature formed to adorn and be admired, and thus violently thwarted from her nature by the necessity of circumstance and opinion. The deed was quickly discovered, and, in spite of the most earnest prayers made to the Pope by the highest persons in Rome, the criminals were put to death. The old man had during his life repeatedly bought his pardon from the Pope for capital crimes of the most enormous and unspeakable kind, at the price of a hundred thousand crowns ; the death therefore of his victims can scarcely be accounted for by the love of justice. The Pope, among other motives for

severity, probably felt that whoever killed the Count
Cenci deprived his treasury of a certain and copious
source of revenue.[1] Such a story, if told so as to
present to the reader all the feelings of those who once
acted it, their hopes and fears, their confidences and
misgivings, their various interests, passions and opinions,
acting upon and with each other, yet all conspiring to
one tremendous end, would be as a light to make
apparent some of the most dark and secret caverns
of the human heart.

On my arrival at Rome I found that the story of the
Cenci was a subject not to be mentioned in Italian
society without awakening a deep and breathless
interest ; and that the feelings of the company never
failed to incline to a romantic pity for the wrongs, and
a passionate exculpation of the horrible deed to which
they urged her, who has been mingled two centuries
with the common dust. All ranks of people knew the
outlines of this history, and participated in the over-
whelming interest which it seems to have the magic
of exciting in the human heart. I had a copy of Guido's
picture of Beatrice which is preserved in the Colonna
Palace, and my servant instantly recognized it as the
portrait of *La Cenci*.

This national and universal interest which the story
produces and has produced for two centuries and among
all ranks of people in a great City, where the imagination
is kept for ever active and awake, first suggested to me
the conception of its fitness for a dramatic purpose.
In fact it is a tragedy which has already received, from
its capacity of awakening and sustaining the sympathy
of men, approbation and success. Nothing remained,
as I imagined, but to clothe it to the apprehensions

---

[1] The Papal Government formerly took the most extraordinary
precautions against the publicity of facts which offer so tragical a
demonstration of its own wickedness and weakness ; so that the
communication of the MS. had become, until very lately, a matter
of some difficulty.

of my countrymen in such language and action as would bring it home to their hearts. The deepest and the sublimest tragic compositions, *King Lear* and the two plays in which the tale of Œdipus is told, were stories which already existed in tradition, as matters of popular belief and interest, before Shakespeare and Sophocles made them familiar to the sympathy of all succeeding generations of mankind.

This story of the Cenci is indeed eminently fearful and monstrous : anything like a dry exhibition of it on the stage would be insupportable. The person who would treat such a subject must increase the ideal, and diminish the actual horror of the events, so that the pleasure which arises from the poetry which exists in these tempestuous sufferings and crimes may mitigate the pain of the contemplation of the moral deformity from which they spring. There must also be nothing attempted to make the exhibition subservient to what is vulgarly termed a moral purpose. The highest moral purpose aimed at in the highest species of the drama, is the teaching the human heart, through its sympathies and antipathies, the knowledge of itself ; in proportion to the possession of which knowledge, every human being is wise, just, sincere, tolerant and kind. If dogmas can do more, it is well : but a drama is no fit place for the enforcement of them. Undoubtedly, no person can be truly dishonoured by the act of another ; and the fit return to make to the most enormous injuries is kindness and forbearance, and a resolution to convert the injurer from his dark passions by peace and love. Revenge, retaliation, atonement, are pernicious mistakes. If Beatrice had thought in this manner she would have been wiser and better ; but she would never have been a tragic character : the few whom such an exhibition would have interested, could never have been sufficiently interested for a dramatic purpose, from the want of finding sympathy in their interest among the mass who surround them. It is in the restless and anatomizing casuistry with which men seek the justification of Beatrice, yet feel that she has done what needs justification ; it is in the superstitious horror with which they contemplate alike her wrongs and their revenge ; that the dramatic character of what she did and suffered consists.

I have endeavoured as nearly as possible to represent the characters as they probably were, and have sought to avoid the error of making them actuated by my own conceptions of right or wrong, false or true—thus under a thin veil converting names and actions of the sixteenth century into cold impersonations of my own mind. They are represented as Catholics, and as Catholics deeply tinged with religion. To a Protestant apprehension there will appear something unnatural in the earnest and perpetual sentiment of the relations between God and men which pervade the tragedy of the Cenci. It will especially be startled at the combination of an undoubting persuasion of the truth of the popular religion with a cool and determined perseverance in enormous guilt. But religion in Italy is not, as in Protestant countries, a cloke to be worn on particular days ; or a passport which those who do not wish to be railed at carry with them to exhibit ; or a gloomy passion for penetrating the impenetrable mysteries of our being, which terrifies its possessor at the darkness of the abyss to the brink of which it has conducted him. Religion co-exists, as it were, in the mind of an Italian Catholic, with a faith in that of which all men have the most certain knowledge. It is interwoven with the whole fabric of life. It is adoration, faith, submission, penitence, blind admiration ; not a rule for moral conduct. It has no necessary connexion with any one virtue. The most atrocious villain may be rigidly devout, and, without any shock to established faith, confess himself to be so. Religion pervades intensely the whole frame of society, and is, according to the temper of the mind which it inhabits, a passion, a persuasion, an excuse, a refuge ; never a check. Cenci himself built a chapel in the court of his Palace, and dedicated it to St. Thomas the Apostle, and established masses for the peace of his soul. Thus in the first scene of the fourth act Lucretia's design in exposing herself to the consequences of an expostulation with Cenci, after having administered the opiate, was to induce him by a feigned tale to confess himself before death ; this being esteemed by Catholics as essential to salvation ; and she only relinquishes her purpose when she perceives that her perseverance would expose Beatrice to new outrages.

I have avoided with great care in writing this play the introduction of what is commonly called mere poetry, and I imagine there will scarcely be found a detached simile or a single isolated description, unless Beatrice's description of the chasm appointed for her father's murder should be judged to be of that nature.[1]

In a dramatic composition the imagery and the passion should interpenetrate one another, the former being reserved simply for the full development and illustration of the latter. Imagination is as the immortal God which should assume flesh for the redemption of mortal passion. It is thus that the most remote and the most familiar imagery may alike be fit for dramatic purposes when employed in the illustration of strong feeling, which raises what is low, and levels to the apprehension that which is lofty, casting over all the shadow of its own greatness. In other respects, I have written more carelessly ; that is, without an over-fastidious and learned choice of words. In this respect I entirely agree with those modern critics who assert that in order to move men to true sympathy we must use the familiar language of men, and that our great ancestors the ancient English poets are the writers,

---

[1] An idea in this speech was suggested by a most sublime passage in *El Purgatorio de San Patricio* of Calderon ; the only plagiarism which I have intentionally committed in the whole piece.

a study of whom might incite us to do that for our own age which they have done for theirs. But it must be the real language of men in general and not that of any particular class to whose society the writer happens to belong. So much for what I have attempted; I need not be assured that success is a very different matter; particularly for one whose attention has but newly been awakened to the study of dramatic literature.

I endeavoured whilst at Rome to observe such monuments of this story as might be accessible to a stranger. The portrait of Beatrice at the Colonna Palace is admirable as a work of art; it was taken by Guido during her confinement in prison. But it is most interesting as a just representation of one of the loveliest specimens of the workmanship of Nature. There is a fixed and pale composure upon the features: she seems sad and stricken down in spirit, yet the despair thus expressed is lightened by the patience of gentleness. Her head is bound with folds of white drapery from which the yellow strings of her golden hair escape, and fall about her neck. The moulding of her face is exquisitely delicate; the eyebrows are distinct and arched: the lips have that permanent meaning of imagination and sensibility which suffering has not repressed and which it seems as if death scarcely could extinguish. Her forehead is large and clear; her eyes, which we are told were remarkable for their vivacity, are swollen with weeping and lustreless, but beautifully tender and serene. In the whole mien there is a simplicity and dignity which, united with her exquisite loveliness and deep sorrow, are inexpressibly pathetic. Beatrice Cenci appears to have been one of those rare persons in whom energy and gentleness dwell together without destroying one another: her nature was simple and profound. The crimes and miseries in which she was an actor and a sufferer are as the mask and the mantle in which circumstances clothed her for her impersonation on the scene of the world.

The Cenci Palace is of great extent ; and though in part modernized, there yet remains a vast and gloomy pile of feudal architecture in the same state as during the dreadful scenes which are the subject of this tragedy. The Palace is situated in an obscure corner of Rome, near the quarter of the Jews, and from the upper windows you see the immense ruins of Mount Palatine half hidden under their profuse overgrowth of trees. There is a court in one part of the Palace (perhaps that in which Cenci built the Chapel to St. Thomas), supported by granite columns and adorned with antique friezes of fine workmanship, and built up, according to the ancient Italian fashion, with balcony over balcony of open-work. One of the gates of the Palace formed of immense stones and leading through a passage, dark and lofty and opening into gloomy subterranean chambers, struck me particularly.

Of the Castle of Petrella, I could obtain no further information than that which is to be found in the manuscript.

DRAMATIS PERSONÆ

COUNT FRANCESCO CENCI
GIACOMO, } his Sons
BERNARDO,
CARDINAL CAMILLO
ORSINO, a Prelate

SAVELLA, the Pope's Legate
OLIMPIO, } Assassins
MARZIO,
ANDREA, Servant to Cenci

Nobles—Judges—Guards—Servants

LUCRETIA, Wife of Cenci, and Step-mother of
his children

BEATRICE, his Daughter

The SCENE *lies principally in Rome, but changes during the fourth Act
to Petrella, a castle among the Apulian Apennines*

TIME. *During the Pontificate of Clement VIII.*

THE CENCI

ACT I

SCENE I. *An Apartment in the Cenci Palace*

Enter COUNT CENCI, *and* CARDINAL CAMILLO

CAMILLO

THAT matter of the murder is hushed up
If you consent to yield his Holiness
Your fief that lies beyond the Pincian gate.—
It needed all my interest in the conclave
To bend him to this point : he said that you
Bought perilous impunity with your gold ;
That crimes like yours if once or twice compounded
Enriched the Church, and respited from hell
An erring soul which might repent and live :—
But that the glory and the interest
Of the high throne he fills, little consist
With making it a daily mart of guilt
As manifold and hideous as the deeds
Which you scarce hide from men's revolted eyes.

CENCI

The third of my possessions—let it go !
Aye, I once heard the nephew of the Pope
Had sent his architect to view the ground,
Meaning to build a villa on my vines
The next time I compounded with his uncle :
I little thought he should outwit me so !
Henceforth no witness—not the lamp—shall see

That which the vassal threatened to divulge
Whose throat is choked with dust for his reward.
The deed he saw could not have rated higher
Than his most worthless life :—it angers me !
Respited me from Hell !—So may the Devil
Respite their souls from Heaven. No doubt Pope
    Clement,
And his most charitable nephews, pray
That the Apostle Peter and the saints
Will grant for their sake that I long enjoy
Strength, wealth, and pride, and lust, and length of days
Wherein to act the deeds which are the stewards
Of their revenue.—But much yet remains
To which they show no title.

CAMILLO

                        Oh, Count Cenci !
So much that thou mightst honourably live
And reconcile thyself with thine own heart
And with thy God, and with the offended world.
How hideously look deeds of lust and blood
Through those snow-white and venerable hairs !—
Your children should be sitting round you now,
But that you fear to read upon their looks
The shame and misery you have written there.
Where is your wife ?   Where is your gentle daughter ?
Methinks her sweet looks, which make all things else
Beauteous and glad, might kill the fiend within you.
Why is she barred from all society
But her own strange and uncomplaining wrongs ?
Talk with me, Count,—you know I mean you well.
I stood beside your dark and fiery youth
Watching its bold and bad career, as men
Watch meteors, but it vanished not—I marked
Your desperate and remorseless manhood ; now
Do I behold you in dishonoured age,
Charged with a thousand unrepented crimes.

Yet I have ever hoped you would amend,
And in that hope have saved your life three times.

CENCI

For which Aldobrandino owes you now
My fief beyond the Pincian.—Cardinal,
One thing, I pray you, recollect henceforth,
And so we shall converse with less restraint.
A man you knew spoke of my wife and daughter—
He was accustomed to frequent my house ;
So the next day *his* wife and daughter came
And asked if I had seen him ; and I smiled :
I think they never saw him any more.

CAMILLO

Thou execrable man, beware !—

CENCI
                                    Of thee ?
Nay, this is idle :—We should know each other.
As to my character for what men call crime,
Seeing I please my senses as I list,
And vindicate that right with force or guile,
It is a public matter, and I care not
If I discuss it with you.   I may speak
Alike to you and my own conscious heart—
For you give out that you have half reformed me,
Therefore strong vanity will keep you silent
If fear should not ; both will, I do not doubt.
All men delight in sensual luxury,
All men enjoy revenge ; and most exult
Over the tortures they can never feel—
Flattering their secret peace with others' pain.
But I delight in nothing else.   I love
The sight of agony, and the sense of joy,
When this shall be another's, and that mine.
And I have no remorse and little fear,

Which are, I think, the checks of other men.
This mood has grown upon me, until now
Any design my captious fancy makes
The picture of its wish, and it forms none
But such as men like you would start to know,
Is as my natural food and rest debarred
Until it be accomplished.

CAMILLO

Art thou not
Most miserable ?

CENCI

Why, miserable ?—
No.—I am what your theologians call
Hardened ;—which they must be in impudence,
So to revile a man's peculiar taste.
True, I was happier than I am, while yet
Manhood remained to act the thing I thought ;
While lust was sweeter than revenge ; and now
Invention palls :—Aye, we must all grow old—
And but that there yet remains a deed to act
Whose horror might make sharp an appetite
Duller than mine—I'd do,—I know not what.
When I was young I thought of nothing else
But pleasure ; and I fed on honey sweets :
Men, by St. Thomas ! cannot live like bees,
And I grew tired :—yet, till I killed a foe,
And heard his groans, and heard his children's
          groans,
Knew I not what delight was else on earth,
Which now delights me little.   I the rather
Look on such pangs as terror ill conceals,
The dry fixed eyeball ; the pale quivering lip,
Which tell me that the spirit weeps within
Tears bitterer than the bloody sweat of Christ.
I rarely kill the body, which preserves,
Like a strong prison, the soul within my power,

Wherein I feed it with the breath of fear
For hourly pain.

CAMILLO

          Hell's most abandoned fiend
Did never, in the drunkenness of guilt,
Speak to his heart as now you speak to me ;
I thank my God that I believe you not.

Enter ANDREA

ANDREA

My Lord, a gentleman from Salamanca
Would speak with you.

CENCI

          Bid him attend me in
The grand saloon.   [*Exit* ANDREA.

CAMILLO

          Farewell ; and I will pray
Almighty God that thy false, impious words.
Tempt not his spirit to abandon thee.

                         [*Exit* CAMILLO.

CENCI

The third of my possessions !   I must use
Close husbandry, or gold, the old man's sword,
Falls from my withered hand.   But yesterday
There came an order from the Pope to make
Fourfold provision for my cursèd sons ;
Whom I had sent from Rome to Salamanca,
Hoping some accident might cut them off ;
And meaning if I could to starve them there.
I pray thee, God, send some quick death upon
     them !

Bernardo and my wife could not be worse
If dead and damned :—then, as to Beatrice—
                    (*looking around him suspiciously*)
I think they cannot hear me at that door ;
What if they should ?   And yet I need not speak
Though the heart triumphs with itself in words.
O, thou most silent air, that shalt not hear
What now I think !   Thou, pavement, which I
    tread
Towards her chamber,—let your echoes talk
Of my imperious step scorning surprise,
But not of my intent !—Andrea !

Enter ANDREA

ANDREA
                    My Lord ?

CENCI

Bid Beatrice attend me in her chamber
This evening :—no, at midnight and alone.

                                        [*Exeunt.*

SCENE II.   *A Garden of the Cenci Palace*

Enter BEATRICE *and* ORSINO, *as in
conversation*

BEATRICE
                    Pervert not truth,
Orsino.   You remember where we held
That conversation ;—nay, we see the spot
Even from this cypress ;—two long years are past
Since, on an April midnight, underneath
The moonlight ruins of mount Palatine,
I did confess to you my secret mind.

ORSINO

You said you loved me then.

BEATRICE

You are a priest
Speak to me not of love.

ORSINO

I may obtain
The dispensation of the Pope to marry.
Because I am a priest do you believe
Your image, as the hunter some struck deer,
Follows me not whether I wake or sleep ?

BEATRICE

As I have said, speak to me not of love ;
Had you a dispensation I have not ;
Nor will I leave this home of misery
Whilst my poor Bernard, and that gentle lady
To whom I owe life, and these virtuous thoughts,
Must suffer what I still have strength to share.
Alas, Orsino ! All the love that once
I felt for you is turned to bitter pain.
Ours was a youthful contract, which you first
Broke, by assuming vows no Pope will loose.
And thus I love you still, but holily,
Even as a sister or a spirit might ;
And so I swear a cold fidelity.
And it is well perhaps we shall not marry.
You have a sly, equivocating vein
That suits me not.—Ah, wretched that I am !
Where shall I turn ? Even now you look on me
As you were not my friend, and as if you
Discovered that I thought so, with false smiles
Making my true suspicion seem your wrong.

5

Ah !   No, forgive me ; sorrow makes me seem
Sterner than else my nature might have been ;
I have a weight of melancholy thoughts,
And they forbode,—but what can they forbode
Worse than I now endure ?

ORSINO

               All will be well.
Is the petition yet prepared ?   You know
My zeal for all you wish, sweet Beatrice ;
Doubt not but I will use my utmost skill
So that the Pope attend to your complaint.

BEATRICE

Your zeal for all I wish ;—Ah me, you are cold !
Your utmost skill . . . speak but one word . . .
    (*aside*) Alas !
Weak and deserted creature that I am,
Here I stand bickering with my only friend !
                        (*To* ORSINO)
This night my father gives a sumptuous feast,
Orsino ; he has heard some happy news
From Salamanca, from my brothers there,
And with this outward show of love he mocks
His inward hate.   'Tis bold hypocrisy,
For he would gladlier celebrate their deaths,
Which I have heard him pray for on his knees :
Great God ! that such a father should be mine !
But there is mighty preparation made,
And all our kin, the Cenci, will be there,
And all the chief nobility of Rome.
And he has bidden me and my pale Mother
Attire ourselves in festival array.
Poor lady !   She expects some happy change
In his dark spirit from this act ; I none.
At supper I will give you the petition :
Till when—farewell.

ORSINO

Farewell.   [*Exit* BEATRICE.
                              I know the Pope
Will ne'er absolve me from my priestly vow
But by absolving me from the revenue
Of many a wealthy see ; and, Beatrice,
I think to win thee at an easier rate.
Nor shall he read her eloquent petition :
He might bestow her on some poor relation
Of his sixth cousin, as he did her sister,
And I should be debarred from all access.
Then as to what she suffers from her father,
In all this there is much exaggeration :—
Old men are testy and will have their way ;
A man may stab his enemy, or his vassal,
And live a free life as to wine or women,
And with a peevish temper may return
To a dull home, and rate his wife and children ;
Daughters and wives call this foul tyranny.
I shall be well content if on my conscience
There rest no heavier sin than what they suffer
From the devices of my love—A net
From which she shall escape not.   Yet I fear
Her subtle mind, her awe-inspiring gaze,
Whose beams anatomize me nerve by nerve
And lay me bare, and make me blush to see
My hidden thoughts.—Ah, no !   A friendless girl
Who clings to me, as to her only hope :—
I were a fool, not less than if a panther
Were panic-stricken by the antelope's eye,
If she escape me.
                                        [*Exit.*

SCENE III. *A magnificent Hall in the Cenci Palace. A Banquet*

Enter CENCI, LUCRETIA, BEATRICE, ORSINO, CAMILLO, Nobles

CENCI

Welcome, my friends and kinsmen ; welcome ye,
Princes and Cardinals, pillars of the church,
Whose presence honours our festivity.
I have too long lived like an anchorite,
And in my absence from your merry meetings
An evil word is gone abroad of me ;
But I do hope that you, my noble friends,
When you have shared the entertainment here,
And heard the pious cause for which 'tis given,
And we have pledged a health or two together,
Will think me flesh and blood as well as you ;
Sinful indeed, for Adam made all so,
But tender-hearted, meek and pitiful.

FIRST GUEST

In truth, my Lord, you seem too light of heart,
Too sprightly and companionable a man,
To act the deeds that rumour pins on you.
                                                    (*To his companion*)
I never saw such blithe and open cheer
In any eye !

SECOND GUEST

                    Some most desired event,
In which we all demand a common joy,
Has brought us hither ; let us hear it, Count.

CENCI

It is indeed a most desired event.

If when a parent from a parent's heart
Lifts from this earth to the great father of all
A prayer, both when he lays him down to sleep,
And when he rises up from dreaming it ;
One supplication, one desire, one hope,
That he would grant a wish for his two sons,
Even all that he demands in their regard——
And suddenly beyond his dearest hope,
It is accomplished, he should then rejoice,
And call his friends and kinsmen to a feast,
And task their love to grace his merriment,
Then honour me thus far—for I am he.

BEATRICE (*to* LUCRETIA)

Great God ! How horrible ! Some dreadful ill
Must have befallen my brothers.

LUCRETIA

Fear not, child,
He speaks too frankly.

BEATRICE

Ah ! My blood runs cold.
I fear that wicked laughter round his eye,
Which wrinkles up the skin even to the hair.

CENCI

Here are the letters brought from Salamanca ;
Beatrice, read them to your mother.   God !
I thank thee !   In one night didst thou perform,
By ways inscrutable, the thing I sought.
My disobedient and rebellious sons
Are dead !—Why dead !—What means this change of cheer ?
You hear me not, I tell you they are dead ;
And they will need no food or raiment more :

The tapers that did light them the dark way
Are their last cost.   The Pope, I think, will not
Expect I should maintain them in their coffins.
Rejoice with me—my heart is wondrous glad.

BEATRICE

(LUCRETIA *sinks, half fainting ;* BEATRICE
supports her)

It is not true !—Dear lady, pray look up.
Had it been true, there is a God in Heaven,—
He would not live to boast of such a boon.
Unnatural man, thou knowest that it is false.

CENCI

Aye, as the word of God ; whom here I call
To witness that I speak the sober truth ;—
And whose most favouring Providence was shown
Even in the manner of their deaths.   For Rocco
Was kneeling at the mass, with sixteen others,
When the church fell and crushed him to a mummy ;
The rest escaped unhurt.   Cristofano
Was stabbed in error by a jealous man,
Whilst she he loved was sleeping with his rival ;
All in the self-same hour of the same night ;
Which shows that Heaven has special care of me.
I beg those friends who love me, that they mark
The day a feast upon their calendars.
It was the twenty-seventh of December :
Aye, read the letters if you doubt my oath.
    [*The assembly appears confused ; several of the
        guests rise.*

FIRST GUEST

Oh, horrible !   I will depart.—

SECOND GUEST

                    And I.—

THIRD GUEST

No, stay !

I do believe it is some jest ; though faith !
'Tis mocking us somewhat too solemnly.
I think his son has married the Infanta,
Or found a mine of gold in El dorado ;
'Tis but to season some such news ; stay, stay !
I see 'tis only raillery by his smile.

CENCI

(filling a bowl of wine, and lifting it up)

Oh, thou bright wine whose purple splendour leaps
And bubbles gaily in this golden bowl
Under the lamp-light, as my spirits do,
To hear the death of my accursèd sons !
Could I believe thou wert their mingled blood,
Then would I taste thee like a sacrament,
And pledge with thee the mighty Devil in Hell,
Who, if a father's curses, as men say,
Climb with swift wings after their children's souls,
And drag them from the very throne of Heaven,
Now triumphs in my triumph !—But thou art
Superfluous ; I have drunken deep of joy,
And I will taste no other wine to-night.
Here, Andrea ! Bear the bowl around.

A GUEST *(rising)*

Thou wretch !

Will none among this noble company
Check the abandoned villain ?

CAMILLO

For God's sake

Let me dismiss the guests ! You are insane,
Some ill will come of this.

SECOND GUEST
Seize, silence him!

FIRST GUEST

I will!

THIRD GUEST

And I!

CENCI

(*addressing those who rise with a threatening gesture*)
Who moves? Who speaks?
(*turning to the Company*) 'Tis nothing,
Enjoy yourselves.—Beware! For my revenge
Is as the sealed commission of a king
That kills, and none dare name the murderer.
[*The Banquet is broken up; several of the guests
are departing.*

BEATRICE

I do entreat you, go not, noble guests;
What, although tyranny and impious hate
Stand sheltered by a father's hoary hair?
What, if 'tis he who clothed us in these limbs
Who tortures them, and triumphs? What, if we
The desolate and the dead, were his own flesh,
His children and his wife, whom he is bound
To love and shelter? Shall we therefore find
No refuge in this merciless wide world?
Oh, think what deep wrongs must have blotted out
First love, then reverence in a child's prone mind,
Till it thus vanquish shame and fear! O, think!
I have borne much, and kissed the sacred hand
Which crushed us to the earth, and thought its stroke
Was perhaps some paternal chastisement!
Have excused much, doubted; and when no doubt
Remained, have sought by patience, love and tears

To soften him, and when this could not be
I have knelt down through the long sleepless nights
And lifted up to God, the father of all,
Passionate prayers : and when these were not heard
I have still borne,—until I meet you here,
Princes and kinsmen, at this hideous feast
Given at my brothers' deaths.   Two yet remain,
His wife remains and I, whom if ye save not,
Ye may soon share such merriment again
As fathers make over their children's graves.
Oh ! Prince Colonna, thou art our near kinsman,
Cardinal, thou art the Pope's chamberlain,
Camillo, thou art chief justiciary,
Take us away !

CENCI

(*He has been conversing with* CAMILLO *during the first
    part of* BEATRICE'S *speech ; he hears the conclusion,
    and now advances*)
                    I hope my good friends here
Will think of their own daughters—or perhaps
Of their own throats—before they lend an ear
To this wild girl.

BEATRICE (*not noticing the words of* CENCI)
                    Dare no one look on me ?
None answer ?   Can one tyrant overbear
The sense of many best and wisest men ?
Or is it that I sue not in some form
Of scrupulous law, that ye deny my suit ?
Oh, God !   That I were buried with my brothers !
And that the flowers of this departed spring
Were fading on my grave !   And that my father
Were celebrating now one feast for all !

CAMILLO

A bitter wish for one so young and gentle ;
Can we do nothing ?

COLONNA

Nothing that I see.
Count Cenci were a dangerous enemy :
Yet I would second any one.

A CARDINAL

And I.

CENCI

Retire to your chamber, insolent girl !

BEATRICE

Retire thou, impious man !   Aye, hide thyself
Where never eye can look upon thee more !
Wouldst thou have honour and obedience
Who art a torturer ?   Father, never dream,
Though thou mayst overbear this company,
But ill must come of ill.—Frown not on me !
Haste, hide thyself, lest with avenging looks
My brothers' ghosts should hunt thee from thy seat !
Cover thy face from every living eye,
And start if thou but hear a human step ;
Seek out some dark and silent corner,—there,
Bow thy white head before offended God,
And we will kneel around, and fervently
Pray that he pity both ourselves and thee.

CENCI

My friends, I do lament this insane girl
Has spoilt the mirth of our festivity.
Good night, farewell ; I will not make you longer
Spectators of our dull domestic quarrels.
Another time.—

[*Exeunt all but* CENCI *and* BEATRICE.

My brain is swimming round ;
Give me a bowl of wine !   (*To* BEATRICE) Thou painted
    viper !
Beast that thou art !   Fair and yet terrible !
I know a charm shall make thee meek and tame,
Now get thee from my sight !   [*Exit* BEATRICE.
                Here, Andrea,
Fill up this goblet with Greek wine.   I said
I would not drink this evening ; but I must ;
For, strange to say, I feel my spirits fail
With thinking what I have decreed to do.—
                (*Drinking the wine*)
Be thou the resolution of quick youth
Within my veins, and manhood's purpose stern,
And age's firm, cold, subtle villainy ;
As if thou wert indeed my children's blood
Which I did thirst to drink !   The charm works well ;
It must be done ; it shall be done, I swear !
                      [*Exit.*

END OF THE FIRST ACT

ACT II

SCENE I.   *An Apartment in the Cenci Palace*

Enter LUCRETIA *and* BERNARDO

LUCRETIA

Weep not, my gentle boy ; he struck but me
Who have borne deeper wrongs.   In truth, if he
Had killed me, he had done a kinder deed.
O, God Almighty, do thou look upon us,
We have no other friend but only thee !
Yet weep not ; though I love you as my own,
I am not your true mother.

BERNARDO

       Oh more, more,
Than ever mother was to any child,
That have you been to me ! Had he not been
My father, do you think that I should weep ?

LUCRETIA

Alas ! Poor boy, what else couldst thou have done ?

Enter BEATRICE

BEATRICE (*in a hurried voice*)

Did he pass this way ? Have you seen him, brother ?
Ah ! No, that is his step upon the stairs ;
'Tis nearer now ; his hand is on the door ;
Mother, if I to thee have ever been
A duteous child, now save me ! Thou, great God,
Whose image upon earth a father is,
Dost thou indeed abandon me ? He comes ;
The door is opening now ; I see his face ;
He frowns on others, but he smiles on me,
Even as he did after the feast last night.

Enter a Servant

Almighty God, how merciful thou art !
'Tis but Orsino's servant.—Well, what news ?

SERVANT

My master bids me say, the Holy Father
Has sent back your petition thus unopened.
        (*Giving a paper*)
And he demands at what hour 'twere secure
To visit you again ?

LUCRETIA

At the Ave Mary. [*Exit* Servant.
So, daughter, our last hope has failed ; Ah me !
How pale you look ; you tremble, and you stand
Wrapped in some fixed and fearful meditation,
As if one thought were over strong for you :
Your eyes have a chill glare ; O, dearest child !
Are you gone mad ? If not, pray speak to me.

BEATRICE

You see I am not mad ; I speak to you.

LUCRETIA

You talked of something that your father did
After that dreadful feast ? Could it be worse
Than when he smiled, and cried, My sons are dead !
And every one looked in his neighbour's face
To see if others were as white as he ?
At the first word he spoke I felt the blood
Rush to my heart, and fell into a trance ;
And when it passed I sat all weak and wild ;
Whilst you alone stood up, and with strong words
Checked his unnatural pride ; and I could see
The devil was rebuked that lives in him.
Until this hour thus have you ever stood
Between us and your father's moody wrath
Like a protecting presence : your firm mind
Has been our only refuge and defence :
What can have thus subdued it ? What can now
Have given you that cold melancholy look,
Succeeding to your unaccustomed fear ?

BEATRICE

What is it that you say ? I was just thinking
'Twere better not to struggle any more.

Men, like my father, have been dark and bloody,
Yet never—O ! Before worse comes of it
'Twere wise to die : it ends in that at last.

LUCRETIA

Oh, talk not so, dear child ! Tell me at once
What did your father do or say to you ?
He stayed not after that accursèd feast
One moment in your chamber.—Speak to me.

BERNARDO

Oh, sister, sister, prithee, speak to us !

BEATRICE

(speaking very slowly, with a forced calmness)

It was one word, Mother, one little word ;
One look, one smile. *(wildly)*
　　　　　　　Oh ! He has trampled me
Under his feet, and made the blood stream down
My pallid cheeks. And he has given us all
Ditch water, and the fever-stricken flesh
Of buffaloes, and bade us eat or starve,
And we have eaten.—He has made me look
On my beloved Bernardo, when the rust
Of heavy chains has gangrened his sweet limbs,
And I have never yet despaired—but now !
What could I say ? *(recovering herself)*
　　　　　　　Ah ! No, 'tis nothing new.
The sufferings we all share have made me wild :
He only struck and cursed me as he passed ;
He said, he looked, he did ;—nothing at all
Beyond his wont, yet it disordered me.
Alas ! I am forgetful of my duty ;
I should preserve my senses for your sake.

LUCRETIA

Nay, Beatrice ; have courage, my sweet girl ;
If any one despairs it should be I
Who loved him once, and now must live with him
Till God in pity call for him or me.
For you may, like your sister, find some husband,
And smile, years hence, with children round your
    knees
Whilst I, then dead, and all this hideous coil
Shall be remembered only as a dream.

BEATRICE

Talk not to me, dear lady, of a husband.
Did you not nurse me when my mother died ?
Did you not shield me and that dearest boy ?
And had we any other friend but you
In infancy, with gentle words and looks,
To win our father not to murder us ?
And shall I now desert you ?   May the ghost
Of my dead mother plead against my soul
If I abandon her who filled the place
She left, with more, even, than a mother's love !

BERNARDO

And I am of my sister's mind.   Indeed
I would not leave you in this wretchedness,
Even though the Pope should make me free to live
In some blithe place, like others of my age,
With sports, and delicate food, and the fresh air.
Oh, never think that I will leave you, Mother !

LUCRETIA

My dear, dear children !

Enter CENCI, *suddenly*

CENCI

What, Beatrice here !
Come hither !   (*She shrinks back, and covers her face.*)
                Nay, hide not your face, 'tis fair ;
Look up !   Why, yesternight you dared to look
With disobedient insolence upon me,
Bending a stern and an enquiring brow
On what I meant ; whilst I then sought to hide
That which I came to tell you—but in vain.

BEATRICE

(*wildly, staggering towards the door*)
Oh, that the earth would gape !   Hide me, oh God !

CENCI

Then it was I whose inarticulate words
Fell from my lips, and who with tottering steps
Fled from your presence, as you now from mine.
Stay, I command you—from this day and hour
Never again, I think, with fearless eye,
And brow superior, and unaltered cheek,
And that lip made for tenderness or scorn,
Shalt thou strike dumb the meanest of mankind ;
Me least of all.   Now get thee to thy chamber !
Thou too, loathed image of thy cursèd mother,
                                        (*to* BERNARDO)
Thy milky, meek face makes me sick with hate !
                        [*Exeunt* BEATRICE *and* BERNARDO.
(*Aside.*)   So much has passed between us as must make
Me bold, her fearful.   'Tis an awful thing
To touch such mischief as I now conceive :
So men sit shivering on the dewy bank,
And try the chill stream with their feet ; once in . . .
How the delighted spirit pants for joy !

LUCRETIA

(*advancing timidly towards him*)

Oh, husband ! Pray forgive poor Beatrice,—
She meant not any ill.

CENCI

Nor you perhaps ?
Nor that young imp, whom you have taught by rote
Parricide with his alphabet ? Nor Giacomo ?
Nor those two most unnatural sons, who stirred
Enmity up against me with the Pope ?
Whom in one night merciful God cut off :
Innocent lambs ! They thought not any ill.
You were not here conspiring ? You said nothing
Of how I might be dungeoned as a madman ;
Or be condemned to death for some offence,
And you would be the witnesses ?—This failing,
How just it were to hire assassins, or
Put sudden poison in my evening drink ?
Or smother me when overcome by wine ?
Seeing we had no other judge but God,
And he had sentenced me, and there were none
But you to be the executioners
Of his decree enregistered in heaven ?
Oh, no ! You said not this ?

LUCRETIA

So help me God,
I never thought the things you charge me with !

CENCI

If you dare speak that wicked lie again
I'll kill you. What ! It was not by your counsel
That Beatrice disturbed the feast last night ?
You did not hope to stir some enemies
Against me, and escape, and laugh to scorn

What every nerve of you now trembles at ?
You judged that men were bolder than they are ;
Few dare to stand between their grave and me.

LUCRETIA

Look not so dreadfully !   By my salvation
I knew not aught that Beatrice designed ;
Nor do I think she designed anything
Until she heard you talk of her dead brothers.

CENCI

Blaspheming liar !   You are damned for this !
But I will take you where you may persuade
The stones you tread on to deliver you :
For men shall there be none but those who dare
All things—not question that which I command.
On Wednesday next I shall set out : you know
That savage rock, the Castle of Petrella :
'Tis safely walled, and moated round about :
Its dungeons underground, and its thick towers
Never told tales ; though they have heard and seen
What might make dumb things speak.—Why do you
       linger ?
Make speediest preparation for the journey !
                                        [*Exit* LUCRETIA.
The all-beholding sun yet shines ; I hear
A busy stir of men about the streets ;
I see the bright sky through the window-panes :
It is a garish, broad, and peering day ;
Loud, light, suspicious, full of eyes and ears,
And every little corner, nook and hole
Is penetrated with the insolent light.
Come darkness !   Yet, what is the day to me ?
And wherefore should I wish for night, who do
A deed which shall confound both night and day ?
'Tis she shall grope through a bewildering mist
Of horror : if there be a sun in heaven

She shall not dare to look upon its beams ;
Nor feel its warmth.   Let her then wish for night ;
The act I think shall soon extinguish all
For me : I bear a darker deadlier gloom
Than the earth's shade, or interlunar air,
Or constellations quenched in murkiest cloud,
In which I walk secure and unbeheld
Towards my purpose.—Would that it were done !

[Exit.

SCENE II.   *A Chamber in the Vatican*

Enter CAMILLO *and* GIACOMO, *in conversation*

CAMILLO

There is an obsolete and doubtful law
By which you might obtain a bare provision
Of food and clothing—

GIACOMO

                    Nothing more ?   Alas !
Bare must be the provision which strict law
Awards, and agèd, sullen avarice pays.
Why did my father not apprentice me
To some mechanic trade ?   I should have then
Been trained in no highborn necessities
Which I could meet not by my daily toil.
The eldest son of a rich nobleman
Is heir to all his incapacities ;
He has wide wants, and narrow powers.   If you,
Cardinal Camillo, were reduced at once
From thrice-driven beds of down, and delicate food,
An hundred servants, and six palaces,
To that which nature doth indeed require ?—

CAMILLO

Nay, there is reason in your plea ; 'twere hard.

GIACOMO

'Tis hard for a firm man to bear : but I
Have a dear wife, a lady of high birth,
Whose dowry in ill hour I lent my father
Without a bond or witness to the deed :
And children, who inherit her fine senses,
The fairest creatures in this breathing world ;
And she and they reproach me not.   Cardinal,
Do you not think the Pope would interpose
And stretch authority beyond the law ?

CAMILLO

Though your peculiar case is hard, I know
The Pope will not divert the course of law.
After that impious feast the other night
I spoke with him, and urged him then to check
Your father's cruel hand ; he frowned and said,
" Children are disobedient, and they sting
Their fathers' hearts to madness and despair,
Requiting years of care with contumely.
I pity the Count Cenci from my heart ;
His outraged love perhaps awakened hate,
And thus he is exasperated to ill.
In the great war between the old and young
I, who have white hairs and a tottering body,
Will keep at least blameless neutrality."

Enter ORSINO

You, my good Lord Orsino, heard those words.

ORSINO

What words ?

GIACOMO

Alas, repeat them not again !
There then is no redress for me, at least
None but that which I may achieve myself,
Since I am driven to the brink.—But, say,
My innocent sister and my only brother
Are dying underneath my father's eye.
The memorable torturers of this land,
Galeaz Visconti, Borgia, Ezzelin,
Never inflicted on the meanest slave
What these endure ; shall they have no protection ?

CAMILLO

Why, if they would petition to the Pope
I see not how he could refuse it—yet
He holds it of most dangerous example
In aught to weaken the paternal power,
Being, as 'twere, the shadow of his own.
I pray you now excuse me.   I have business
That will not bear delay.   [*Exit* CAMILLO.

GIACOMO

But you, Orsino,
Have the petition : wherefore not present it ?

ORSINO

I have presented it, and backed it with
My earnest prayers, and urgent interest ;
It was returned unanswered.   I doubt not
But that the strange and execrable deeds
Alleged in it—in truth they might well baffle
Any belief—have turned the Pope's displeasure
Upon the accusers from the criminal :
So I should guess from what Camillo said.

GIACOMO

My friend, that palace-walking devil Gold

Has whispered silence to his Holiness :
And we are left, as scorpions ringed with fire.
What should we do but strike ourselves to death ?
For he who is our murderous persecutor
Is shielded by a father's holy name,
Or I would—   (*Stops abruptly.*)

ORSINO

What ?   Fear not to speak your thought.
Words are but holy as the deeds they cover :
A priest who has forsworn the God he serves ;
A judge who makes Truth weep at his decree ;
A friend who should weave counsel, as I now,
But as the mantle of some selfish guile ;
A father who is all a tyrant seems,
Were the profaner for his sacred name.

GIACOMO

Ask me not what I think ; the unwilling brain
Feigns often what it would not ; and we trust
Imagination with such phantasies
As the tongue dares not fashion into words,—
Which have no words,—their horror makes them dim
To the mind's eye.—My heart denies itself
To think what you demand.

ORSINO

But a friend's bosom
Is as the inmost cave of our own mind
Where we sit shut from the wide gaze of day,
And from the all-communicating air.
You look what I suspected—

GIACOMO

Spare me now !
I am as one lost in a midnight wood,

Who dares not ask some harmless passenger
The path across the wilderness, lest he,
As my thoughts are, should be—a murderer.
I know you are my friend, and all I dare
Speak to my soul that will I trust with thee.
But now my heart is heavy, and would take
Lone counsel from a night of sleepless care.
Pardon me, that I say farewell—farewell!
I would that to my own suspected self
I could address a word so full of peace.

ORSINO

Farewell!—Be your thoughts better or more bold.
                                        [*Exit* GIACOMO.
I had disposed the Cardinal Camillo
To feed his hope with cold encouragement:
It fortunately serves my close designs
That 'tis a trick of this same family
To analyse their own and other minds.
Such self-anatomy shall teach the will
Dangerous secrets: for it tempts our powers,
Knowing what must be thought, and may be done,
Into the depth of darkest purposes:
So Cenci fell into the pit; even I,
Since Beatrice unveiled me to myself,
And made me shrink from what I cannot shun,
Show a poor figure to my own esteem,
To which I grow half reconciled.   I'll do
As little mischief as I can; that thought
Shall fee the accuser conscience.
                    (*after a pause*)   Now what harm
If Cenci should be murdered?—Yet, if murdered,
Wherefore by me?   And what if I could take
The profit, yet omit the sin and peril
In such an action?   Of all earthly things
I fear a man whose blows outspeed his words;
And such is Cenci: and while Cenci lives

His daughter's dowry were a secret grave
If a priest wins her.—Oh, fair Beatrice !
Would that I loved thee not, or loving thee
Could but despise danger and gold and all
That frowns between my wish and its effect,
Or smiles beyond it !   There is no escape. . . .
Her bright form kneels beside me at the altar,
And follows me to the resort of men,
And fills my slumber with tumultuous dreams,
So when I wake my blood seems liquid fire ;
And if I strike my damp and dizzy head
My hot palm scorches it : her very name,
But spoken by a stranger, makes my heart
Sicken and pant ; and thus unprofitably
I clasp the phantom of unfelt delights
Till weak imagination half possesses
The self-created shadow.   Yet much longer
Will I not nurse this life of feverous hours :
From the unravelled hopes of Giacomo
I must work out my own dear purposes.
I see, as from a tower, the end of all :
Her father dead ; her brother bound to me
By a dark secret, surer than the grave ;
Her mother scared and unexpostulating
From the dread manner of her wish achieved :
And she !—Once more take courage, my faint heart ;
What dares a friendless maiden matched with thee ?
I have such foresight as assures success :
Some unbeheld divinity doth ever,
When dread events are near, stir up men's minds
To black suggestions ; and he prospers best,
Not who becomes the instrument of ill,
But who can flatter the dark spirit, that makes
Its empire and its prey of other hearts
Till it become his slave . . . as I will do.   [*Exit.*

END OF THE SECOND ACT

ACT III

Scene I. *An Apartment in the Cenci Palace*

Lucretia, *to her enter* Beatrice

Beatrice

(She enters staggering, and speaks wildly)

Reach me that handkerchief !—My brain is hurt ;
My eyes are full of blood ; just wipe them for me. . . .
I see but indistinctly. . . .

Lucretia

My sweet child,
You have no wound ; 'tis only a cold dew
That starts from your dear brow. . . . Alas ! Alas !
What has befallen ?

Beatrice

How comes this hair undone ?
Its wandering strings must be what blind me so,
And yet I tied it fast.—O, horrible !
The pavement sinks under my feet ！ The walls
Spin round ！ I see a woman weeping there,
And standing calm and motionless, whilst I
Slide giddily as the world reels. . . . My God !
The beautiful blue heaven is flecked with blood !
The sunshine on the floor is black ！ The air
Is changed to vapours such as the dead breathe
In charnel pits ！ Pah ！ I am choked ！ There creeps
A clinging, black, contaminating mist
About me . . . 'tis substantial, heavy, thick,
I cannot pluck it from me, for it glues
My fingers and my limbs to one another,
And eats into my sinews, and dissolves
My flesh to a pollution, poisoning

The subtle, pure, and inmost spirit of life !
My God ! I never knew what the mad felt
Before ; for I am mad beyond all doubt !
(*More wildly.*)　No, I am dead !　These putrefying limbs
Shut round and sepulchre the panting soul
Which would burst forth into the wandering air ! (*a pause*)
What hideous thought was that I had even now ?
'Tis gone ; and yet its burthen remains here
O'er these dull eyes . . . upon this weary heart !
O, world ! O, life ! O, day ! O, misery !

LUCRETIA

What ails thee, my poor child ?　She answers not :
Her spirit apprehends the sense of pain,
But not its cause ; suffering has dried away
The source from which it sprung. . . .

BEATRICE (*franticly*)

　　　　　　　　　　　　Like Parricide . . .
Misery has killed its father : yet its father
Never like mine. . . . O, God ! What thing am I ?

LUCRETIA

My dearest child, what has your father done ?

BEATRICE (*doubtfully*)

Who art thou, questioner ?　I have no father.
(*Aside.*)　She is the madhouse nurse who tends on me,
It is a piteous office.
(*To* LUCRETIA, *in a slow, subdued voice.*)　Do you know
I thought I was that wretched Beatrice
Men speak of, whom her father sometimes hales
From hall to hall by the entangled hair ;
At others, pens up naked in damp cells
Where scaly reptiles crawl, and starves her there,
Till she will eat strange flesh.　This woful story

So did I overact in my sick dreams,
That I imagined . . . no, it cannot be !
Horrible things have been in this wild world,
Prodigious mixtures, and confusions strange
Of good and ill ; and worse have been conceived
Than ever there was found a heart to do.
But never fancy imaged such a deed
As . . .   (*Pauses, suddenly recollecting herself.*)
          Who art thou ?   Swear to me, ere I die
With fearful expectation, that indeed
Thou art not what thou seemest . . . Mother !

LUCRETIA

                                              Oh !
My sweet child, know you . . .

BEATRICE

                              Yet speak it not :
For then if this be truth, that other too
Must be a truth, a firm enduring truth,
Linked with each lasting circumstance of life,
Never to change, never to pass away.
Why so it is.   This is the Cenci Palace ;
Thou art Lucretia ; I am Beatrice.
I have talked some wild words, but will no more.
Mother, come near me : from this point of time,
I am . . .   (*Her voice dies away faintly.*)

LUCRETIA

          Alas !   What has befallen thee, child ?
What has thy father done ?

BEATRICE

                        What have I done ?
Am I not innocent ?   Is it my crime
That one with white hair, and imperious brow,

Who tortured me from my forgotten years,
As parents only dare, should call himself
My father, yet should be !—Oh, what am I ?
What name, what place, what memory shall be mine ?
What retrospects, outliving even despair ?

LUCRETIA

He is a violent tyrant, surely, child :
We know that death alone can make us free ;
His death or ours.   But what can he have done
Of deadlier outrage or worse injury ?
Thou art unlike thyself ; thine eyes shoot forth
A wandering and strange spirit.   Speak to me,
Unlock those pallid hands whose fingers twine
With one another.

BEATRICE

                    'Tis the restless life
Tortured within them.   If I try to speak
I shall go mad.   Aye, something must be done ;
What, yet I know not . . . something which shall make
The thing that I have suffered but a shadow
In the dread lightning which avenges it ;
Brief, rapid, irreversible, destroying
The consequence of what it cannot cure.
Some such thing is to be endured or done :
When I know what, I shall be still and calm,
And never anything will move me more.
But now !—Oh blood, which art my father's blood,
Circling through these contaminated veins,
If thou, poured forth on the polluted earth,
Could wash away the crime, and punishment
By which I suffer . . . no, that cannot be !
Many might doubt there were a God above
Who sees and permits evil, and so die :
That faith no agony shall obscure in me.

LUCRETIA

It must indeed have been some bitter wrong ;
Yet what, I dare not guess.   Oh, my lost child,
Hide not in proud impenetrable grief
Thy sufferings from my fear.

BEATRICE

I hide them not.
What are the words which you would have me speak ?
I, who can feign no image in my mind
Of that which has transformed me : I, whose thought
Is like a ghost shrouded and folded up
In its own formless horror : of all words,
That minister to mortal intercourse,
Which wouldst thou hear ?   For there is none to tell
My misery : if another ever knew
Aught like to it, she died as I will die,
And left it, as I must, without a name.
Death ! Death ! Our law and our religion call thee
A punishment and a reward. . . . Oh, which
Have I deserved ?

LUCRETIA

The peace of innocence ;
Till in your season you be called to heaven.
Whate'er you may have suffered, you have done
No evil.   Death must be the punishment
Of crime, or the reward of trampling down
The thorns which God has strewed upon the path
Which leads to immortality.

BEATRICE

Aye, death . . .
The punishment of crime.   I pray thee, God,
Let me not be bewildered while I judge.
If I must live day after day, and keep

These limbs, the unworthy temple of thy spirit,
As a foul den from which what thou abhorrest
May mock thee, unavenged . . . it shall not be!
Self-murder . . . no, that might be no escape,
For thy decree yawns like a Hell between
Our will and it :—O ! In this mortal world
There is no vindication and no law
Which can adjudge and execute the doom
Of that through which I suffer.

Enter ORSINO

(*She approaches him solemnly.*)   Welcome, Friend !
I have to tell you that, since last we met,
I have endured a wrong so great and strange,
That neither life nor death can give me rest.
Ask me not what it is, for there are deeds
Which have no form, sufferings which have no tongue.

ORSINO

And what is he who has thus injured you ?

BEATRICE

The man they call my father : a dread name.

ORSINO

It cannot be. . . .

BEATRICE

What it can be, or not,
Forbear to think.   It is, and it has been ;
Advise me how it shall not be again.
I thought to die ; but a religious awe
Restrains me, and the dread lest death itself
Might be no refuge from the consciousness
Of what is yet unexpiated.   Oh, speak !

ORSINO

Accuse him of the deed, and let the law
Avenge thee.

BEATRICE

Oh, ice-hearted counsellor !
If I could find a word that might make known
The crime of my destroyer ; and that done,
My tongue should like a knife tear out the secret
Which cankers my heart's core ; aye, lay all bare
So that my unpolluted fame should be
With vilest gossips a stale mouthèd story ;
A mock, a bye-word, an astonishment :—
If this were done, which never shall be done,
Think of the offender's gold, his dreaded hate,
And the strange horror of the accuser's tale,
Baffling belief, and overpowering speech ;
Scarce whispered, unimaginable, wrapped
In hideous hints. . . . Oh, most assured redress !

ORSINO

You will endure it then ?

BEATRICE

Endure ?—Orsino,
It seems your counsel is small profit.
(*Turns from him, and speaks half to herself.*)   Aye,
All must be suddenly resolved and done.
What is this undistinguishable mist
Of thoughts, which rise, like shadow after shadow,
Darkening each other ?

ORSINO

Should the offender live ?
Triumph in his misdeed ? and make, by use,
His crime, whate'er it is, dreadful no doubt,
Thine element ; until thou mayest become
Utterly lost ; subdued even to the hue
Of that which thou permittest ?

BEATRICE (*to herself*)

Mighty death !
Thou double-visaged shadow !   Only judge !
Rightfullest arbiter !   (*She retires absorbed in thought.*)

LUCRETIA

If the lightning
Of God has e'er descended to avenge . . .

ORSINO

Blaspheme not !   His high Providence commits
Its glory on this earth, and their own wrongs
Into the hands of men ; if they neglect
To punish crime . . .

LUCRETIA

But if one, like this wretch,
Should mock with gold, opinion, law and power ?
If there be no appeal to that which makes
The guiltiest tremble ?   If because our wrongs,
For that they are unnatural, strange and monstrous,
Exceed all measure of belief ?   Oh, God !
If, for the very reasons which should make
Redress most swift and sure, our injurer triumphs ?
And we, the victims, bear worse punishment
Than that appointed for their torturer ?

ORSINO

Think not
But that there is redress where there is wrong,
So we be bold enough to seize it.

LUCRETIA

How ?
If there were any way to make all sure,
I know not . . . but I think it might be good
To . . .

ORSINO

Why, his late outrage to Beatrice ;
For it is such, as I but faintly guess,
As makes remorse dishonour, and leaves her
Only one duty, how she may avenge :
You, but one refuge from ills ill endured ;
Me, but one counsel . . .

LUCRETIA

For we cannot hope
That aid, or retribution, or resource
Will arise thence, where every other one
Might find them with less need.

(BEATRICE *advances*.)

ORSINO

Then . . .

BEATRICE

Peace, Orsino !
And, honoured Lady, while I speak, I pray,
That you put off, as garments overworn,
Forbearance and respect, remorse and fear,
And all the fit restraints of daily life,
Which have been borne from childhood, but which now
Would be a mockery to my holier plea.
As I have said, I have endured a wrong,
Which, though it be expressionless, is such
As asks atonement ; both for what is past,
And lest I be reserved, day after day,
To load with crimes an overburthened soul,
And be . . . what ye can dream not.   I have prayed
To God, and I have talked with my own heart,
And have unravelled my entangled will,
And have at length determined what is right.
Art thou my friend, Orsino ?   False or true ?
Pledge thy salvation ere I speak.

6

ORSINO

I swear
To dedicate my cunning, and my strength,
My silence, and whatever else is mine,
To thy commands.

LUCRETIA

You think we should devise
His death ?

BEATRICE

And execute what is devised;
And suddenly.   We must be brief and bold.

ORSINO

And yet most cautious.

LUCRETIA

For the jealous laws
Would punish us with death and infamy
For that which it became themselves to do.

BEATRICE

Be cautious as ye may, but prompt.   Orsino,
What are the means ?

ORSINO

I know two dull, fierce outlaws,
Who think man's spirit as a worm's, and they
Would trample out, for any slight caprice,
The meanest or the noblest life.   This mood
Is marketable here in Rome.   They sell
What we now want.

LUCRETIA

To-morrow before dawn,
Cenci will take us to that lonely rock,
Petrella, in the Apulian Apennines.
If he arrive there . . .

BEATRICE

He must not arrive.

ORSINO

Will it be dark before you reach the tower ?

LUCRETIA

The sun will scarce be set.

BEATRICE

But I remember
Two miles on this side of the fort, the road
Crosses a deep ravine ; 'tis rough and narrow,
And winds with short turns down the precipice ;
And in its depth there is a mighty rock,
Which has, from unimaginable years,
Sustained itself with terror and with toil
Over a gulph, and with the agony
With which it clings seems slowly coming down ;
Even as a wretched soul hour after hour
Clings to the mass of life ; yet clinging, leans ;
And leaning, makes more dark the dread abyss
In which it fears to fall : beneath this crag
Huge as despair, as if in weariness,
The melancholy mountain yawns . . . below,
You hear but see not an impetuous torrent
Raging among the caverns, and a bridge
Crosses the chasm ; and high above there grow,
With intersecting trunks, from crag to crag,
Cedars, and yews, and pines ; whose tangled hair
Is matted in one solid roof of shade
By the dark ivy's twine.   At noon-day here
'Tis twilight, and at sunset blackest night.

ORSINO

Before you reach that bridge make some excuse
For spurring on your mules, or loitering
Until . . .

BEATRICE

What sound is that ?

LUCRETIA

Hark !　No, it cannot be a servant's step ;
It must be Cenci, unexpectedly
Returned. . . .　Make some excuse for being here.

BEATRICE (*to* ORSINO, *as she goes out*)

That step we hear approach must never pass
The bridge of which we spoke.

　　　　　　　　[*Exeunt* LUCRETIA *and* BEATRICE.

ORSINO

　　　　　　　　What shall I do ?
Cenci must find me here, and I must bear
The imperious inquisition of his looks
As to what brought me hither : let me mask
Mine own in some inane and vacant smile.

Enter GIACOMO, *in a hurried manner*

How !　Have you ventured hither ?　Know you then
That Cenci is from home ?

GIACOMO

　　　　　　　　I sought him here ;
And now must wait till he returns.

ORSINO

　　　　　　　　Great God !
Weigh you the danger of this rashness ?

GIACOMO

　　　　　　　　Aye !
Does my destroyer know his danger ?　We
Are now no more, as once, parent and child,

But man to man ; the oppressor to the oppressed ;
The slanderer to the slandered ; foe to foe :
He has cast Nature off, which was his shield,
And Nature casts him off, who is her shame ;
And I spurn both.   Is it a father's throat
Which I will shake, and say, I ask not gold ;
I ask not happy years ; nor memories
Of tranquil childhood ; nor home-sheltered love ;
Though all these hast thou torn from me, and more ;
But only my fair fame ; only one hoard
Of peace, which I thought hidden from thy hate,
Under the penury heaped on me by thee,
Or I will . . . God can understand and pardon :
Why should I speak with man ?

ORSINO

Be calm, dear friend

GIACOMO

Well, I will calmly tell you what he did.
This old Francesco Cenci, as you know,
Borrowed the dowry of my wife from me,
And then denied the loan ; and left me so
In poverty, the which I sought to mend
By holding a poor office in the state.
It had been promised to me, and already
I bought new clothing for my ragged babes,
And my wife smiled ; and my heart knew repose.
When Cenci's intercession, as I found,
Conferred this office on a wretch, whom thus
He paid for vilest service.   I returned
With this ill news, and we sate sad together
Solacing our despondency with tears
Of such affection and unbroken faith
As temper life's worst bitterness ; when he,
As he is wont, came to upbraid and curse,
Mocking our poverty, and telling us
Such was God's scourge for disobedient sons.

And then, that I might strike him dumb with shame,
I spoke of my wife's dowry ; but he coined
A brief yet specious tale, how I had wasted
The sum in secret riot ; and he saw
My wife was touched, and he went smiling forth.
And when I knew the impression he had made,
And felt my wife insult with silent scorn
My ardent truth, and look averse and cold,
I went forth too : but soon returned again ;
Yet not so soon but that my wife had taught
My children her harsh thoughts, and they all cried,
" Give us clothes, father ! Give us better food !
What you in one night squander were enough
For months ! " I looked, and saw that home was hell.
And to that hell will I return no more
Until mine enemy has rendered up
Atonement, or, as he gave life to me
I will, reversing nature's law . . .

ORSINO

Trust me,
The compensation which thou seekest here
Will be denied.

GIACOMO

Then . . . Are you not my friend ?
Did you not hint at the alternative,
Upon the brink of which you see I stand,
The other day when we conversed together ?
My wrongs were then less. That word parricide,
Although I am resolved, haunts me like fear.

ORSINO

It must be fear itself, for the bare word
Is hollow mockery. Mark, how wisest God
Draws to one point the threads of a just doom,
So sanctifying it : what you devise
Is, as it were, accomplished.

GIACOMO

Is he dead ?

ORSINO

His grave is ready.   Know that since we met
Cenci has done an outrage to his daughter.

GIACOMO

What outrage ?

ORSINO

That she speaks not, but you may
Conceive such half conjectures as I do,
From her fixed paleness, and the lofty grief
Of her stern brow bent on the idle air,
And her severe unmodulated voice,
Drowning both tenderness and dread ; and last
From this ; that whilst her step-mother and I,
Bewildered in our horror, talked together
With obscure hints, both self-misunderstood
And darkly guessing, stumbling, in our talk,
Over the truth, and yet to its revenge,
She interrupted us, and with a look
Which told before she spoke it, he must die : .

GIACOMO

It is enough.   My doubts are well appeased ;
There is a higher reason for the act
Than mine ; there is a holier judge than me,
A more unblamed avenger.   Beatrice,
Who in the gentleness of thy sweet youth
Hast never trodden on a worm, or bruised
A living flower, but thou hast pitied it
With needless tears !   Fair sister, thou in whom
Men wondered how such loveliness and wisdom
Did not destroy each other !   Is there made
Ravage of thee ?   O, heart, I ask no more
Justification !   Shall I wait, Orsino,
Till he return, and stab him at the door ?

ORSINO

Not so ; some accident might interpose
To rescue him from what is now most sure :
And you are unprovided where to fly,
How to excuse or to conceal.   Nay, listen :
All is contrived ; success is so assured
That . . .

Enter BEATRICE

BEATRICE

'Tis my brother's voice !   You know me not ?

GIACOMO

My sister, my lost sister !

BEATRICE

Lost indeed !
I see Orsino has talked with you, and
That you conjecture things too horrible
To speak, yet far less than the truth.   Now, stay not,
He might return : yet kiss me ; I shall know
That then thou hast consented to his death.
Farewell, farewell !   Let piety to God,
Brotherly love, justice and clemency,
And all things that make tender hardest hearts
Make thine hard, brother.   Answer not . . . farewell.
                              [*Exeunt severally.*

SCENE II.   *A mean apartment in* GIACOMO'S
        House.   GIACOMO *alone*

GIACOMO

'Tis midnight, and Orsino comes not yet.
                    (*Thunder, and the sound of a storm.*)
What ! can the everlasting elements
Feel with a worm like man ?   If so the shaft

Of mercy-wingèd lightning would not fall
On stones and trees.   My wife and children sleep :
They are now living in unmeaning dreams :
But I must wake, still doubting if that deed
Be just which was most necessary.   O,
Thou unreplenished lamp ! whose narrow fire
Is shaken by the wind, and on whose edge
Devouring darkness hovers !   Thou small flame,
Which, as a dying pulse rises and falls,
Still flickerest up and down, how very soon,
Did I not feed thee, wouldst thou fail and be
As thou hadst never been !   So wastes and sinks
Even now, perhaps, the life that kindled mine :
But that no power can fill with vital oil,
That broken lamp of flesh.   Ha ! 'tis the blood
Which fed these veins that ebbs till all is cold :
It is the form that moulded mine that sinks
Into the white and yellow spasms of death :
It is the soul by which mine was arrayed
In God's immortal likeness which now stands
Naked before Heaven's judgment-seat !
              (*A bell strikes.*)   One !   Two !
The hours crawl on ; and when my hairs are white,
My son will then perhaps be waiting thus,
Tortured between just hate and vain remorse ;
Chiding the tardy messenger of news
Like those which I expect.   I almost wish
He be not dead, although my wrongs are great ;
Yet . . .'tis Orsino's step . . .

Enter ORSINO

Speak !

ORSINO

I am come

To say he has escaped.

GIACOMO

Escaped !

6 a

ORSINO

And safe
Within Petrella.   He passed by the spot
Appointed for the deed an hour too soon.

GIACOMO

Are we the fools of such contingencies ?
And do we waste in blind misgivings thus
The hours when we should act ?   Then wind and thunder,
Which seemed to howl his knell, is the loud laughter
With which Heaven mocks our weakness !   I henceforth
Will ne'er repent of aught designed or done
But my repentance.

ORSINO

See, the lamp is out.

GIACOMO

If no remorse is ours when the dim air
Has drank this innocent flame, why should we quail
When Cenci's life, that light by which ill spirits
See the worst deeds they prompt, shall sink for ever ?
No, I am hardened.

ORSINO

Why, what need of this ?
Who feared the pale intrusion of remorse
In a just deed ?   Although our first plan failed,
Doubt not but he will soon be laid to rest.
But light the lamp ; let us not talk i' the dark.

GIACOMO (*lighting the lamp*)

And yet once quenched I cannot thus relume
My father's life : do you not think his ghost
Might plead that argument with God ?

ORSINO

Once gone
You cannot now recall your sister's peace ;
Your own extinguished years of youth and hope ;
Nor your wife's bitter words ; nor all the taunts
Which, from the prosperous, weak misfortune takes ;
Nor your dead mother ; nor . . .

GIACOMO

O, speak no more !
I am resolved, although this very hand
Must quench the life that animated it.

ORSINO

There is no need of that.   Listen : you know
Olimpio, the castellan of Petrella
In old Colonna's time ; him whom your father
Degraded from his post ?   And Marzio,
That desperate wretch, whom he deprived last year
Of a reward of blood, well earned and due ?

GIACOMO

I knew Olimpio ; and they say he hated
Old Cenci so, that in his silent rage
His lips grew white only to see him pass.
Of Marzio I know nothing.

ORSINO

Marzio's hate
Matches Olimpio's.   I have sent these men,
But in your name, and as at your request,
To talk with Beatrice and Lucretia.

GIACOMO

Only to talk ?

ORSINO

The moments which even now
Pass onward to to-morrow's midnight hour
May memorize their flight with death : ere then
They must have talked, and may perhaps have done,
And made an end. . . .

GIACOMO
                        Listen !   What sound is that ?

ORSINO

The house-dog moans, and the beams crack : naught else.

GIACOMO

It is my wife complaining in her sleep :
I doubt not she is saying bitter things
Of me ; and all my children round her dreaming
That I deny them sustenance.

ORSINO
                                    Whilst he
Who truly took it from them, and who fills
Their hungry rest with bitterness, now sleeps
Lapped in bad pleasures, and triumphantly
Mocks thee in visions of successful hate
Too like the truth of day.

GIACOMO
                            If e'er he wakes
Again, I will not trust to hireling hands. . . .

ORSINO

Why, that were well.   I must be gone ; good night :
When next we meet—may all be done !

GIACOMO
                                        And all

Forgotten : Oh, that I had never been !   [*Exeunt.*

END OF THE THIRD ACT

ACT IV

SCENE I. *An Apartment in the Castle of Petrella*

Enter CENCI

CENCI

She comes not ; yet I left her even now
Vanquished and faint.   She knows the penalty
Of her delay : yet what if threats are vain ?
Am I not now within Petrella's moat ?
Or fear I still the eyes and ears of Rome ?
Might I not drag her by the golden hair ?
Stamp on her ?   Keep her sleepless till her brain
Be overworn ?   Tame her with chains and famine ?
Less would suffice.   Yet so to leave undone
What I most seek !   No, tis her stubborn will
Which by its own consent shall stoop as low
As that which drags it down.

Enter LUCRETIA

                    Thou loathèd wretch !
Hide thee from my abhorrence ; fly, begone !
Yet stay !   Bid Beatrice come hither.

LUCRETIA
                              Oh,
Husband !   I pray for thine own wretched sake
Heed what thou dost.   A man who walks like thee
Through crimes, and through the danger of his crimes,
Each hour may stumble o'er a sudden grave.
And thou art old ; thy hairs are hoary-grey ;
As thou wouldst save thyself from death and hell,
Pity thy daughter ; give her to some friend
In marriage : so that she may tempt thee not
To hatred, or worse thoughts, if worse there be.

CENCI

What ! like her sister who has found a home
To mock my hate from with prosperity ?
Strange ruin shall destroy both her and thee
And all that yet remain.   My death may be
Rapid, her destiny outspeeds it.   Go,
Bid her come hither, and before my mood
Be changed, lest I should drag her by the hair.

LUCRETIA

She sent me to thee, husband.   At thy presence
She fell, as thou dost know, into a trance ;
And in that trance she heard a voice which said,
" Cenci must die !   Let him confess himself !
Even now the accusing Angel waits to hear
If God, to punish his enormous crimes,
Harden his dying heart ! "

CENCI

Why—such things are . . .
No doubt divine revelings may be made.
'Tis plain I have been favoured from above,
For when I cursed my sons they died.—Aye . . . so . . .
As to the right or wrong that's talk . . . repentance . . .
Repentance is an easy moment's work
And more depends on God than me.   Well . . . well . . .
I must give up the greater point, which was
To poison and corrupt her soul.

(*A pause ;* LUCRETIA *approaches anxiously, and
then shrinks back as he speaks.*)
One, two ;
Aye . . . Rocco and Cristofano my curse
Strangled : and Giacomo, I think, will find
Life a worse Hell than that beyond the grave :
Beatrice shall, if there be skill in hate,
Die in despair, blaspheming : to Bernardo,

He is so innocent, I will bequeath
The memory of these deeds, and make his youth
The sepulchre of hope, where evil thoughts
Shall grow like weeds on a neglected tomb.
When all is done, out in the wide Campagna,
I will pile up my silver and my gold ;
My costly robes, paintings and tapestries ;
My parchments and all records of my wealth,
And make a bonfire in my joy, and leave
Of my possessions nothing but my name ;
Which shall be an inheritance to strip
Its wearer bare as infamy. That done,
My soul, which is a scourge, will I resign
Into the hands of him who wielded it ;
Be it for its own punishment or theirs,
He will not ask it of me till the lash
Be broken in its last and deepest wound ;
Until its hate be all inflicted. Yet,
Lest death outspeed my purpose, let me make
Short work and sure . . .   (*Going.*)

LUCRETIA (*stops him*)
                    Oh, stay ! It was a feint :
She had no vision, and she heard no voice.
I said it but to awe thee.

CENCI
                    That is well.
Vile palterer with the sacred truth of God,
Be thy soul choked with that blaspheming lie !
For Beatrice worse terrors are in store
To bend her to my will.

LUCRETIA
                    Oh ! to what will ?
What cruel sufferings more than she has known
Canst thou inflict ?

CENCI

Andrea ! go call my daughter,
And if she comes not tell her that I come.
What sufferings ? I will drag her, step by step,
Through infamies unheard of among men :
She shall stand shelterless in the broad noon
Of public scorn, for acts blazoned abroad,
One among which shall be . . . What ? Canst thou
    guess ?
She shall become, (for what she most abhors
Shall have a fascination to entrap
Her loathing will,) to her own conscious self
All she appears to others ; and when dead,
As she shall die unshrived and unforgiven,
A rebel to her father and her God,
Her corpse shall be abandoned to the hounds ;
Her name shall be the terror of the earth ;
Her spirit shall approach the throne of God
Plague-spotted with my curses. I will make
Body and soul a monstrous lump of ruin.

Enter ANDREA

ANDREA

The Lady Beatrice . . .

CENCI

Speak, pale slave ! What
Said she ?

ANDREA

My Lord, 'twas what she looked ; she said
" Go tell my father that I see the gulph
Of Hell between us two, which he may pass,
I will not."   [*Exit* ANDREA.

CENCI

Go thou quick, Lucretia,

Tell her to come ; yet let her understand
Her coming is consent : and say, moreover,
That if she come not I will curse her.

[*Exit* LUCRETIA.

Ha !

With what but with a father's curse doth God
Panic-strike armèd victory, and make pale
Cities in their prosperity ?   The world's Father
Must grant a parent's prayer against his child
Be he who asks even what men call me.
Will not the deaths of her rebellious brothers
Awe her before I speak ?   For I on them
Did imprecate quick ruin, and it came.

Enter LUCRETIA

Well ; what ?   Speak, wretch !

LUCRETIA

She said, " I cannot come ;
Go tell my father that I see a torrent
Of his own blood raging between us."

CENCI (*kneeling*)

God !

Hear me !   If this most specious mass of flesh,
Which thou hast made my daughter ; this my blood,
This particle of my divided being ;
Or rather, this my bane and my disease,
Whose sight infects and poisons me ; this devil
Which, sprung from me as from a hell, was meant
To aught good use ; if her bright loveliness
Was kindled to illumine this dark world ;
If nursed by thy selectest dew of love
Such virtues blossom in her as should make
The peace of life, I pray thee for my sake,
As thou the common God and Father art
Of her, and me, and all ; reverse that doom !

Earth, in the name of God, let her food be
Poison, until she be encrusted round
With leprous stains ! Heaven, rain upon her head
The blistering drops of the Maremma's dew,
Till she be speckled like a toad ; parch up
Those love-enkindled lips, warp those fine limbs
To loathèd lameness ! All-beholding sun,
Strike in thine envy those life-darting eyes
With thine own blinding beams !

LUCRETIA

                Peace ! Peace !
For thine own sake unsay those dreadful words.
When high God grants he punishes such prayers.

CENCI

(leaping up, and throwing his right hand towards
Heaven)

He does his will, I mine ! This in addition,
That if she have a child . . .

LUCRETIA

                Horrible thought !

CENCI

That if she ever have a child ; and thou,
Quick Nature ! I adjure thee by thy God,
That thou be fruitful in her, and increase
And multiply, fulfilling his command,
And my deep imprecation ! May it be
A hideous likeness of herself, that as
From a distorting mirror, she may see
Her image mixed with what she most abhors,
Smiling upon her from her nursing breast.
And that the child may from its infancy
Grow, day by day, more wicked and deformed,
Turning her mother's love to misery :

And that both she and it may live until
It shall repay her care and pain with hate,
Or what may else be more unnatural
So he may hunt her through the clamorous scoffs
Of the loud world to a dishonoured grave.
Shall I revoke this curse ? Go, bid her come
Before my words are chronicled in heaven.

[Exit LUCRETIA.

I do not feel as if I were a man,
But like a fiend appointed to chastise
The offences of some unremembered world.
My blood is running up and down my veins ;
A fearful pleasure makes it prick and tingle :
I feel a giddy sickness of strange awe ;
My heart is beating with an expectation
Of horrid joy.

Enter LUCRETIA

What ? Speak !

LUCRETIA

                    She bids thee curse ;
And if thy curses, as they cannot do
Could kill her soul . . . .

CENCI

                    She would not come. 'Tis well,
I can do both : first take what I demand,
And then extort concession. To thy chamber !
Fly ere I spurn thee : and beware this night
That thou cross not my footsteps. It were safer
To come between the tiger and his prey.

[Exit LUCRETIA.

It must be late ; mine eyes grow weary dim
With unaccustomed heaviness of sleep.
Conscience ! Oh, thou most insolent of lies !
They say that sleep, that healing dew of heaven,

Steeps not in balm the foldings of the brain
Which thinks thee an impostor.   I will go
First to belie thee with an hour of rest,
Which will be deep and calm, I feel : and then . . .
O, multitudinous Hell, the fiends will shake
Thine arches with the laughter of their joy !
There shall be lamentation heard in Heaven
As o'er an angel fallen ; and upon Earth
All good shall droop and sicken, and ill things
Shall with a spirit of unnatural life
Stir and be quickened . . . even as I am now.

[*Exit*.

SCENE II.   *Before the Castle of Petrella*

Enter BEATRICE *and* LUCRETIA *above
on the Ramparts*

BEATRICE

They come not yet.

LUCRETIA

'Tis scarce midnight.

BEATRICE

How slow
Behind the course of thought, even sick with speed,
Lags leaden-footed time !

LUCRETIA

The minutes pass . . .
If he should wake before the deed is done ?

BEATRICE

O, Mother !   He must never wake again.
What thou hast said persuades me that our act

Will but dislodge a spirit of deep hell
Out of a human form.

LUCRETIA

'Tis true he spoke
Of death and judgment with strange confidence
For one so wicked ; as a man believing
In God, yet recking not of good or ill,
And yet to die without confession ! . . .

BEATRICE

Oh !
Believe that Heaven is merciful and just,
And will not add our dread necessity
To the amount of his offences.

Enter OLIMPIO *and* MARZIO *below*

LUCRETIA

See,
They come.

BEATRICE

All mortal things must hasten thus
To their dark end.   Let us go down.
[*Exeunt* LUCRETIA *and* BEATRICE *from above.*

OLIMPIO

How feel you to this work ?

MARZIO

As one who thinks
A thousand crowns excellent market price
For an old murderer's life.   Your cheeks are pale.

OLIMPIO

It is the white reflexion of your own,
Which you call pale.

MARZIO

Is that their natural hue ?

OLIMPIO

Or 'tis my hate and the deferred desire
To wreak it, which extinguishes their blood.

MARZIO

You are inclined then to this business ?

OLIMPIO

Aye.
If one should bribe me with a thousand crowns
To kill a serpent which had stung my child,
I could not be more willing.

Enter BEATRICE *and* LUCRETIA *below*
Noble ladies !

BEATRICE

Are ye resolved ?

OLIMPIO

Is he asleep ?

MARZIO

Is all
Quiet ?

LUCRETIA

I mixed an opiate with his drink :
He sleeps so soundly . . .

BEATRICE

That his death will be
But as a change of sin-chastising dreams,
A dark continuance of the Hell within him,

Which God extinguish ! But ye are resolved ?
Ye know it is a high and holy deed ?

OLIMPIO

We are resolved.

MARZIO

As to the how this act
Be warranted, it rests with you.

BEATRICE

Well, follow !

OLIMPIO

Hush ! Hark ! What noise is that ?

MARZIO

Ha ! some one comes !

BEATRICE

Ye conscience-stricken cravens, rock to rest
Your baby hearts. It is the iron gate,
Which ye left open, swinging to the wind,
That enters whistling as in scorn. Come, follow !
And be your steps like mine, light, quick and bold.

[*Exeunt.*

SCENE III. *An Apartment in the Castle*

Enter BEATRICE *and* LUCRETIA

LUCRETIA

They are about it now.

BEATRICE

Nay, it is done.

LUCRETIA

I have not heard him groan.

BEATRICE
　　　　　　　He will not groan

LUCRETIA

What sound is that ?

BEATRICE
　　　　　　　List ! 'tis the tread of feet

About his bed.

LUCRETIA
　　　　My God !
If he be now a cold stiff corpse . . .

BEATRICE
　　　　　　　　O, fear not

What may be done, but what is left undone :
The act seals all.

Enter OLIMPIO *and* MARZIO
　　　　Is it accomplished ?

MARZIO
　　　　　　　　　What ?

OLIMPIO

Did you not call ?

BEATRICE
When ?

OLIMPIO
　　　　Now.

BEATRICE
　　　　　　　I ask if all is over ?

OLIMPIO

We dare not kill an old and sleeping man ;
His thin grey hair, his stern and reverent brow,
His veinèd hands crossed on his heaving breast,
And the calm innocent sleep in which he lay,
Quelled me.　Indeed, indeed, I cannot do it.

MARZIO

But I was bolder ; for I chid Olimpio,
And bade him bear his wrongs to his own grave
And leave me the reward.   And now my knife
Touched the loose wrinkled throat, when the old man
Stirred in his sleep, and said, " God ! hear, O, hear,
A father's curse !   What, art thou not our father ? "
And then he laughed.   I knew it was the ghost
Of my dead father speaking through his lips,
And could not kill him.

BEATRICE

Miserable slaves !
Where, if ye dare not kill a sleeping man,
Found ye the boldness to return to me
With such a deed undone ?   Base palterers !
Cowards and traitors !   Why, the very conscience
Which ye would sell for gold and for revenge
Is an equivocation : it sleeps over
A thousand daily acts disgracing men ;
And when a deed where mercy insults heaven . . .
Why do I talk ?

(*Snatching a dagger from one of them and raising it.*)
Hadst thou a tongue to say,
She murdered her own father, I must do it !
But never dream ye shall outlive him long !

OLIMPIO

Stop, for God's sake !

MARZIO

I will go back and kill him.

OLIMPIO

Give me the weapon, we must do thy will.

BEATRICE

Take it !   Depart !   Return !
                    [*Exeunt* OLIMPIO *and* MARZIO.

How pale thou art !
We do but that which 'twere a deadly crime
To leave undone.

LUCRETIA

Would it were done !

BEATRICE

Even whilst
That doubt is passing through your mind, the world
Is conscious of a change.   Darkness and hell
Have swallowed up the vapour they sent forth
To blacken the sweet light of life.   My breath
Comes, methinks, lighter, and the jellied blood
Runs freely through my veins.   Hark !

Enter OLIMPIO *and* MARZIO

He is . . . .

OLIMPIO

Dead !

MARZIO

We strangled him that there might be no blood ;
And then we threw his heavy corpse i' the garden
Under the balcony ; 'twill seem it fell.

BEATRICE (*giving them a bag of coin*)

Here, take this gold, and hasten to your homes.
And, Marzio, because thou wast only awed
By that which made me tremble, wear thou this !
(*Clothes him in a rich mantle.*)
It was the mantle which my grandfather
Wore in his high prosperity, and men
Envied his state : so may they envy thine.
Thou wert a weapon in the hand of God
To a just use.   Live long and thrive !   And, mark,
If thou hast crimes, repent : this deed is none.
(*A horn is sounded.*)

LUCRETIA

Hark, 'tis the castle horn ; my God ! it sounds
Like the last trump.

BEATRICE

Some tedious guest is coming.

LUCRETIA

The drawbridge is let down ; there is a tramp
Of horses in the court ; fly, hide yourselves !

[*Exeunt* OLIMPIO *and* MARZIO.

BEATRICE

Let us retire to counterfeit deep rest ;
I scarcely need to counterfeit it now :
The spirit which doth reign within these limbs
Seems strangely undisturbed.   I could even sleep
Fearless and calm : all ill is surely past.

[*Exeunt.*

SCENE IV.   *Another Apartment in the Castle*

Enter on one side the Legate SAVELLA, *introduced by a*
Servant, *and on the other* LUCRETIA *and* BERNARDO

SAVELLA

Lady, my duty to his Holiness
Be my excuse that thus unseasonably
I break upon your rest.   I must speak with
Count Cenci ; doth he sleep ?

LUCRETIA

(*in a hurried and confused manner*)

I think he sleeps ;
Yet wake him not, I pray, spare me awhile,
He is a wicked and a wrathful man ;

Should he be roused out of his sleep to-night,
Which is, I know, a hell of angry dreams,
It were not well ; indeed it were not well.
Wait till day break . . . (*Aside.*) O, I am deadly sick !

SAVELLA

I grieve thus to distress you, but the Count
Must answer charges of the gravest import,
And suddenly ; such my commission is.

LUCRETIA (*with increased agitation*)

I dare not rouse him : I know none who dare. . . .
'Twere perilous ; . . . you might as safely waken
A serpent ; or a corpse in which some fiend
Were laid to sleep.

SAVELLA

Lady, my moments here
Are counted. I must rouse him from his sleep,
Since none else dare.

LUCRETIA (*aside*)

O, terror ! O, despair !
(*To Bernardo.*) Bernardo, conduct you the Lord
Legate to
Your father's chamber.

[*Exeunt* SAVELLA *and* BERNARDO.

Enter BEATRICE

BEATRICE

'Tis a messenger
Come to arrest the culprit who now stands
Before the throne of unappealable God.
Both Earth and Heaven, consenting arbiters,
Acquit our deed.

LUCRETIA

Oh, agony of fear !
Would that he yet might live ! Even now I heard

The Legate's followers whisper as they passed
They had a warrant for his instant death.
All was prepared by unforbidden means
Which we must pay so dearly, having done.
Even now they search the tower, and find the body;
Now they suspect the truth ; now they consult
Before they come to tax us with the fact :
O, horrible, 'tis all discovered !

BEATRICE

       Mother,
What is done wisely, is done well. Be bold
As thou art just. 'Tis like a truant child
To fear that others know what thou hast done,
Even from thine own strong consciousness, and thus
Write on unsteady eyes and altered cheeks
All thou wouldst hide. Be faithful to thyself,
And fear no other witness but thy fear.
For if, as cannot be, some circumstance
Should rise in accusation, we can blind
Suspicion with such cheap astonishment,
Or overbear it with such guiltless pride,
As murderers cannot feign. The deed is done,
And what may follow now regards not me.
I am as universal as the light ;
Free as the earth-surrounding air ; as firm
As the world's centre. Consequence, to me,
Is as the wind which strikes the solid rock
But shakes it not.   (*A cry within and tumult.*)

VOICES

Murder ! Murder ! Murder !

Enter BERNARDO *and* SAVELLA

SAVELLA (*to his followers*)

Go search the castle round ; sound the alarm !
Look to the gates that none escape !

BEATRICE

                                        What now ?

BERNARDO

I know not what to say . . . my father's dead.

BEATRICE

How ; dead ! he only sleeps ; you mistake, brother.
His sleep is very calm, very like death ;
'Tis wonderful how well a tyrant sleeps.
He is not dead ?

BERNARDO

Dead ; murdered.

LUCRETIA (*with extreme agitation*)

                                    Oh, no, no
He is not murdered though he may be dead ;
I have alone the keys of those apartments.

SAVELLA

Ha !   Is it so ?

BERNARDO

            My Lord, I pray excuse us ;
We will retire ; my mother is not well :
She seems quite overcome with this strange horror.
                    [*Exeunt* LUCRETIA *and* BEATRICE.

SAVELLA

Can you suspect who may have murdered him ?

BERNARDO

I know not what to think.

SAVELLA

                        Can you name any
Who had an interest in his death ?

BERNARDO

Alas !
I can name none who had not, and those most
Who most lament that such a deed is done ;
My mother, and my sister, and myself.

SAVELLA

'Tis strange !   There were clear marks of violence.
I found the old man's body in the moonlight
Hanging beneath the window of his chamber,
Among the branches of a pine : he could not
Have fallen there, for all his limbs lay heaped
And effortless ; 'tis true there was no blood. . . .
Favour me, Sir,—it much imports your house
That all should be made clear,—to tell the ladies
That I request their presence.

[Exit BERNARDO.

Enter Guards *bringing in* MARZIO

GUARD

We have one.

OFFICER

My Lord, we found this ruffian and another
Lurking among the rocks ; there is no doubt
But that they are the murderers of Count Cenci :
Each had a bag of coin ; this fellow wore
A gold-inwoven robe, which shining bright
Under the dark rocks to the glimmering moon
Betrayed them to our notice : the other fell
Desperately fighting.

SAVELLA

What does he confess ?

OFFICER

He keeps firm silence : but these lines found on him
May speak.

SAVELLA

Their language is at least sincere.   (*Reads.*)

TO THE LADY BEATRICE

" That the atonement of what my nature sickens to
conjecture may soon arrive, I send thee, at thy brother's
desire, those who will speak and do more than I dare
write. . . . Thy devoted servant, ORSINO."

Enter LUCRETIA, BEATRICE, *and* BERNARDO

Knowest thou this writing, Lady ?

BEATRICE

No.

SAVELLA

Nor thou ?

LUCRETIA

(*Her conduct throughout the scene is marked by
extreme agitation*)

Where was it found ?   What is it ?   It should be
Orsino's hand !   It speaks of that strange horror
Which never yet found utterance, but which made
Between that hapless child and her dead father
A gulph of obscure hatred.

SAVELLA

Is it so ?

Is it true, Lady, that thy father did
Such outrages as to awaken in thee
Unfilial hate ?

BEATRICE

Not hate—'twas more than hate :
This is most true, yet wherefore question me ?

SAVELLA

There is a deed demanding question done ;
Thou hast a secret which will answer not.

BEATRICE

What sayest ?   My Lord, your words are bold and rash.

SAVELLA

I do arrest all present in the name
Of the Pope's Holiness.   You must to Rome.

LUCRETIA

O, not to Rome !   Indeed we are not guilty.

BEATRICE

Guilty !   Who dares talk of guilt ?   My Lord,
I am more innocent of parricide
Than is a child born fatherless. . . . Dear Mother,
Your gentleness and patience are no shield
For this keen-judging world, this two-edged lie,
Which seems, but is not.   What ! will human laws,—
Rather will ye who are their ministers,—
Bar all access to retribution first,
And then, when heaven doth interpose to do
What ye neglect, arming familiar things
To the redress of an unwonted crime,
Make ye the victims who demanded it
Culprits ?   'Tis ye are culprits !   That poor wretch
Who stands so pale, and trembling, and amazed,
If it be true he murdered Cenci, was
A sword in the right hand of justest God.
Wherefore should I have wielded it ?   Unless
The crimes which mortal tongue dare never name
God therefore scruples to avenge.

SAVELLA

                              You own
That you desired his death ?

BEATRICE

                              It would have been

7

A crime no less than his, if for one moment
That fierce desire had faded in my heart.
'Tis true I did believe, and hope, and pray,
Aye, I even knew,—for God is wise and just,—
That some strange sudden death hung over him.
'Tis true that this did happen, and most true
There was no other rest for me on earth,
No other hope in Heaven . . . now what of this ?

SAVELLA

Strange thoughts beget strange deeds ; and here are
    both :
I judge thee not.

BEATRICE

                    And yet, if you arrest me,
You are the judge and executioner
Of that which is the life of life : the breath
Of accusation kills an innocent name,
And leaves for lame acquittal the poor life
Which is a mask without it. 'Tis most false
That I am guilty of foul parricide ;
Although I must rejoice, for justest cause,
That other hands have sent my father's soul
To ask the mercy he denied to me.
Now leave us free : stain not a noble house
With vague surmises of rejected crime ;
Add to our sufferings and your own neglect
No heavier sum : let them have been enough :
Leave us the wreck we have.

SAVELLA

                        I dare not, Lady.
I pray that you prepare yourselves for Rome :
There the Pope's further pleasure will be known.

LUCRETIA

O, not to Rome ! O, take us not to Rome !

BEATRICE

Why not to Rome, dear mother ? There as here
Our innocence is as an armèd heel
To trample accusation. God is there
As here, and with his shadow ever clothes
The innocent, the injured and the weak ;
And such are we. Cheer up, dear Lady, lean
On me ; collect your wandering thoughts. My Lord,
As soon as you have taken some refreshment,
And had all such examinations made
Upon the spot, as may be necessary
To the full understanding of this matter,
We shall be ready. Mother ; will you come ?

LUCRETIA

Ha ! they will bind us to the rack, and wrest
Self-accusation from our agony !
Will Giacomo be there ? Orsino ? Marzio ?
All present ; all confronted ; all demanding
Each from the other's countenance the thing
Which is in every heart ! O, misery !

[She faints, and is borne out.

SAVELLA

She faints : an ill appearance this.

BEATRICE

My Lord,
She knows not yet the uses of the world.
She fears that power is as a beast which grasps
And loosens not : a snake whose look transmutes
All things to guilt which is its nutriment.
She cannot know how well the supine slaves
Of blind authority read the truth of things
When written on a brow of guilenessness :
She sees not yet triumphant Innocence
Stand at the judgment-seat of mortal man,

A judge and an accuser of the wrong
Which drags it there.　Prepare yourself, my Lord ;
Our suite will join yours in the court below.

　　　　　　　　　　　　　　　　　　　　　[Exeunt.

END OF THE FOURTH ACT

ACT V

Scene I. *An Apartment in* Orsino's *Palace*

Enter Orsino *and* Giacomo

Giacomo

Do evil deeds thus quickly come to end ?
O, that the vain remorse which must chastise
Crimes done, had but as loud a voice to warn
As its keen sting is mortal to avenge !
O, that the hour when present had cast off
The mantle of its mystery, and shown
The ghastly form with which it now returns
When its scared game is roused, cheering the hounds
Of conscience to their prey ! Alas ! Alas !
It was a wicked thought, a piteous deed,
To kill an old and hoary-headed father.

Orsino

It has turned out unluckily, in truth.

Giacomo

To violate the sacred doors of sleep ;
To cheat kind nature of the placid death
Which she prepares for overwearied age ;
To drag from Heaven an unrepentant soul
Which might have quenched in reconciling prayers
A life of burning crimes . . .

Orsino

　　　　　　　　　　You cannot say
I urged you to the deed.

GIACOMO

O, had I never
Found in thy smooth and ready countenance
The mirror of my darkest thoughts ; hadst thou
Never with hints and questions made me look
Upon the monster of my thought, until
It grew familiar to desire . . .

ORSINO

'Tis thus
Men cast the blame of their unprosperous acts
Upon the abettors of their own resolve ;
Or anything but their weak, guilty selves.
And yet, confess the truth, it is the peril
In which you stand that gives you this pale sickness
Of penitence ; confess 'tis fear disguised
From its own shame that takes the mantle now
Of thin remorse.   What if we yet were safe ?

GIACOMO

How can that be ?   Already Beatrice,
Lucretia and the murderer are in prison.
I doubt not officers are, whilst we speak,
Sent to arrest us.

ORSINO

I have all prepared
For instant flight.   We can escape even now,
So we take fleet occasion by the hair.

GIACOMO

Rather expire in tortures, as I may.
What ! will you cast by self-accusing flight
Assured conviction upon Beatrice ?
She who, alone in this unnatural work,
Stands like God's angel ministered upon
By fiends ; avenging such a nameless wrong
As turns black parricide to piety ;

Whilst we for basest ends . . . I fear, Orsino,
While I consider all your words and looks,
Comparing them with your proposal now,
That you must be a villain.   For what end
Could you engage in such a perilous crime,
Training me on with hints, and signs, and smiles,
Even to this gulph ?   Thou art no liar ?   No,
Thou art a lie !   Traitor and murderer !
Coward and slave !   But, no, defend thyself ;

(Drawing.)

Let the sword speak what the indignant tongue
Disdains to brand thee with.

ORSINO

Put up your weapon.
Is it the desperation of your fear
Makes you thus rash and sudden with a friend,
Now ruined for your sake ?   If honest anger
Have moved you, know, that what I just proposed
Was but to try you.   As for me, I think,
Thankless affection led me to this point,
From which, if my firm temper could repent,
I cannot now recede.   Even whilst we speak
The ministers of justice wait below :
They grant me these brief moments.   Now if you
Have any word of melancholy comfort
To speak to your pale wife, 'twere best to pass
Out at the postern, and avoid them so.

GIACOMO

O, generous friend !   How canst you pardon me ?
Would that my life could purchase thine !

ORSINO

That wish
Now comes a day too late.   Haste : fare thee well !
Hear'st thou not steps along the corridor ?

[*Exit* GIACOMO.

I'm sorry for it ; but the guards are waiting

At his own gate, and such was my contrivance
That I might rid me both of him and them.
I thought to act a solemn comedy
Upon the painted scene of this new world,
And to attain my own peculiar ends
By some such plot of mingled good and ill
As others weave ; but there arose a Power
Which grasped and snapped the threads of my device
And turned it to a net of ruin . . . Ha !

                           (*A shout is heard.*)

Is that my name I hear proclaimed abroad ?
But I will pass, wrapped in a vile disguise ;
Rags on my back, and a false innocence
Upon my face, through the misdeeming crowd
Which judges by what seems. 'Tis easy then
For a new name and for a country new,
And a new life, fashioned on old desires,
To change the honours of abandoned Rome.
And these must be the masks of that within,
Which must remain unaltered. . . . Oh, I fear
That what is past will never let me rest !
Why, when none else is conscious, but myself,
Of my misdeeds, should my own heart's contempt
Trouble me ?   Have I not the power to fly
My own reproaches ?   Shall I be the slave
Of . . . what ?   A word ? which those of this false world
Employ against each other, not themselves ;
As men wear daggers not for self-defence.
But if I am mistaken, where shall I
Find the disguise to hide me from myself,
As now I skulk from every other eye ?   [*Exit.*

SCENE II. *A Hall of Justice.* CAMILLO, *Judges, etc.,*
    are discovered seated ; MARZIO *is led in*

FIRST JUDGE

Accused, do you persist in your denial ?

I ask you, are you innocent, or guilty ?
I demand who were the participators
In your offence ?   Speak truth and the whole truth.

MARZIO

My God ! I did not kill him ; I know nothing ;
Olimpio sold the robe to me from which
You would infer my guilt.

SECOND JUDGE
                    Away with him !

FIRST JUDGE

Dare you, with lips yet white from the rack's kiss
Speak false ?   Is it so soft a questioner,
That you would bandy lover's talk with it
Till it wind out your life and soul ?   Away !

MARZIO

Spare me !   O, spare !   I will confess.

FIRST JUDGE
                            Then speak.

MARZIO

I strangled him in his sleep.

FIRST JUDGE
                    Who urged you to it ?

MARZIO

His own son Giacomo, and the young prelate
Orsino sent me to Petrella ; there
The ladies Beatrice and Lucretia
Tempted me with a thousand crowns, and I
And my companion forthwith murdered him.
Now let me die.

FIRST JUDGE

This sounds as bad as truth.   Guards, there,
Lead forth the prisoners !

Enter LUCRETIA, BEATRICE, *and* GIACOMO, *guarded*

      Look upon this man ;
When did you see him last ?

BEATRICE

      We never saw him.

MARZIO

You know me too well, Lady Beatrice.

BEATRICE

I know thee ! How ? Where ? When ?

MARZIO

       You know 'twas I
Whom you did urge with menaces and bribes
To kill your father. When the thing was done
You clothed me in a robe of woven gold
And bade me thrive : how I have thriven, you see.
You, my Lord Giacomo, Lady Lucretia,
You know that what I speak is true.

  (BEATRICE *advances towards him ; he covers his*
   face and shrinks back.)

         O, dart
The terrible resentment of those eyes
On the dead earth ! Turn them away from me !
They wound : 'twas torture forced the truth. My Lords,
Having said this let me be led to death.

BEATRICE

Poor wretch, I pity thee : yet stay awhile.

CAMILLO

Guards, lead him not away.

BEATRICE

      Cardinal Camillo,
You have a good repute for gentleness
And wisdom : can it be that you sit here

7 a

To countenance a wicked farce like this ?—
When some obscure and trembling slave is dragged
From sufferings which might shake the sternest heart
And bade to answer, not as he believes,
But as those may suspect or do desire,
Whose questions thence suggest their own reply :
And that in peril of such hideous torments
As merciful God spares even the damned.   Speak now
The thing you surely know, which is that you,
If your fine frame were stretched upon that wheel,
And you were told : " Confess that you did poison
Your little nephew ; that fair blue-eyed child
Who was the loadstar of your life : "—and though
All see, since his most swift and piteous death,
That day and night, and heaven and earth, and time,
And all the things hoped for or done therein,
Are changed to you, through your exceeding grief,
Yet you would say, " I confess anything : "
And beg from your tormentors, like that slave,
The refuge of dishonourable death.
I pray thee, Cardinal, that thou assert
My innocence.

CAMILLO (much moved)

What shall we think, my Lords ?
Shame on these tears !   I thought the heart was frozen
Which is their fountain.   I would pledge my soul
That she is guiltless.

JUDGE

Yet she must be tortured.

CAMILLO

I would as soon have tortured mine own nephew
(If he now lived he would be just her age ;
His hair, too, was her colour, and his eyes
Like hers in shape, but blue and not so deep)
As that most perfect image of God's love
That ever came sorrowing upon the earth.
She is as pure as speechless infancy !

JUDGE

Well, be her purity on your head, my Lord,
If you forbid the rack. His Holiness
Enjoined us to pursue this monstrous crime
By the severest forms of law ; nay, even
To stretch a point against the criminals.
The prisoners stand accused of parricide
Upon such evidence as justifies
Torture.

BEATRICE

What evidence ? This man's ?

JUDGE

Even so.

BEATRICE (*to* MARZIO)

Come near. And who art thou thus chosen forth
Out of the multitude of living men
To kill the innocent ?

MARZIO

I am Marzio,

Thy father's vassal.

BEATRICE

Fix thine eyes on mine ;
Answer to what I ask.   (*Turning to the* Judges.)
I prithee mark
His countenance : unlike bold calumny
Which sometimes dares not speak the thing it looks,
He dares not look the thing he speaks, but bends
His gaze on the blind earth.
           (*To* MARZIO.) What ! wilt thou say
That I did murder my own father ?

MARZIO

Oh !

Spare me ! My brain swims round. . . . I cannot
    speak. . . .
It was that horrid torture forced the truth.

Take me away ! Let her not look on me !
I am a guilty miserable wretch ;
I have said all I know ; now, let me die !

BEATRICE

My Lords, if by my nature I had been
So stern, as to have planned the crime alleged,
Which your suspicions dictate to this slave,
And the rack makes him utter do you think
I should have left this two-edged instrument
Of my misdeed ; this man, this bloody knife
With my own name engraven on the heft,
Lying unsheathed amid a world of foes,
For my own death ?   That with such horrible need
For deepest silence, I should have neglected
So trivial a precaution, as the making
His tomb the keeper of a secret written
On a thief's memory ?   What is his poor life ?
What are a thousand lives ?   A parricide
Had trampled them like dust ; and, see, he lives !
(*Turning to* MARZIO.)   And thou . . .

MARZIO

Oh, spare me ! Speak to me no more !
That stern yet piteous look, those solemn tones,
Wound worse than torture.
(*To the* Judges.)   I have told it all ;
For pity's sake lead me away to death.

CAMILLO

Guards, lead him nearer the Lady Beatrice,
He shrinks from her regard like autumn's leaf
From the keen breath of the serenest north.

BEATRICE

Oh, thou who tremblest on the giddy verge
Of life and death, pause ere thou answerest me ;
So mayst thou answer God with less dismay :

What evil have we done thee ?   I, alas !
Have lived but on this earth a few sad years
And so my lot was ordered, that a father
First turned the moments of awakening life
To drops, each poisoning youth's sweet hope ; and then
Stabbed with one blow my everlasting soul ;
And my untainted fame ; and even that peace
Which sleeps within the core of the heart's heart ;
But the wound was not mortal ; so my hate
Became the only worship I could lift
To our great father, who in pity and love,
Armed thee, as thou dost say, to cut him off ;
And thus his wrong becomes my accusation ;
And art thou the accuser ?   If thou hopest
Mercy in heaven, show justice upon earth :
Worse than a bloody hand is a hard heart.
If thou hast done murders, made thy life's path
Over the trampled laws of God and man,
Rush not before thy Judge, and say : " My maker,
I have done this and more ; for there was one
Who was most pure and innocent on earth ;
And because she endured what never any
Guilty or innocent endured before :
Because her wrongs could not be told, not thought ;
Because thy hand at length did rescue her ;
I with my words killed her and all her kin."
Think, I adjure you, what it is to slay
The reverence living in the minds of men
Towards our ancient house, and stainless fame !
Think what it is to strangle infant pity,
Cradled in the belief of guileless looks,
Till it become a crime to suffer.   Think
What 'tis to blot with infamy and blood
All that which shows like innocence, and is,
Hear me, great God ! I swear, most innocent,
So that the world lose all discrimination
Between the sly, fierce, wild regard of guilt,
And that which now compels thee to reply

To what I ask : Am I, or am I not
A parricide ?

MARZIO
Thou art not !

JUDGE
                              What is this ?

MARZIO
I here declare those whom I did accuse
Are innocent.   'Tis I alone am guilty.

JUDGE
Drag him away to torments ; let them be
Subtle and long drawn out, to tear the folds
Of the heart's inmost cell.   Unbind him not
Till he confess.

MARZIO
                    Torture me as ye will :
A keener pang has wrung a higher truth
From my last breath.   She is most innocent !
Bloodhounds, not men, glut yourselves well with me ;
I will not give you that fine piece of nature
To rend and ruin.   [*Exit* MARZIO, *guarded.*

CAMILLO
What say ye now, my Lords ?

JUDGE
Let tortures strain the truth till it be white
As snow thrice sifted by the frozen wind.

CAMILLO
Yet stained with blood.

JUDGE (*to* BEATRICE)
                    Know you this paper, Lady ?

BEATRICE
Entrap me not with questions.   Who stands here
As my accuser ?   Ha ! wilt thou be he,

Who art my judge ?   Accuser, witness, judge,
What, all in one ?   Here is Orsino's name ;
Where is Orsino ?   Let his eye meet mine.
What means this scrawl ?   Alas !   Ye know not what,
And therefore on the chance that it may be
Some evil, will ye kill us ?

Enter an Officer

OFFICER
                Marzio's dead.

JUDGE

What did he say ?

OFFICER
                Nothing.   As soon as we
Had bound him on the wheel, he smiled on us,
As one who baffles a deep adversary ;
And holding his breath, died.

JUDGE
                    There remains nothing
But to apply the question to those prisoners,
Who yet remain stubborn.

CAMILLO
                I overrule
Further proceedings, and in the behalf
Of these most innocent and noble persons
Will use my interest with the Holy Father.

JUDGE

Let the Pope's pleasure then be done.   Meanwhile
Conduct these culprits each to separate cells ;
And be the engines ready : for this night
If the Pope's resolution be as grave,
Pious, and just as once, I'll wring the truth
Out of those nerves and sinews, groan by groan.
                                        [*Exeunt.*

SCENE III. *The Cell of a Prison.* BEATRICE *is discovered asleep on a Couch*

Enter BERNARDO

BERNARDO

How gently slumber rests upon her face,
Like the last thoughts of some day sweetly spent
Closing in night and dreams, and so prolonged.
After such torments as she bore last night,
How light and soft her breathing comes. Ay, me !
Methinks that I shall never sleep again.
But I must shake the heavenly dew of rest
From this sweet folded flower, thus . . . wake ! awake !
What, sister, canst thou sleep ?

BEATRICE (*awaking*)

                  I was just dreaming
That we were all in Paradise. Thou knowest
This cell seems like a kind of Paradise
After our father's presence.

BERNARDO

                Dear, dear sister,
Would that thy dream were not a dream ! O, God !
How shall I tell ?

BEATRICE

What wouldst thou tell, sweet brother ?

BERNARDO

Look not so calm and happy, or even whilst
I stand considering what I have to say
My heart will break.

BEATRICE

             See now, thou mak'st me weep :
How very friendless thou wouldst be, dear child,
If I were dead. Say what thou hast to say.

BERNARDO

They have confessed ; they could endure no more
The tortures . . .

BEATRICE

      Ha ! What was there to confess ?
They must have told some weak and wicked lie
To flatter their tormentors.   Have they said
That they were guilty ?   O, white innocence,
That thou shouldst wear the mask of guilt to hide
Thine awful and serenest countenance
From those who know thee not !

Enter Judge *with* LUCRETIA *and* GIACOMO, *guarded*

            Ignoble hearts !
For some brief spasms of pain, which are at least
As mortal as the limbs through which they pass,
Are centuries of high splendour laid in dust ?
And that eternal honour which should live
Sunlike, above the reek of mortal fame,
Changed to a mockery and a bye-word ?   What !
Will you give up these bodies to be dragged
At horses' heels, so that our hair should sweep
The footsteps of the vain and senseless crowd,
Who, that they may make our calamity
Their worship and their spectacle, will leave
The churches and the theatres as void
As their own hearts ?   Shall the light multitude
Fling, at their choice, curses or faded pity,
Sad funeral flowers to deck a living corpse,
Upon us as we pass to pass away,
And leave . . . what memory of our having been ?
Infamy, blood, terror, despair ?   O thou,
Who wert a mother to the parentless,
Kill not thy child !   Let not her wrongs kill thee !
Brother, lie down with me upon the rack,
And let us each be silent as a corpse ;
It soon will be as soft as any grave.

'Tis but the falsehood it can wring from fear
Makes the rack cruel.

GIACOMO

They will tear the truth
Even from thee at last, those cruel pains :
For pity's sake say thou art guilty now.

LUCRETIA

O, speak the truth ! Let us all quickly die ;
And after death, God is our judge, not they ;
He will have mercy on us.

BERNARDO

If indeed
It can be true, say so, dear sister mine ;
And then the Pope will surely pardon you,
And all be well.

JUDGE

Confess, or I will warp
Your limbs with such keen tortures . . .

BEATRICE

Tortures ! Turn
The rack henceforth into a spinning wheel !
Torture your dog, that he may tell when last
He lapped the blood his master shed . . . not me !
My pangs are of the mind, and of the heart,
And of the soul ; aye, of the inmost soul,
Which weeps within tears as of burning gall
To see, in this ill world where none are true,
My kindred false to their deserted selves.
And with considering all the wretched life
Which I have lived, and its now wretched end,
And the small justice shown by Heaven and Earth
To me or mine ; and what a tyrant thou art,
And what slaves these ; and what a world we make,
The oppressor and the oppressed . . . such pangs compel
My answer. What is it thou wouldst with me ?

JUDGE

Art thou not guilty of thy father's death?

BEATRICE

Or wilt thou rather tax high-judging God
That he permitted such an act as that
Which I have suffered, and which he beheld;
Made it unutterable, and took from it
All refuge, all revenge, all consequence,
But that which thou hast called my father's death?
Which is or is not what men call a crime,
Which either I have done, or have not done;
Say what ye will. I shall deny no more.
If ye desire it thus, thus let it be,
And so an end of all. Now do your will;
No other pains shall force another word.

JUDGE

She is convicted, but has not confessed.
Be it enough. Until their final sentence
Let none have converse with them. You, young Lord,
Linger not here!

BEATRICE

O, tear him not away!

JUDGE

Guards, do your duty.

BERNARDO (*embracing* BEATRICE)
Oh, would ye divide

Body from soul?

OFFICER

That is the headsman's business.
[*Exeunt all but* LUCRETIA, BEATRICE, *and* GIACOMO.

GIACOMO

Have I confessed? Is it all over now?
No hope! No refuge! O, weak, wicked tongue
Which hast destroyed me, would that thou hadst been

Cut out and thrown to dogs first ! to have killed
My father first, and then betrayed my sister ;
Aye, thee ! the one thing innocent and pure
In this black guilty world, to that which I
So well deserve ! My wife ! my little ones !
Destitute, helpless, and I . . . Father ! God !
Canst thou forgive even the unforgiving,
When their full hearts break thus, thus ! . . .

(Covers his face and weeps.)

LUCRETIA

O, my child !
To what a dreadful end are we all come !
Why did I yield ? Why did I not sustain
Those torments ? Oh, that I were all dissolved
Into these fast and unavailing tears,
Which flow and feel not !

BEATRICE

What 'twas weak to do,
'Tis weaker to lament, once being done ;
Take cheer ! The God who knew my wrong, and made
Our speedy act the angel of his wrath,
Seems, and but seems to have abandoned us.
Let us not think that we shall die for this.
Brother, sit near me ; give me your firm hand,
You had a manly heart. Bear up ! Bear up !
O, dearest Lady, put your gentle head
Upon my lap, and try to sleep awhile :
Your eyes look pale, hollow and overworn,
With heaviness of watching and slow grief.
Come, I will sing you some low, sleepy tune,
Not cheerful, nor yet sad ; some dull old thing,
Some outworn and unused monotony,
Such as our country gossips sing and spin,
Till they almost forget they live : lie down !
So, that will do. Have I forgot the words ?
Faith ! They are sadder than I thought they were.

SONG

False friend, wilt thou smile or weep
When my life is laid asleep ?
Little cares for a smile or a tear
The clay-cold corpse upon the bier !
   Farewell ! Heigho !
   What is this whispers low ?
There is a snake in thy smile, my dear ;
And bitter poison within thy tear.

Sweet sleep, were death like to thee,
Or if thou couldst mortal be,
I would close these eyes of pain ;
When to wake ? Never again.
   O, World ! Farewell !
   Listen to the passing bell !
It says, thou and I must part,
With a light and a heavy heart.

         [*The scene closes.*

SCENE IV. *A Hall of the Prison*

Enter CAMILLO *and* BERNARDO

CAMILLO

The Pope is stern ; not to be moved or bent.
He looked as calm and keen as is the engine
Which tortures and which kills, exempt itself
From aught that it inflicts ; a marble form,
A rite, a law, a custom : not a man.
He frowned, as if to frown had been the trick
Of his machinery, on the advocates
Presenting the defences, which he tore
And threw behind, muttering with hoarse, harsh voice :
" Which among ye defended their old father
Killed in his sleep ? " Then to another : " Thou

Dost this in virtue of thy place ; 'tis well."
He turned to me then, looking deprecation,
And said these three words, coldly : " They must die."

BERNARDO

And yet you left him not ?

CAMILLO

              I urged him still ;
Pleading, as I could guess, the devilish wrong
Which prompted your unnatural parent's death.
And he replied : " Paolo Santa Croce
Murdered his mother yester evening,
And he is fled. Parricide grows so rife,
That soon, for some just cause no doubt, the young
Will strangle us all, dozing in our chairs.
Authority, and power, and hoary hair
Are grown crimes capital. You are my nephew,
You come to ask their pardon ; stay a moment ;
Here is their sentence ; never see me more
Till, to the letter, it be all fulfilled."

BERNARDO

O, God, not so ! I did believe indeed
That all you said was but sad preparation
For happy news. O, there are words and looks
To bend the sternest purpose ! Once I knew them,
Now I forget them at my dearest need.
What think you if I seek him out, and bathe
His feet and robe with hot and bitter tears ?
Importune him with prayers, vexing his brain
With my perpetual cries, until in rage
He strike me with his pastoral cross, and trample
Upon my prostrate head, so that my blood
May stain the senseless dust on which he treads,
And remorse waken mercy ? I will do it !
O, wait till I return !

                             [Rushes out.

CAMILLO

Alas ! poor boy !
A wreck-devoted seaman thus might pray
To the deaf sea.

Enter LUCRETIA, BEATRICE, *and* GIACOMO, *guarded*

BEATRICE

I hardly dare to fear
That thou bring'st other news than a just pardon.

CAMILLO

May God in heaven be less inexorable
To the Pope's prayers, than he has been to mine.
Here is the sentence and the warrant.

BEATRICE (*wildly*)

Oh,
My God ! Can it be possible I have
To die so suddenly ? So young to go
Under the obscure, cold, rotting, wormy ground !
To be nailed down into a narrow place ;
To see no more sweet sunshine ; hear no more
Blithe voice of living thing ; muse not again
Upon familiar thoughts, sad, yet thus lost—
How fearful ! to be nothing ! Or to be . . .
What ? O, where am I ? Let me not go mad !
Sweet Heaven, forgive weak thoughts ! If there should be
No God, no Heaven, no Earth in the void world ;
The wide, grey, lampless, deep, unpeopled world !
If all things then should be . . . my father's spirit,
His eye, his voice, his touch surrounding me ;
The atmosphere and breath of my dead life !
If sometimes, as a shape more like himself,
Even the form which tortured me on earth,
Masked in grey hairs and wrinkles, he should come
And wind me in his hellish arms, and fix
His eyes on mine, and drag me down, down, down !

For was he not alone omnipotent
On Earth, and ever present ?   Even though dead,
Does not his spirit live in all that breathe,
And work for me and mine still the same ruin,
Scorn, pain, despair ?   Who ever yet returned
To teach the laws of death's untrodden realm ?
Unjust perhaps as those which drive us now,
O, whither, whither ?

LUCRETIA

        Trust in God's sweet love,
The tender promises of Christ : ere night,
Think, we shall be in Paradise.

BEATRICE

           'Tis past !
Whatever comes my heart shall sink no more.
And yet, I know not why, your words strike chill :
How tedious, false and cold seem all things.   I
Have met with much injustice in this world ;
No difference has been made by God or man,
Or any power moulding my wretched lot,
'Twixt good or evil, as regarded me.
I am cut off from the only world I know,
From light, and life, and love, in youth's sweet prime.
You do well telling me to trust in God,—
I hope I do trust in him.   In whom else
Can any trust ?   And yet my heart is cold.

    [During the latter speeches GIACOMO *has retired*
        conversing with CAMILLO, *who now goes out ;*
        GIACOMO *advances.*

GIACOMO

Know you not, Mother . . . Sister, know you not ?
Bernardo even now is gone to implore
The Pope to grant our pardon.

LUCRETIA

          Child, perhaps

It will be granted.   We may all then live
To make these woes a tale for distant years :
O, what a thought !   It gushes to my heart
Like the warm blood.

BEATRICE

Yet both will soon be cold.
O, trample out that thought !   Worse than despair,
Worse than the bitterness of death, is hope :
It is the only ill which can find place
Upon the giddy, sharp and narrow hour
Tottering beneath us.   Plead with the swift frost
That it should spare the eldest flower of spring :
Plead with awakening earthquake, o'er whose couch
Even now a city stands, strong, fair and free ;
Now stench and blackness yawn, like death.   O, plead
With famine, or wind-walking Pestilence,
Blind lightning, or the deaf sea, not with man !
Cruel, cold, formal man ; righteous in words,
In deeds a Cain.   No, Mother, we must die :
Since such is the reward of innocent lives ;
Such the alleviation of worst wrongs.
And whilst our murderers live, and hard, cold men,
Smiling and slow, walk through a world of tears
To death as to life's sleep ; 'twere just the grave
Were some strange joy for us.   Come, obscure Death,
And wind me in thine all-embracing arms !
Like a fond mother hide me in thy bosom,
And rock me to the sleep from which none wake.
Live ye, who live, subject to one another
As we were once, who now . . .

BERNARDO *rushes in*

BERNARDO

Oh, horrible !
That tears, that looks, that hope poured forth in prayer,
Even till the heart is vacant and despairs,
Should all be vain !   The ministers of death

Are waiting round the doors. I thought I saw
Blood on the face of one . . . what if 'twere fancy ?
Soon the heart's blood of all I love on earth
Will sprinkle him, and he will wipe it off
As if 'twere only rain. O, life ! O, world !
Cover me ! let me be no more ! To see
That perfect mirror of pure innocence
Wherein I gazed, and grew happy and good,
Shivered to dust ! To see thee, Beatrice,
Who made all lovely thou didst look upon . . .
Thee, light of life . . . dead, dark ! while I say, sister,
To hear I have no sister ; and thou, Mother,
Whose love was as a bond to all our loves . . .
Dead ! The sweet bond broken !

Enter CAMILLO *and* Guards

                                   They come ! Let me
Kiss those warm lips before their crimson leaves
Are blighted . . . white . . . cold. Say farewell, before
Death chokes that gentle voice ! O, let me hear
You speak !

BEATRICE

        Farewell, my tender brother. Think
Of our sad fate with gentleness, as now :
And let mild, pitying thoughts lighten for thee
Thy sorrow's load. Err not in harsh despair,
But tears and patience. One thing more, my child,
For thine own sake be constant to the love
Thou bearest us ; and to the faith that I,
Though wrapped in a strange cloud of crime and shame,
Lived ever holy and unstained. And though
Ill tongues shall wound me, and our common name
Be as a mark stamped on thine innocent brow
For men to point at as they pass, do thou
Forbear, and never think a thought unkind
Of those, who perhaps love thee in their graves.
So mayest thou die as I do ; fear and pain
Being subdued. Farewell ! Farewell ! Farewell !

BERNARDO

I cannot say, farewell !

CAMILLO

O, Lady Beatrice !

BEATRICE

Give yourself no unnecessary pain,
My dear Lord Cardinal.   Here, Mother, tie
My girdle for me, and bind up this hair
In any simple knot ; aye, that does well.
And yours I see is coming down.   How often
Have we done this for one another ; now
We shall not do it any more.   My Lord,
We are quite ready.   Well, 'tis very well.

PROMETHEUS UNBOUND

A LYRICAL DRAMA
IN FOUR ACTS

PREFACE

THE Greek tragic writers, in selecting as their subject any portion of their national history or mythology, employed in their treatment of it a certain arbitrary discretion. They by no means conceived themselves bound to adhere to the common interpretation or to imitate in story as in title their rivals and predecessors. Such a system would have amounted to a resignation of those claims to preference over their competitors which incited the composition. The Agamemnonian story was exhibited on the Athenian theatre with as many variations as dramas.

I have presumed to employ a similar licence. The *Prometheus Unbound* of Æschylus supposed the reconciliation of Jupiter with his victim as the price of the disclosure of the danger threatened to his empire by the consummation of his marriage with Thetis. Thetis, according to this view of the subject, was given in marriage to Peleus, and Prometheus, by the permission of Jupiter, delivered from his captivity by Hercules. Had I framed my story on this model, I should have done no more than have attempted to restore the lost drama of Æschylus; an ambition which, if my preference to this mode of treating the subject had incited me to cherish, the recollection of the high comparison such an attempt would challenge might well abate. But, in truth, I was averse from a catastrophe so feeble as that of reconciling the Champion with the Oppressor of mankind. The moral interest of the fable, which is so powerfully sustained by the sufferings and endurance of Prometheus, would be annihilated if we could conceive of him as unsaying his high language and quailing before his successful and perfidious adversary. The only imaginary being resembling in any degree Prometheus, is Satan; and Prometheus is, in my judgment, a more poetical character than Satan, because, in addition to courage, and majesty, and firm and patient opposition to omnipotent force, he is susceptible of being described as exempt from the taints of ambition, envy, revenge, and a desire for personal aggrandizement, which, in the Hero of *Paradise Lost,* interfere with the interest. The character of Satan engenders in the mind a pernicious casuistry which leads us to weigh his faults with his wrongs, and to excuse the former because the latter exceed all measure. In the minds of those who consider that magnificent fiction with a religious feeling it engenders something worse. But Prometheus is, as it were, the type of the highest perfection of moral and intellectual nature, impelled by the purest and the truest motives to the best and noblest ends.

This Poem was chiefly written upon the mountainous ruins of the Baths of Caracalla, among the flowery glades, and thickets of odoriferous blossoming trees, which are extended in ever winding labyrinths upon its immense platforms and dizzy arches suspended in the air. The bright blue sky of Rome, and the effect of the vigorous awakening spring in that divinest climate, and the new life with which it drenches the spirits even to intoxication, were the inspiration of this drama.

The imagery which I have employed will be found, in many instances, to have been drawn from the operations of the human mind, or from those external actions by which they are expressed. This is unusual in modern poetry, although Dante and Shakespeare are full of instances of the same kind: Dante indeed more than any other poet, and with greater success. But the Greek poets, as writers to whom no resource of awakening the sympathy of their contemporaries was unknown, were in the habitual use of this power; and it is the study of their works, (since a higher merit would probably be denied me,) to which I am willing that my readers should impute this singularity.

One word is due in candour to the degree in which the study of contemporary writings may have tinged my composition, for such has been a topic of censure with regard to poems far more popular, and indeed more deservedly popular, than mine. It is impossible that any one who inhabits the same age with such writers as those who stand in the foremost ranks of our own, can conscientiously assure himself that his language and tone of thought may not have been modified by the study of the productions of those extraordinary intellects. It is true that, not the spirit of their genius, but the forms in which it has manifested itself, are due less to the peculiarities of their own minds than to the peculiarity of the moral and intellectual condition of the minds among which they have been produced. Thus a number of writers possess the form, whilst they want the spirit of those whom, it is alleged, they imitate ; because the former is the endowment of the age in which they live, and the latter must be the uncommunicated lightning of their own mind.

The peculiar style of intense and comprehensive imagery which distinguishes the modern literature of England, has not been, as a general power, the product of the imitation of any particular writer. The mass of capabilities remains at every period materially the same ; the circumstances which awaken it to action perpetually change. If England were divided into forty republics, each equal in population and extent to Athens, there is no reason to suppose but that, under institutions not more perfect than those of Athens, each would produce philosophers and poets equal to those who (if we except Shakespeare) have never been surpassed. We owe the great writers of the golden age of our literature to that fervid awakening of the public mind which shook to dust the oldest and most oppressive form of the Christian religion. We owe Milton to the progress and development of the same spirit : the sacred Milton was, let it ever be remembered, a republican, and a bold enquirer into morals and religion. The great writers of our own age are, we have reason to suppose, the companions and forerunners of some unimagined change in our social condition or the opinions which cement it. The cloud of mind is discharging its collected lightning, and the equilibrium between institutions and opinions is now restoring, or is about to be restored.

As to imitation, poetry is a mimetic art. It creates, but it creates by combination and representation. Poetical abstractions are beautiful and new, not because the portions of which they are composed had no previous existence in the mind of man or in nature, but because the whole produced by their combination has some intelligible and beautiful analogy with those sources of emotion and thought, and with the contemporary condition of them : one great poet is a masterpiece of nature which another not only ought to study but must study. He might as wisely and as easily determine that his mind should no longer be the mirror of all that is lovely in the visible universe, as exclude from his contemplation the beautiful which exists in the writings of a great contemporary. The pretence of doing it would be a presumption in any but the greatest ; the effect, even in him, would be strained, unnatural, and ineffectual. A poet is the combined product of such internal powers as modify the nature of others, and of such external influences as excite and sustain these powers ; he is not one, but both. Every man's mind is, in this respect, modified by all the objects of nature and art ; by every word and every suggestion which he ever admitted to act upon his consciousness ; it is the mirror upon which all forms are reflected, and in which they compose one form. Poets, not otherwise than philosophers, painters, sculptors, and musicians, are, in one sense, the creators, and, in another, the creations, of their age. From this subjection the loftiest do not escape. There is a similarity between Homer and Hesiod, between Æschylus and Euripides, between Virgil and Horace, between Dante and Petrarch, between Shakespeare and Fletcher, between Dryden and Pope ; each has a generic resemblance under which their specific distinctions are arranged. If this similarity be the result of imitation, I am willing to confess that I have imitated.

Let this opportunity be conceded to me of acknowledging that I have, what a Scotch philosopher characteristically terms, " a passion for reforming the world : " what passion incited him to write and publish his book, he omits to explain. For my part I had rather be damned with Plato and Lord Bacon, than go to Heaven with Paley and Malthus. But it is a mistake to suppose that I dedicate my poetical compositions solely to the direct enforcement of reform, or that I consider them in any degree as containing a reasoned system on the theory of human life. Didactic poetry is my abhorrence ; nothing can be equally well expressed in prose that is not tedious and supererogatory in verse. My purpose has hitherto been simply to familiarize the highly refined imagination of the more select classes of poetical readers with beautiful idealisms of moral excellence ; aware that until the mind can love, and admire, and trust, and hope, and endure, reasoned principles of moral conduct are seeds cast upon the highway of life which the unconscious passenger tramples into dust, although they would bear the harvest of his happiness. Should I live to accomplish what I purpose, that is, produce a systematical history of what appear to me to be the genuine elements of human society, let not the advocates of injustice and superstition flatter themselves that I should take Æschylus rather than Plato as my model.

The having spoken of myself with unaffected freedom

will need little apology with the candid ; and let the uncandid consider that they injure me less than their own hearts and minds by misrepresentation. Whatever talents a person may possess to amuse and instruct others, be they ever so inconsiderable, he is yet bound to exert them : if his attempt be ineffectual, let the punishment of an unaccomplished purpose have been sufficient ; let none trouble themselves to heap the dust of oblivion upon his efforts ; the pile they raise will betray his grave which might otherwise have been unknown.

DRAMATIS PERSONÆ

PROMETHEUS
DEMOGORGON
JUPITER
THE EARTH
OCEAN
APOLLO
MERCURY
HERCULES
ASIA
PANTHEA } Oceanides
IONE
THE PHANTASM OF JUPITER
THE SPIRIT OF THE EARTH
THE SPIRIT OF THE MOON
SPIRITS OF THE HOURS
SPIRITS. ECHOES. FAUNS. FURIES

PROMETHEUS UNBOUND

ACT I

SCENE. *A Ravine of Icy Rocks in the Indian Caucasus.*
PROMETHEUS *is discovered bound to the Precipice.*
PANTHEA *and* IONE *are seated at his feet.* TIME,
Night. During the Scene, Morning slowly breaks.

PROMETHEUS

MONARCH of Gods and Dæmons, and all Spirits
But One, who throng those bright and rolling worlds
Which Thou and I alone of living things
Behold with sleepless eyes ! regard this Earth
Made multitudinous with thy slaves, whom thou
Requitest for knee-worship, prayer, and praise,
And toil, and hecatombs of broken hearts,
With fear and self-contempt and barren hope.
Whilst me, who am thy foe, eyeless in hate,
Hast thou made reign and triumph, to thy scorn,
O'er mine own misery and thy vain revenge.
Three thousand years of sleep-unsheltered hours,
And moments aye divided by keen pangs
Till they seemed years, torture and solitude,
Scorn and despair,—these are mine empire.
More glorious far than that which thou surveyest
From thine unenvied throne, O, Mighty God !
Almighty, had I deigned to share the shame
Of thine ill tyranny, and hung not here
Nailed to this wall of eagle-baffling mountain,
Black, wintry, dead, unmeasured ; without herb
Insect, or beast, or shape or sound of life.
Ah me ! alas, pain, pain ever, for ever !

No change, no pause, no hope ! Yet I endure.
I ask the Earth, have not the mountains felt ?
I ask yon Heaven, the all-beholding Sun,
Has it not seen ?   The Sea, in storm or calm,
Heaven's ever-changing Shadow, spread below,
Have its deaf waves not heard my agony ?
Ah me ! alas, pain, pain ever, for ever !

The crawling glaciers pierce me with the spears
Of their moon-freezing crystals, the bright chains
Eat with their burning cold into my bones.
Heaven's wingèd hound, polluting from thy lips
His beak in poison not his own, tears up
My heart ; and shapeless sights come wandering by,
The ghastly people of the realm of dream,
Mocking me : and the Earthquake-fiends are charged
To wrench the rivets from my quivering wounds
When the rocks split and close again behind :
While from their loud abysses howling throng
The genii of the storm, urging the rage
Of whirlwind, and afflict me with keen hail.
And yet to me welcome is day and night,
Whether one breaks the hoar-frost of the morn,
Or starry, dim, and slow, the other climbs
The leaden-coloured east ; for then they lead
The wingless, crawling hours, one among whom
—As some dark Priest hales the reluctant victim—
Shall drag thee, cruel King, to kiss the blood
From these pale feet, which then might trample thee
If they disdained not such a prostrate slave.
Disdain ! Ah no ! I pity thee.   What ruin
Will hunt thee undefended through the wide Heaven !
How will thy soul, cloven to its depth with terror,
Gape like a hell within !   I speak in grief,
Not exultation, for I hate no more,
As then ere misery made me wise.   The curse
Once breathed on thee I would recall.   Ye Mountains,
Whose many-voicèd Echoes, through the mist

Of cataracts, flung the thunder of that spell !
Ye icy Springs, stagnant with wrinkling frost,
Which vibrated to hear me, and then crept
Shuddering through India ! Thou serenest Air,
Through which the Sun walks burning without beams !
And ye swift Whirlwinds, who on poisèd wings
Hung mute and moveless o'er yon hushed abyss,
As thunder, louder than your own, made rock
The orbèd world ! If then my words had power,
Though I am changed so that aught evil wish
Is dead within ; although no memory be
Of what is hate, let them not lose it now !
What was that curse ? for ye all heard me speak.

FIRST VOICE : *from the Mountains*
Thrice three hundred thousand years
   O'er the Earthquake's couch we stood :
Oft, as men convulsed with fears,
   We trembled in our multitude.

SECOND VOICE : *from the Springs*
Thunder-bolts had parched our water,
   We had been stained with bitter blood,
And had run mute, 'mid shrieks of slaughter,
   Through a city and a solitude.

THIRD VOICE : *from the Air*
I had clothed, since Earth uprose,
   Its wastes in colours not their own,
And oft had my serene repose
   Been cloven by many a rending groan.

FOURTH VOICE : *from the Whirlwinds*
We had soared beneath these mountains
   Unresting ages ; nor had thunder,
Nor yon volcano's flaming fountains,
   Nor any power above or under
   Ever made us mute with wonder.

FIRST VOICE

But never bowed our snowy crest
As at the voice of thine unrest.

SECOND VOICE

Never such a sound before
To the Indian waves we bore.
A pilot asleep on the howling sea
Leaped up from the deck in agony,
And heard, and cried, " Ah, woe is me ! "
And died as mad as the wild waves be.

THIRD VOICE

By such dread words from Earth to Heaven
My still realm was never riven :
When its wound was closed, there stood
Darkness o'er the day like blood.

FOURTH VOICE

And we shrank back : for dreams of ruin
To frozen caves our flight pursuing
Made us keep silence—thus—and thus—
Though silence is a hell to us.

THE EARTH

The tongueless Caverns of the craggy hills
Cried, " Misery ! " then ; the hollow Heaven replied,
" Misery ! "   And the Ocean's purple waves,
Climbing the land, howled to the lashing winds,
And the pale nations heard it, " Misery ! "

PROMETHEUS

I hear a sound of voices : not the voice
Which I gave forth.   Mother, thy sons and thou
Scorn him, without whose all-enduring will
Beneath the fierce omnipotence of Jove,
Both they and thou had vanished, like thin mist

Unrolled on the morning wind.   Know ye not me,
The Titan?   He who made his agony
The barrier to your else all-conquering foe?
Oh, rock-embosomed lawns, and snow-fed streams,
Now seen athwart frore vapours, deep below,
Through whose o'ershadowing woods I wandered once
With Asia, drinking life from her loved eyes;
Why scorns the spirit which informs ye, now
To commune with me?   me alone, who checked,
As one who checks a fiend-drawn charioteer,
The falsehood and the force of him who reigns
Supreme, and with the groans of pining slaves
Fills your dim glens and liquid wildernesses:
Why answer ye not, still?   Brethren!

THE EARTH

They dare not.

PROMETHEUS

Who dares?   for I would hear that curse again.
Ha, what an awful whisper rises up!
'Tis scarce like sound: it tingles through the frame
As lightning tingles, hovering ere it strike.
Speak, Spirit! from thine inorganic voice
I only know that thou art moving near
And love.   How cursed I him?

THE EARTH

How canst thou hear
Who knowest not the language of the dead?

PROMETHEUS

Thou art a living spirit: speak as they.

THE EARTH

I dare not speak like life, lest Heaven's fell King
Should hear, and link me to some wheel of pain
More torturing than the one whereon I roll.
Subtle thou art and good, and though the Gods

Hear not this voice, yet thou art more than God
Being wise and kind : earnestly hearken now.

PROMETHEUS

Obscurely through my brain, like shadows dim,
Sweep awful thoughts, rapid and thick.   I feel
Faint, like one mingled in entwining love ;
Yet 'tis not pleasure.

THE EARTH
                            No, thou canst not hear :
Thou art immortal, and this tongue is known
Only to those who die.

PROMETHEUS
                            And what art thou,
O, melancholy Voice ?

THE EARTH
                            I am the Earth,
Thy mother ; she within whose stony veins,
To the last fibre of the loftiest tree
Whose thin leaves trembled in the frozen air,
Joy ran, as blood within a living frame,
When thou didst from her bosom, like a cloud
Of glory, arise, a spirit of keen joy !
And at thy voice her pining sons uplifted
Their prostrate brows from the polluting dust,
And our almighty Tyrant with fierce dread
Grew pale, until his thunder chained thee here.
Then, see those million worlds which burn and roll
Around us : their inhabitants beheld
My spherèd light wane in wide Heaven ; the sea
Was lifted by strange tempest, and new fire
From earthquake-rifted mountains of bright snow
Shook its portentous hair beneath Heaven's frown ;
Lightning and Inundation vexed the plains ;
Blue thistles bloomed in cities ; foodless toads
Within voluptuous chambers panting crawled :

When Plague had fallen on man, and beast, and worm,
And Famine ; and black blight on herb and tree ;
And in the corn, and vines, and meadow-grass,
Teemed ineradicable poisonous weeds
Draining their growth, for my wan breast was dry
With grief ; and the thin air, my breath, was stained
With the contagion of a mother's hate
Breathed on her child's destroyer ; aye, I heard
Thy curse, the which, if thou rememberest not,
Yet my innumerable seas and streams,
Mountains, and caves, and winds, and yon wide air,
And the inarticulate people of the dead,
Preserve, a treasured spell.   We meditate
In secret joy and hope those dreadful words
But dare not speak them.

PROMETHEUS

Venerable mother !
All else who live and suffer take from thee
Some comfort ; flowers, and fruits, and happy sounds,
And love, though fleeting ; these may not be mine.
But mine own words, I pray, deny me not.

THE EARTH

They shall be told.   Ere Babylon was dust,
The Magus Zoroaster, my dead child,
Met his own image walking in the garden.
That apparition, sole of men, he saw.
For know there are two worlds of life and death :
One that which thou beholdest ; but the other
Is underneath the grave, where do inhabit
The shadows of all forms that think and live
Till death unite them and they part no more ;
Dreams and the light imaginings of men,
And all that faith creates or love desires,
Terrible, strange, sublime and beauteous shapes.
There thou art, and dost hang, a writhing shade,
'Mid whirlwind-peopled mountains ; all the gods

Are there, and all the powers of nameless worlds,
Vast, sceptred phantoms ; heroes, men, and beasts ;
And Demogorgon, a tremendous gloom ;
And he, the supreme Tyrant, on his throne
Of burning gold.   Son, one of these shall utter
The curse which all remember.   Call at will
Thine own ghost, or the ghost of Jupiter,
Hades or Typhon, or what mightier Gods
From all-prolific Evil, since thy ruin,
Have sprung, and trampled on my prostrate sons.
Ask, and they must reply : so the revenge
Of the Supreme may sweep through vacant shades,
As rainy wind through the abandoned gate
Of a fallen palace.

PROMETHEUS

       Mother, let not aught
Of that which may be evil, pass again
My lips, or those of aught resembling me.
Phantasm of Jupiter, arise, appear !

IONE

My wings are folded o'er mine ears :
   My wings are crossèd o'er mine eyes :
Yet through their silver shade appears,
   And through their lulling plumes arise,
A Shape, a throng of sounds ;
   May it be no ill to thee
O thou of many wounds !
Near whom, for our sweet sister's sake,
Ever thus we watch and wake.

PANTHEA

The sound is of whirlwind underground,
   Earthquake, and fire, and mountains cloven ;
The shape is awful like the sound,
   Clothed in dark purple, star-inwoven.
A sceptre of pale gold

To stay steps proud, o'er the slow cloud
His veinèd hand doth hold.
Cruel he looks, but calm and strong,
Like one who does, not suffers wrong.

PHANTASM OF JUPITER

Why have the secret powers of this strange world
Driven me, a frail and empty phantom, hither
On direst storms ?   What unaccustomed sounds
Are hovering on my lips, unlike the voice
With which our pallid race hold ghastly talk
In darkness ?   And, proud sufferer, who art thou ?

PROMETHEUS

Tremendous Image, as thou art must be
He whom thou shadowest forth.   I am his foe,
The Titan.   Speak the words which I would hear,
Although no thought inform thine empty voice.

THE EARTH

Listen !   And though your echoes must be mute,
Grey mountains, and old woods, and haunted springs,
Prophetic caves, and isle-surrounding streams,
Rejoice to hear what yet ye cannot speak.

PHANTASM

A spirit seizes me and speaks within :
It tears me as fire tears a thunder-cloud.

PANTHEA

See, how he lifts his mighty looks, the Heaven
Darkens above.

IONE

He speaks !   O shelter me !

PROMETHEUS

I see the curse on gestures proud and cold,
And looks of firm defiance, and calm hate,
And such despair as mocks itself with smiles,
Written as on a scroll : yet speak : Oh, speak !

PHANTASM

Fiend, I defy thee ! with a calm, fixed mind,
 All that thou canst inflict I bid thee do ;
Foul Tyrant both of Gods and Human-kind,
 One only being shalt thou not subdue.
Rain then thy plagues upon me here,
Ghastly disease, and frenzying fear ;
And let alternate frost and fire
Eat into me, and be thine ire
Lightning, and cutting hail, and legioned forms
Of furies, driving by upon the wounding storms.

Aye, do thy worst. Thou art omnipotent.
 O'er all things but thyself I gave thee power,
And my own will. Be thy swift mischiefs sent
 To blast mankind, from yon ætherial tower.
Let thy malignant spirit move
In darkness over those I love :
On me and mine I imprecate
The utmost torture of thy hate ;
And thus devote to sleepless agony,
This undeclining head while thou must reign on high.

But thou, who art the God and Lord : O, thou,
 Who fillest with thy soul this world of woe,
To whom all things of Earth and Heaven do bow
 In fear and worship : all-prevailing foe !
I curse thee ! let a sufferer's curse
Clasp thee, his torturer, like remorse ;
Till thine Infinity shall be
A robe of envenomed agony ;
And thine Omnipotence a crown of pain,
To cling like burning gold round thy dissolving brain.

Heap on thy soul, by virtue of this Curse,
 Ill deeds, then be thou damned, beholding good ;
Both infinite as is the universe,
 And thou, and thy self-torturing solitude.
An awful image of calm power

Though now thou sittest, let the hour
Come, when thou must appear to be
That which thou art internally.
And after many a false and fruitless crime
Scorn track thy lagging fall through boundless space
  and time.

PROMETHEUS

Were these my words, O Parent ?

THE EARTH

                    They were thine.
PROMETHEUS

It doth repent me : words are quick and vain ;
Grief for awhile is blind, and so was mine.
I wish no living thing to suffer pain.

THE EARTH

Misery, Oh misery to me,
That Jove at length should vanquish thee.
Wail, howl aloud, Land and Sea,
The Earth's rent heart shall answer ye.
Howl, Spirits of the living and the dead,
Your refuge, your defence lies fallen and vanquishèd.

FIRST ECHO

Lies fallen and vanquishèd !

SECOND ECHO

Fallen and vanquishèd !

IONE

Fear not : 'tis but some passing spasm ;
  The Titan is unvanquished still.
But see, where through the azure chasm
  Of yon forked and snowy hill
Trampling the slant winds on high
  With golden-sandalled feet, that glow

Under plumes of purple dye,
Like rose-ensanguined ivory,
   A Shape comes now,
Stretching on high from his right hand
   A serpent-cinctured wand.

PANTHEA

'Tis Jove's world-wandering herald, Mercury.

IONE

And who are those with hydra tresses
   And iron wings that climb the wind,
Whom the frowning God represses
   Like vapours steaming up behind,
Clanging loud, an endless crowd—

PANTHEA

These are Jove's tempest-walking hounds,
Whom he gluts with groans and blood,
When charioted on sulphurous cloud
   He bursts Heaven's bounds.

IONE

Are they now led, from the thin dead
On new pangs to be fed ?

PANTHEA

The Titan looks as ever, firm, not proud.

FIRST FURY

Ha ! I scent life !

SECOND FURY

Let me but look into his eyes !

THIRD FURY

The hope of torturing him smells like a heap
Of corpses, to a death-bird after battle.

FIRST FURY

Darest thou delay, O Herald ! take cheer, Hounds
Of Hell : what if the Son of Maia soon
Should make us food and sport—who can please long
The Omnipotent ?

MERCURY

Back to your towers of iron,
And gnash, beside the streams of fire and wail,
Your foodless teeth.   Geryon, arise ! and Gorgon,
Chimæra, and thou Sphinx, subtlest of fiends
Who ministered to Thebes Heaven's poisoned wine,
Unnatural love, and more unnatural hate :
These shall perform your task.

FIRST FURY

Oh, mercy ! mercy !
We die with our desire : drive us not back !

MERCURY

Crouch then in silence.

Awful Sufferer
To the unwilling, most unwillingly
I come, by the great Father's will driven down,
To execute a doom of new revenge.
Alas ! I pity thee, and hate myself
That I can do no more : aye from thy sight
Returning, for a season, Heaven seems Hell,
So thy worn form pursues me night and day,
Smiling reproach.   Wise art thou, firm and good,
But vainly wouldst stand forth alone in strife
Against the Omnipotent ; as yon clear lamps
That measure and divide the weary years
From which there is no refuge, long have taught
And long must teach.   Even now thy Torturer arms
With the strange might of unimagined pains
The powers who scheme slow agonies in Hell,
And my commission is to lead them here,

Or what more subtle, foul, or savage fiends
People the abyss, and leave them to their task.
Be it not so ! there is a secret known
To thee, and to none else of living things,
Which may transfer the sceptre of wide Heaven,
The fear of which perplexes the Supreme :
Clothe it in words, and bid it clasp his throne
In intercession ; bend thy soul in prayer,
And like a suppliant in some gorgeous fane,
Let the will kneel within thy haughty heart :
For benefits and meek submission tame
The fiercest and the mightiest.

PROMETHEUS
                                    Evil minds
Change good to their own nature.   I gave all
He has ; and in return he chains me here
Years, ages, night and day : whether the Sun
Split my parched skin, or in the moony night
The crystal-wingèd snow cling round my hair :
Whilst my belovèd race is trampled down
By his thought-executing ministers.
Such is the tyrant's recompense : 'tis just :
He who is evil can receive no good ;
And for a world bestowed, or a friend lost,
He can feel hate, fear, shame ; not gratitude :
He but requites me for his own misdeed.
Kindness to such is keen reproach, which breaks
With bitter stings the light sleep of Revenge.
Submission, thou dost know I cannot try :
For what submission but that fatal word,
The death-seal of mankind's captivity,
Like the Sicilian's hair-suspended sword,
Which trembles o'er his crown, would he accept,
Or could I yield ?   Which yet I will not yield.
Let others flatter Crime, where it sits throned
In brief Omnipotence : secure are they :
For Justice, when triumphant, will weep down

Pity, not punishment, on her own wrongs,
Too much avenged by those who err.   I wait,
Enduring thus, the retributive hour
Which since we spake is even nearer now.
But hark, the hell-hounds clamour : fear delay :
Behold ! Heaven lowers under thy Father's frown.

MERCURY

Oh, that we might be spared,—I to inflict
And thou to suffer !   Once more answer me :
Thou knowest not the period of Jove's power ?

PROMETHEUS

I know but this, that it must come.

MERCURY

Alas !
Thou canst not count thy years to come of pain ?

PROMETHEUS

They last while Jove must reign : nor more, nor less
Do I desire or fear.

MERCURY

Yet pause, and plunge
Into Eternity, where recorded time,
Even all that we imagine, age on age,
Seems but a point, and the reluctant mind
Flags wearily in its unending flight,
Till it sink, dizzy, blind, lost, shelterless ;
Perchance it has not numbered the slow years
Which thou must spend in torture, unreprieved ?

PROMETHEUS

Perchance no thought can count them : yet they pass.

MERCURY

If thou might'st dwell among the Gods the while
Lapped in voluptuous joy ?

PROMETHEUS

I would not quit
This bleak ravine, these unrepentant pains.

MERCURY

Alas ! I wonder at, yet pity thee.

PROMETHEUS

Pity the self-despising slaves of Heaven,
Not me, within whose mind sits peace serene,
As light in the sun, throned : how vain is talk !
Call up the fiends.

IONE

O, sister, look ! White fire
Has cloven to the roots yon huge snow-loaded cedar ;
How fearfully God's thunder howls behind !

MERCURY

I must obey his words and thine : alas !
Most heavily remorse hangs at my heart !

PANTHEA

See where the child of Heaven, with wingèd feet,
Runs down the slanted sunlight of the dawn.

IONE

Dear sister, close thy plumes over thine eyes
Lest thou behold and die : they come : they come :
Blackening the birth of day with countless wings,
And hollow underneath, like death.

FIRST FURY

Prometheus !

SECOND FURY

Immortal Titan !

THIRD FURY

Champion of Heaven's slaves !

PROMETHEUS

He whom some dreadful voice invokes is here,
Prometheus, the chained Titan.   Horrible forms,
What and who are ye ?   Never yet there came
Phantasms so foul through monster-teeming Hell
From the all-miscreative brain of Jove ;
Whilst I behold such execrable shapes,
Methinks I grow like what I contemplate,
And laugh and stare in loathsome sympathy.

FIRST FURY

We are the ministers of pain, and fear,
And disappointment, and mistrust, and hate,
And clinging crime ; and as lean dogs pursue
Through wood and lake some struck and sobbing fawn,
We track all things that weep, and bleed, and live,
When the great King betrays them to our will.

PROMETHEUS

Oh ! many fearful natures in one name,
I know ye ; and these lakes and echoes know
The darkness and the clangour of your wings.
But why more hideous than your lothèd selves
Gather ye up in legions from the deep ?

SECOND FURY

We knew not that : Sisters, rejoice, rejoice !

PROMETHEUS

Can aught exult in its deformity ?

SECOND FURY

The beauty of delight makes lovers glad,
Gazing on one another : so are we.
As from the rose which the pale priestess kneels
To gather for her festal crown of flowers

The aërial crimson falls, flushing her cheek,
So from our victim's destined agony
The shade which is our form invests us round ;
Else we are shapeless as our mother Night.

PROMETHEUS

I laugh your power, and his who sent you here,
To lowest scorn.   Pour forth the cup of pain.

FIRST FURY

Thou thinkest we will rend thee bone from bone,
And nerve from nerve, working like fire within ?

PROMETHEUS

Pain is my element, as hate is thine ;
Ye rend me now : I care not.

SECOND FURY

                    Dost imagine
We will but laugh into thy lidless eyes ?

PROMETHEUS

I weigh not what ye do, but what ye suffer,
Being evil.   Cruel was the power which called
You, or aught else so wretched, into light.

THIRD FURY

Thou think'st we will live through thee, one by one,
Like animal life, and though we can obscure not
The soul which burns within, that we will dwell
Beside it, like a vain loud multitude
Vexing the self-content of wisest men :
That we will be dread thought beneath thy brain,
And foul desire round thine astonished heart
And blood within thy labyrinthine veins
Crawling like agony.

Prometheus

               Why, ye are thus now;
Yet am I king over myself, and rule
The torturing and conflicting throngs within,
As Jove rules you when Hell grows mutinous.

Chorus of Furies

From the ends of the earth, from the ends of the earth,
Where the night has its grave and the morning its birth,
          Come, come, come!
Oh, ye who shake hills with the scream of your mirth,
When cities sink howling in ruin; and ye
Who with wingless footsteps trample the sea,
And close upon Shipwreck and Famine's track,
Sit chattering with joy on the foodless wreck;
          Come, come, come!
    Leave the bed, low, cold, and red,
    Strewed beneath a nation dead;
    Leave the hatred, as in ashes
      Fire is left for future burning:
    It will burst in bloodier flashes
      When ye stir it, soon returning:
    Leave the self-contempt implanted
    In young spirits, sense-enchanted,
      Misery's yet unkindled fuel:
    Leave Hell's secrets half unchanted
      To the maniac dreamer; cruel
    More than ye can be with hate
      Is he with fear.
      Come, come, come!
We are steaming up from Hell's wide gate
    And we burthen the blast of the atmosphere,
    But vainly we toil till ye come here.

Ione

Sister, I hear the thunder of new wings.

PANTHEA

These solid mountains quiver with the sound
Even as the tremulous air : their shadows make
The space within my plumes more black than night.

FIRST FURY

Your call was as a wingèd car
Driven on whirlwinds fast and far ;
It rapt us from red gulphs of war.

SECOND FURY

From wide cities, famine-wasted ;

THIRD FURY

Groans half heard, and blood untasted ;

FOURTH FURY

Kingly conclaves stern and cold,
Where blood with gold is bought and sold ;

FIFTH FURY

From the furnace, white and hot,
In which—

A FURY

Speak not : whisper not :
I know all that ye would tell,
But to speak might break the spell
Which must bend the Invincible,
The stern of thought ;
He yet defies the deepest power of Hell.

FURY

Tear the veil !

ANOTHER FURY

It is torn.

CHORUS

The pale stars of the morn
Shine on a misery, dire to be borne.
Dost thou faint, mighty Titan ?   We laugh thee to scorn.
Dost thou boast the clear knowledge thou wakenedst
    for man ?
Then was kindled within him a thirst which outran
Those perishing waters ; a thirst of fierce fever,
Hope, love, doubt, desire, which consume him for ever.
    One came forth of gentle worth
    Smiling on the sanguine earth ;
    His words outlived him, like swift poison
        Withering up truth, peace, and pity.
    Look ! where round the wide horizon
        Many a million-peopled city
    Vomits smoke in the bright air.
    Mark that outcry of despair !
    'Tis his mild and gentle ghost
        Wailing for the faith he kindled :
    Look again, the flames almost
        To a glow-worm's lamp have dwindled :
    The survivors round the embers
        Gather in dread.
            Joy, joy, joy !
Past ages crowd on thee, but each one remembers,
And the future is dark, and the present is spread
Like a pillow of thorns for thy slumberless head.

SEMICHORUS I

Drops of bloody agony flow
From his white and quivering brow.
Grant a little respite now :
See a disenchanted nation
Springs like day from desolation ;
To Truth its state is dedicate,
And Freedom leads it forth, her mate ;
A legioned band of linkèd brothers
Whom Love calls children——

SEMICHORUS II

'Tis another's :

See how kindred murder kin :
'Tis the vintage-time for death and sin :
Blood, like new wine, bubbles within :
    Till Despair smothers
The struggling world, which slaves and tyrants win.

             [*All the* FURIES *vanish, except one.*

IONE

Hark, sister ! what a low yet dreadful groan
Quite unsuppressed is tearing up the heart
Of the good Titan, as storms tear the deep,
And beasts hear the sea moan in inland caves.
Darest thou observe how the fiends torture him ?

PANTHEA

Alas ! I looked forth twice, but will no more.

IONE

What didst thou see ?

PANTHEA

          A woful sight : a youth
With patient looks nailed to a crucifix.

IONE

What next ?

PANTHEA

        The heaven around, the earth below
Was peopled with thick shapes of human death,
All horrible, and wrought by human hands,
And some appeared the work of human hearts,
For men were slowly killed by frowns and smiles :
And other sights too foul to speak and live
Were wandering by.   Let us not tempt worse fear
By looking forth : those groans are grief enough.

FURY

Behold an emblem : those who do endure
Deep wrongs for man, and scorn, and chains, but heap
Thousandfold torment on themselves and him.

PROMETHEUS

Remit the anguish of that lighted stare ;
Close those wan lips ; let that thorn-wounded brow
Stream not with blood ; it mingles with thy tears !
Fix, fix those tortured orbs in peace and death,
So thy sick throes shake not that crucifix,
So those pale fingers play not with thy gore.
O, horrible !   Thy name I will not speak,
It hath become a curse.   I see, I see
The wise, the mild, the lofty, and the just,
Whom thy slaves hate for being like to thee,
Some hunted by foul lies from their heart's home,
An early-chosen, late-lamented home ;
As hooded ounces cling to the driven hind ;
Some linked to corpses in unwholesome cells :
Some—Hear I not the multitude laugh loud ?—
Impaled in lingering fire : and mighty realms
Float by my feet, like sea-uprooted isles,
Whose sons are kneaded down in common blood
By the red light of their own burning homes.

FURY

Blood thou canst see, and fire ; and canst hear groans ;
Worse things, unheard, unseen, remain behind.

PROMETHEUS

Worse ?

FURY

In each human heart terror survives
The ruin it has gorged : the loftiest fear
All that they would disdain to think were true :
Hypocrisy and custom make their minds

The fanes of many a worship, now outworn.
They dare not devise good for man's estate,
And yet they know not that they do not dare,
The good want power, but to weep barren tears.
The powerful goodness want : worse need for them.
The wise want love ; and those who love want wisdom ;
And all best things are thus confused to ill.
Many are strong and rich, and would be just,
But live among their suffering fellow-men
As if none felt : they know not what they do.

PROMETHEUS

Thy words are like a cloud of wingèd snakes ;
And yet I pity those they torture not.

FURY

Thou pitiest them ? I speak no more !　　　　*[Vanishes.*

PROMETHEUS

　　　　　　　　　　　　　　　　Ah woe !
Ah woe ! Alas ! pain, pain ever, for ever !
I close my tearless eyes, but see more clear
Thy works within my woe-illumèd mind,
Thou subtle tyrant ! Peace is in the grave.
The grave hides all things beautiful and good :
I am a God and cannot find it there,
Nor would I seek it : for, though dread revenge,
This is defeat, fierce king, not victory.
The sights with which thou torturest gird my soul
With new endurance, till the hour arrives
When they shall be no types of things which are.

PANTHEA

Alas ! what sawest thou ?

PROMETHEUS

　　　　　　　　　There are two woes ;
To speak, and to behold ; thou spare me one.

Names are there, Nature's sacred watch-words, they
Were borne aloft in bright emblazonry;
The nations thronged around, and cried aloud,
As with one voice, Truth, liberty, and love!
Suddenly fierce confusion fell from heaven
Among them: there was strife, deceit, and fear:
Tyrants rushed in, and did divide the spoil.
This was the shadow of the truth I saw.

THE EARTH

I felt thy torture, son, with such mixed joy
As pain and virtue give. To cheer thy state
I bid ascend those subtle and fair spirits,
Whose homes are the dim caves of human thought,
And who inhabit, as birds wing the wind,
Its world-surrounding æther: they behold
Beyond that twilight realm, as in a glass,
The future: may they speak comfort to thee!

PANTHEA

Look, sister, where a troop of spirits gather,
Like flocks of clouds in spring's delightful weather,
Thronging in the blue air!

IONE

           And see! more come,
Like fountain-vapours when the winds are dumb,
That climb up the ravine in scattered lines.
And, hark! is it the music of the pines?
Is it the lake? Is it the waterfall?

PANTHEA

'Tis something sadder, sweeter far than all.

CHORUS OF SPIRITS

From unremembered ages we
Gentle guides and guardians be

Of heaven-oppressed mortality ;
And we breathe, and sicken not,
The atmosphere of human thought :
Be it dim, and dank, and grey,
Like a storm-extinguished day,
Travelled o'er by dying gleams ;
   Be it bright as all between
Cloudless skies and windless streams,
   Silent, liquid, and serene ;
As the birds within the wind,
   As the fish within the wave,
As the thoughts of man's own mind
   Float through all above the grave ;
We make there our liquid lair,
Voyaging cloudlike and unpent
Through the boundless element :
Thence we bear the prophecy
Which begins and ends in thee !

IONE

More yet come, one by one : the air around them
Looks radiant as the air around a star.

FIRST SPIRIT

On a battle-trumpet's blast
I fled hither, fast, fast, fast,
'Mid the darkness upward cast.
From the dust of creeds outworn,
From the tyrant's banner torn,
Gathering round me, onward borne,
There was mingled many a cry—
Freedom ! Hope ! Death ! Victory !
Till they faded through the sky ;
And one sound, above, around,
One sound beneath, around, above,
Was moving ; 'twas the soul of love ;
'Twas the hope, the prophecy,
Which begins and ends in thee.

SECOND SPIRIT

A rainbow's arch stood on the sea,
Which rocked beneath, immovably ;
And the triumphant storm did flee,
Like a conqueror, swift and proud,
Between, with many a captive cloud,
A shapeless, dark and rapid crowd,
Each by lightning riven in half :
I heard the thunder hoarsely laugh :
Mighty fleets were strewn like chaff
And spread beneath a hell of death
O'er the white waters.   I alit
On a great ship lightning-split,
And speeded hither on the sigh
Of one who gave an enemy
His plank, then plunged aside to die.

THIRD SPIRIT

I sate beside a sage's bed,
And the lamp was burning red
Near the book where he had fed,
When a Dream with plumes of flame,
To his pillow hovering came,
And I knew it was the same
Which had kindled long ago
Pity, eloquence, and woe ;
And the world awhile below
Wore the shade, its lustre made.
It has borne me here as fleet
As Desire's lightning feet :
I must ride it back ere morrow,
Or the sage will wake in sorrow.

FOURTH SPIRIT

On a poet's lips I slept
Dreaming like a love-adept
In the sound his breathing kept ;

Nor seeks nor finds he mortal blisses,
But feeds on the aërial kisses
Of shapes that haunt thought's wildernesses.
He will watch from dawn to gloom
The lake-reflected sun illume
The yellow bees in the ivy-bloom,
Nor heed nor see, what things they be ;
But from these create he can
Forms more real than living man,
Nurslings of immortality !
One of these awakened me,
And I sped to succour thee.

IONE

Behold'st thou not two shapes from the east and west
Come, as two doves to one belovèd nest,
Twin nurslings of the all-sustaining air
On swift still wings glide down the atmosphere ?
And, hark ! their sweet, sad voices ! 'tis despair
Mingled with love and then dissolved in sound.

PANTHEA

Canst thou speak, sister ? all my words are drowned.

IONE

Their beauty gives me voice.   See how they float
On their sustaining wings of skiey grain,
Orange and azure deepening into gold :
Their soft smiles light the air like a star's fire.

CHORUS OF SPIRITS

Hast thou beheld the form of Love ?

FIFTH SPIRIT

                              As over wide dominions
I sped, like some swift cloud that wings the wide air's
      wildernesses,
That planet-crested shape swept by on lightning-
      braided pinions,

Scattering the liquid joy of life from his ambrosial
  tresses :
His footsteps paved the world with light ; but as I
  passed 'twas fading,
And hollow Ruin yawned behind : great sages bound
  in madness,
And headless patriots, and pale youths who perished,
  unupbraiding,
Gleamed in the night. I wandered o'er, till thou,
  O King of sadness,
Turned by thy smile the worst I saw to recollected
  gladness.

Sixth Spirit

Ah, sister ! Desolation is a delicate thing :
It walks not on the earth, it floats not on the air,
But treads with killing footstep, and fans with silent wing
The tender hopes which in their hearts the best and
  gentlest bear ;
Who, soothed to false repose by the fanning plumes
  above
And the music-stirring motion of its soft and busy feet,
Dream visions of aërial joy, and call the monster, Love,
And wake, and find the shadow Pain, as he whom now
  we greet.

Chorus

  Though Ruin now Love's shadow be,
  Following him, destroyingly,
    On Death's white and wingèd steed,
  Which the fleetest cannot flee,
    Trampling down both flower and weed,
  Man and beast, and foul and fair,
  Like a tempest through the air ;
  Thou shalt quell this horseman grim,
  Woundless though in heart or limb.

Prometheus

Spirits ! how know ye this shall be ?

CHORUS

In the atmosphere we breathe,
As buds grow red when the snow-storms flee,
　From spring gathering up beneath,
Whose mild winds shake the elder brake,
And the wandering herdsmen know
That the white-thorn soon will blow :
Wisdom, Justice, Love, and Peace,
When they struggle to increase,
　　Are to us as soft winds be
　　To shepherd boys, the prophecy
　　Which begins and ends in thee.

IONE

Where are the Spirits fled ?

PANTHEA

　　　　　　Only a sense
Remains of them, like the omnipotence
Of music, when the inspired voice and lute
Languish, ere yet the responses are mute,
Which through the deep and labyrinthine soul,
Like echoes through long caverns, wind and roll.

PROMETHEUS

How fair these air-born shapes ! and yet I feel
Most vain all hope but love ; and thou art far,
Asia ! who, when my being overflowed,
Wert like a golden chalice to bright wine
Which else had sunk into the thirsty dust.
All things are still : alas ! how heavily
This quiet morning weighs upon my heart ;
Though I should dream I could even sleep with grief
If slumber were denied not.   I would fain
Be what it is my destiny to be,
The saviour and the strength of suffering man,
Or sink into the original gulph of things :
There is no agony, and no solace left ;
Earth can console, Heaven can torment no more.

PANTHEA

Hast thou forgotten one who watches thee
The cold dark night, and never sleeps but when
The shadow of thy spirit falls on her ?

PROMETHEUS

I said all hope was vain but love : thou lovest.

PANTHEA

Deeply in truth ; but the eastern star looks white,
And Asia waits in that far Indian vale
The scene of her sad exile ; rugged once
And desolate and frozen, like this ravine ;
But now invested with fair flowers and herbs,
And haunted by sweet airs and sounds, which flow
Among the woods and waters, from the æther
Of her transforming presence, which would fade
If it were mingled not with thine.   Farewell !

END OF THE FIRST ACT

ACT II

SCENE I. *Morning. A lovely Vale in the Indian
Caucasus.* ASIA *alone*

ASIA

From all the blasts of heaven thou hast descended :
Yes, like a spirit, like a thought, which makes
Unwonted tears throng to the horny eyes,
And beatings haunt the desolated heart,
Which should have learnt repose : thou hast descended
Cradled in tempests ; thou dost wake, O Spring !
O child of many winds ! As suddenly
Thou comest as the memory of a dream,
Which now is sad because it hath been sweet ;

Like genius, or like joy which riseth up
As from the earth, clothing with golden clouds
The desert of our life.
This is the season, this the day, the hour ;
At sunrise thou shouldst come, sweet sister mine,
Too long desired, too long delaying, come !
How like death-worms the wingless moments crawl !
The point of one white star is quivering still
Deep in the orange light of widening morn
Beyond the purple mountains : through a chasm
Of wind-divided mist the darker lake
Reflects it : now it wanes : it gleams again
As the waves fade, and as the burning threads
Of woven cloud unravel in pale air :
'Tis lost ! and through yon peaks of cloudlike snow
The roseate sun-light quivers : hear I not
The Æolian music of her sea-green plumes
Winnowing the crimson dawn ?

PANTHEA *enters*

I feel, I see
Those eyes which burn through smiles that fade in tears,
Like stars half quenched in mists of silver dew.
Belovèd and most beautiful, who wearest
The shadow of that soul by which I live,
How late thou art ! the spherèd sun had climbed
The sea ; my heart was sick with hope, before
The printless air felt thy belated plumes.

PANTHEA

Pardon, great Sister ! but my wings were faint
With the delight of a remembered dream,
As are the noon-tide plumes of summer winds
Satiate with sweet flowers.   I was wont to sleep
Peacefully, and awake refreshed and calm
Before the sacred Titan's fall, and thy
Unhappy love, had made, through use and pity,
Both love and woe familiar to my heart

As they had grown to thine : erewhile I slept
Under the glaucous caverns of old Ocean
Within dim bowers of green and purple moss,
Our young Ione's soft and milky arms
Locked then, as now, behind my dark, moist hair,
While my shut eyes and cheek were pressed within
The folded depth of her life-breathing bosom :
But not as now, since I am made the wind
Which fails beneath the music that I bear
Of thy most wordless converse ; since dissolved
Into the sense with which love talks, my rest
Was troubled and yet sweet ; my waking hours
Too full of care and pain.

ASIA

                    Lift up thine eyes,
And let me read thy dream.

PANTHEA

                    As I have said,
With our sea-sister at his feet I slept.
The mountain mists, condensing at our voice
Under the moon, had spread their snowy flakes,
From the keen ice shielding our linkèd sleep.
Then two dreams came. One, I remember not.
But in the other his pale wound-worn limbs
Fell from Prometheus, and the azure night
Grew radiant with the glory of that form
Which lives unchanged within, and his voice fell
Like music which makes giddy the dim brain,
Faint with intoxication of keen joy :
" Sister of her whose footsteps pave the world
With loveliness—more fair than aught but her,
Whose shadow thou art—lift thine eyes on me."
I lifted them : the overpowering light
Of that immortal shape was shadowed o'er
By love ; which, from his soft and flowing limbs,
And passion-parted lips, and keen, faint eyes,

Steamed forth like vaporous fire ; an atmosphere
Which wrapped me in its all-dissolving power,
As the warm æther of the morning sun
Wraps ere it drinks some cloud of wandering dew.
I saw not, heard not, moved not, only felt
His presence flow and mingle through my blood
Till it became his life, and his grew mine,
And I was thus absorbed, until it passed,
And like the vapours when the sun sinks down,
Gathering again in drops upon the pines,
And tremulous as they, in the deep night
My being was condensed ; and as the rays
Of thought were slowly gathered, I could hear
His voice, whose accents lingered ere they died
Like footsteps of weak melody : thy name
Among the many sounds alone I heard
Of what might be articulate ; though still
I listened through the night when sound was none.
Ione wakened then, and said to me :
" Canst thou divine what troubles me to-night ?
I always knew what I desired before,
Nor ever found delight to wish in vain.
But now I cannot tell thee what I seek ;
I know not ; something sweet, since it is sweet
Even to desire ; it is thy sport, false sister ;
Thou hast discovered some enchantment old,
Whose spells have stolen my spirit as I slept
And mingled it with thine : for when just now
We kissed, I felt within thy parted lips
The sweet air that sustained me, and the warmth
Of the life-blood, for loss of which I faint,
Quivered between our intertwining arms."
I answered not, for the Eastern star grew pale,
But fled to thee.

ASIA

       Thou speakest, but thy words
Are as the air : I feel them not : Oh, lift
Thine eyes, that I may read his written soul !

PANTHEA

I lift them though they droop beneath the load
Of that they would express : what canst thou see
But thine own fairest shadow imaged there ?

ASIA

Thine eyes are like the deep, blue, boundless heaven
Contracted to two circles underneath
Their long, fine lashes ; dark, far, measureless,
Orb within orb, and line through line inwoven.

PANTHEA

Why lookest thou as if a spirit passed ?

ASIA

There is a change : beyond their inmost depth
I see a shade, a shape : 'tis He, arrayed
In the soft light of his own smiles, which spread
Like radiance from the cloud-surrounded moon.
Prometheus, it is thine ! depart not yet !
Say not those smiles that we shall meet again
Within that bright pavilion which their beams
Shall build on the waste world ?   The dream is told.
What shape is that between us ?   Its rude hair
Roughens the wind that lifts it, its regard
Is wild and quick, yet 'tis a thing of air,
For through its grey robe gleams the golden dew
Whose stars the noon has quenched not.

DREAM

              Follow !   Follow !

PANTHEA

It is mine other dream.

ASIA

              It disappears.

PANTHEA

It passes now into my mind.   Methought
As we sate here, the flower-infolding buds

Burst on yon lightning-blasted almond-tree,
When swift from the white Scythian wilderness
A wind swept forth wrinkling the Earth with frost :
I looked, and all the blossoms were blown down ;
But on each leaf was stamped, as the blue bells
Of Hyacinth tell Apollo's written grief,
O, FOLLOW, FOLLOW !

ASIA

As you speak, your words
Fill, pause by pause, my own forgotten sleep
With shapes.   Methought among the lawns together
We wandered, underneath the young grey dawn,
And multitudes of dense white fleecy clouds
Were wandering in thick flocks along the mountains
Shepherded by the slow, unwilling wind ;
And the white dew on the new bladed grass,
Just piercing the dark earth, hung silently :
And there was more which I remember not :
But on the shadows of the morning clouds,
Athwart the purple mountain slope, was written
FOLLOW, O, FOLLOW ! as they vanished by,
And on each herb, from which Heaven's dew had
    fallen,
The like was stamped, as with a withering fire.
A wind arose among the pines ; it shook
The clinging music from their boughs, and then
Low, sweet, faint sounds, like the farewell of ghosts,
Were heard : OH, FOLLOW, FOLLOW, FOLLOW ME !
And then I said : " Panthea, look on me."
But in the depth of those belovèd eyes
Still I saw, FOLLOW, FOLLOW !

ECHO

Follow, follow !

PANTHEA

The crags, this clear spring morning, mock our voices
As they were spirit-tongued.

ASIA

It is some being
Around the crags.   What fine clear sounds !   O, list !

ECHOES (*unseen*)

Echoes we : listen !
We cannot stay :
As dew-stars glisten
Then fade away—
Child of Ocean !

ASIA

Hark !   Spirits speak.   The liquid responses
Of their aërial tongues yet sound.

PANTHEA

I hear.

ECHOES

O, follow, follow,
As our voice recedeth
Through the caverns hollow,
Where the forest spreadeth ;

(*More distant*)

O, follow, follow !
Through the caverns hollow,
As the song floats thou pursue,
Where the wild bee never flew,
Through the noon-tide darkness deep,
By the odour-breathing sleep
Of faint night flowers, and the waves
At the fountain-lighted caves,
While our music, wild and sweet,
Mocks thy gently falling feet,
Child of Ocean !

ASIA

Shall we pursue the sound ?   It grows more faint
And distant.

PANTHEA

List ! the strain floats nearer now.

ECHOES

In the world unknown
Sleeps a voice unspoken ;
By thy step alone
Can its rest be broken ;
Child of Ocean !

ASIA

How the notes sink upon the ebbing wind !

ECHOES

O, follow, follow !
Through the caverns hollow,
As the song floats thou pursue,
By the woodland noon-tide dew ;
By the forests, lakes, and fountains
Through the many-folded mountains ;
To the rents, and gulphs, and chasms,
Where the Earth reposed from spasms,
On the day when He and thou
Parted, to commingle now ;
Child of Ocean !

ASIA

Come, sweet Panthea, link thy hand in mine,
And follow, ere the voices fade away.

SCENE II. *A Forest, intermingled with Rocks and
Caverns.* ASIA *and* PANTHEA *pass into it. Two
young Fauns are sitting on a Rock, listening.*

SEMICHORUS I. OF SPIRITS

The path through which that lovely twain
Have passed, by cedar, pine, and yew,

And each dark tree that ever grew,
    Is curtained out from Heaven's wide blue ;
Nor sun, nor moon, nor wind, nor rain,
    Can pierce its interwoven bowers,
Nor aught, save where some cloud of dew,
Drifted along the earth-creeping breeze,
Between the trunks of the hoar trees,
    Hangs each a pearl in the pale flowers
Of the green laurel, blown anew ;
And bends, and then fades silently,
One frail and fair anemone :
Or when some star of many a one
That climbs and wanders through steep night,
Has found the cleft through which alone
Beams fall from high those depths upon
Ere it is borne away, away,
By the swift Heavens that cannot stay,
It scatters drops of golden light,
Like lines of rain that ne'er unite :
And the gloom divine is all around ;
And underneath is the mossy ground.

SEMICHORUS II

There the voluptuous nightingales,
    Are awake through all the broad noon-day.
When one with bliss or sadness fails,
        And through the windless ivy-boughs,
    Sick with sweet love, droops dying away
On its mate's music-panting bosom ;
Another from the swinging blossom,
        Watching to catch the languid close
    Of the last strain, then lifts on high
    The wings of the weak melody,
'Till some new strain of feeling bear
    The song, and all the woods are mute ;
When there is heard through the dim air
The rush of wings, and rising there

Like many a lake-surrounded flute,
Sounds overflow the listener's brain
So sweet, that joy is almost pain.

SEMICHORUS I

There those enchanted eddies play
    Of echoes, music-tongued, which draw,
    By Demogorgon's mighty law,
    With melting rapture, or sweet awe,
All spirits on that secret way ;
    As inland boats are driven to Ocean
Down streams made strong with mountain-thaw :
    And first there comes a gentle sound
    To those in talk or slumber bound,
And wakes the destined.   Soft emotion
Attracts, impels them : those who saw
    Say from the breathing earth behind
    There steams a plume-uplifting wind
Which drives them on their path, while they
    Believe their own swift wings and feet
The sweet desires within obey :
And so they float upon their way,
Until, still sweet, but loud and strong,
The storm of sound is driven along,
    Sucked up and hurrying : as they fleet
    Behind, its gathering billows meet
And to the fatal mountain bear
Like clouds amid the yielding air.

FIRST FAUN

Canst thou imagine where those spirits live
Which make such delicate music in the woods ?
We haunt within the least frequented caves
And closest coverts, and we know these wilds,
Yet never meet them, though we hear them oft :
Where may they hide themselves ?

SECOND FAUN

'Tis hard to tell :
I have heard those more skilled in spirits say,
The bubbles, which the enchantment of the sun
Sucks from the pale faint water-flowers that pave
The oozy bottom of clear lakes and pools,
Are the pavilions where such dwell and float
Under the green and golden atmosphere
Which noon-tide kindles through the woven leaves ;
And when these burst, and the thin fiery air,
The which they breathed within those lucent domes,
Ascends to flow like meteors through the night,
They ride on them, and rein their headlong speed,
And bow their burning crests, and glide in fire
Under the waters of the earth again.

FIRST FAUN

If such live thus, have others other lives,
Under pink blossoms or within the bells
Of meadow flowers, or folded violets deep,
Or on their dying odours, when they die,
Or in the sunlight of the spherèd dew ?

SECOND FAUN

Aye, many more which we may well divine.
But, should we stay to speak, noontide would come,
And thwart Silenus find his goats undrawn,
And grudge to sing those wise and lovely songs
Of fate, and chance, and God, and Chaos old,
And Love, and the chained Titan's woful doom,
And how he shall be loosed, and make the earth
One brotherhood : delightful strains which cheer
Our solitary twilights, and which charm
To silence the unenvying nightingales.

SCENE III. *A Pinnacle of Rock among Mountains.*
ASIA *and* PANTHEA

PANTHEA

Hither the sound has borne us—to the realm
Of Demogorgon, and the mighty portal,
Like a volcano's meteor-breathing chasm,
Whence the oracular vapour is hurled up
Which lonely men drink wandering in their youth,
And call truth, virtue, love, genius, or joy,
That maddening wine of life, whose dregs they drain
To deep intoxication ; and uplift,
Like Mænads who cry aloud, Evoe ! Evoe !
The voice which is contagion to the world.

ASIA

Fit throne for such a Power ! Magnificent !
How glorious art thou, Earth ! And if thou be
The shadow of some spirit lovelier still,
Though evil stain its work, and it should be
Like its creation, weak yet beautiful,
I could fall down and worship that and thee.
Even now my heart adoreth : Wonderful !
Look, sister, ere the vapour dim thy brain :
Beneath is a wide plain of billowy mist,
As a lake, paving in the morning sky,
With azure waves which burst in silver light,
Some Indian vale. Behold it, rolling on
Under the curdling winds, and islanding
The peak whereon we stand, midway, around,
Encinctured by the dark and blooming forests,
Dim twilight-lawns, and stream-illumined caves,
And wind-enchanted shapes of wandering mist ;
And far on high the keen sky-cleaving mountains
From icy spires of sun-like radiance fling
The dawn, as lifted Ocean's dazzling spray,
From some Atlantic islet scattered up,
Spangles the wind with lamp-like water-drops.

The vale is girdled with their walls, a howl
Of cataracts from their thaw-cloven ravines,
Satiates the listening wind, continuous, vast,
Awful as silence.   Hark ! the rushing snow !
The sun-awakened avalanche ! whose mass,
Thrice sifted by the storm, had gathered there
Flake after flake, in heaven-defying minds
As thought by thought is piled, till some great truth
Is loosened, and the nations echo round,
Shaken to their roots, as do the mountains now.

PANTHEA

Look how the gusty sea of mist is breaking
In crimson foam, even at our feet ! it rises
As Ocean at the enchantment of the moon
Round foodless men wrecked on some oozy isle.

ASIA

The fragments of the cloud are scattered up ;
The wind that lifts them disentwines my hair ;
Its billows now sweep o'er mine eyes ; my brain
Grows dizzy ; I see thin shapes within the mist.

PANTHEA

A countenance with beckoning smiles : there burns
An azure fire within its golden locks !
Another and another : hark ! they speak !

SONG OF SPIRITS

To the deep, to the deep,
        Down, down !
Through the shade of sleep,
Through the cloudy strife
Of Death and of Life ;
Through the veil and the bar
Of things which seem and are
Even to the steps of the remotest throne,
        Down, down !

While the sound whirls around,
   Down, down !
As the fawn draws the hound.
As the lightning the vapour,
As a weak moth the taper ;
Death, despair ; love, sorrow ;
Time both ; to-day, to-morrow ;
As steel obeys the spirit of the stone,
   Down, down !

Through the grey, void abysm,
   Down, down !
Where the air is no prism,
And the moon and stars are not,
And the cavern-crags wear not
The radiance of Heaven,
Nor the gloom to Earth given,
Where there is one pervading, one alone.
   Down, down !

In the depth of the deep
   Down, down !
Like veiled lightning asleep,
Like the spark nursed in embers,
The last look Love remembers,
Like a diamond, which shines
On the dark wealth of mines,
A spell is treasured but for thee alone.
   Down, down !

We have bound thee, we guide thee ;
   Down, down !
With the bright form beside thee ;
Resist not the weakness,
Such strength is in meekness
That the Eternal, the Immortal,
Must unloose through life's portal
The snake-like Doom coiled underneath his throne
   By that alone.

SCENE IV. *The Cave of* DEMOGORGON. ASIA *and*
PANTHEA

PANTHEA

What veilèd form sits on that ebon throne ?

ASIA

The veil has fallen.

PANTHEA

I see a mighty darkness
Filling the seat of power, and rays of gloom
Dart round, as light from the meridian sun,
Ungazed upon and shapeless ; neither limb,
Nor form, nor outline ; yet we feel it is
A living Spirit.

DEMOGORGON

Ask what thou wouldst know.

ASIA

What canst thou tell ?

DEMOGORGON

All things thou dar'st demand.

ASIA

Who made the living world ?

DEMOGORGON

God.

ASIA

Who made all
That it contains ? thought, passion, reason, will,
Imagination ?

DEMOGORGON

God : Almighty God.

ASIA

Who made that sense which, when the winds of spring

In rarest visitation, or the voice
Of one belovèd heard in youth alone,
Fills the faint eyes with falling tears which dim
The radiant looks of unbewailing flowers,
And leaves this peopled earth a solitude
When it returns no more ?

DEMOGORGON
Merciful God.

ASIA
And who made terror, madness, crime, remorse
Which from the links of the great chain of things,
To every thought within the mind of man
Sway and drag heavily, and each one reels
Under the load towards the pit of death ;
Abandoned hope, and love that turns to hate ;
And self-contempt, bitterer to drink than blood ;
Pain, whose unheeded and familiar speech
Is howling, and keen shrieks, day after day ;
And Hell, or the sharp fear of Hell ?

DEMOGORGON
He reigns.

ASIA
Utter his name ; a world pining in pain
Asks but his name : curses shall drag him down.

DEMOGORGON
He reigns.

ASIA
I feel, I know it : who ?

DEMOGORGON
He reigns.

ASIA
Who reigns ?   There was the Heaven and Earth at first,
And Light and Love ; then Saturn, from whose throne

Time fell, an envious shadow : such the state
Of the earth's primal spirits beneath his sway,
As the calm joy of flowers and living leaves
Before the wind or sun has withered them,
And semivital worms ; but he refused
The birthright of their being, knowledge, power,
The skill which wields the elements, the thought
Which pierces this dim universe like light,
Self-empire, and the majesty of love ;
For thirst of which they fainted.   Then Prometheus
Gave wisdom, which is strength, to Jupiter,
And with this law alone, " Let man be free,"
Clothed him with the dominion of wide Heaven.
To know nor faith, nor love, nor law ; to be
Omnipotent but friendless is to reign ;
And Jove now reigned ; for on the race of man
First famine, and then toil, and then disease,
Strife, wounds, and ghastly death unseen before,
Fell ; and the unseasonable seasons drove
With alternating shafts of frost and fire
Their shelterless, pale tribes to mountain caves :
And in their desert hearts fierce wants he sent,
And mad disquietudes, and shadows idle
Of unreal good, which levied mutual war,
So ruining the lair wherein they raged.
Prometheus saw, and waked the legioned hopes
Which sleep within folded Elysian flowers,
Nepenthe, Moly, Amaranth, fadeless blooms,
That they might hide with thin and rainbow wings
The shape of Death ; and Love he sent to bind
The disunited tendrils of that vine
Which bears the wine of life, the human heart ;
And he tamed fire which, like some beast of prey,
Most terrible, but lovely, played beneath
The frown of man ; and tortured to his will
Iron and gold, the slaves and signs of power,
And gems and poisons, and all subtlest forms
Hidden beneath the mountains and the waves.

He gave man speech, and speech created thought,
Which is the measure of the universe ;
And Science struck the thrones of earth and heaven,
Which shook, but fell not ; and the harmonious mind
Poured itself forth in all-prophetic song ;
And music lifted up the listening spirit
Until it walked, exempt from mortal care,
Godlike, o'er the clear billows of sweet sound ;
And human hands first mimicked and then mocked,
With moulded limbs more lovely than its own,
The human form, till marble grew divine ;
And mothers, gazing, drank the love men see
Reflected in their race, behold, and perish.
He told the hidden power of herbs and springs,
And Disease drank and slept.   Death grew like sleep.
He taught the implicated orbits woven
Of the wide-wandering stars ; and how the sun
Changes his lair, and by what secret spell
The pale moon is transformed, when her broad eye
Gazes not on the interlunar sea :
He taught to rule, as life directs the limbs,
The tempest-wingèd chariots of the Ocean,
And the Celt knew the Indian.   Cities then
Were built, and through their snow-like columns flowed
The warm winds, and the azure æther shone,
And the blue sea and shadowy hills were seen.
Such, the alleviations of his state,
Prometheus gave to man, for which he hangs
Withering in destined pain : but who reigns down
Evil, the immedicable plague, which, while
Man looks on his creation like a God
And sees that it is glorious, drives him on
The wreck of his own will, the scorn of earth,
The outcast, the abandoned, the alone ?
Not Jove : while yet his frown shook heaven, aye, when
His adversary from adamantine chains
Cursed him, he trembled like a slave.   Declare
Who is his master ?   Is he too a slave ?

DEMOGORGON

All spirits are enslaved which serve things evil :
Thou knowest if Jupiter be such or no.

ASIA

Whom calledst thou God ?

DEMOGORGON

                          I spoke but as ye speak,
For Jove is the supreme of living things.

ASIA

Who is the master of the slave ?

DEMOGORGON

                         If the abysm
Could vomit forth its secrets.   But a voice
Is wanting, the deep truth is imageless ;
For what would it avail to bid thee gaze
On the revolving world ?   What to bid speak
Fate, Time, Occasion, Chance and Change ?   To these
All things are subject but eternal Love.

ASIA

So much I asked before, and my heart gave
The response thou hast given ; and of such truths
Each to itself must be the oracle.
One more demand ; and do thou answer me
As mine own soul would answer, did it know
That which I ask.   Prometheus shall arise
Henceforth the sun of this rejoicing world :
When shall the destined hour arrive ?

DEMOGORGON

                       Behold !

ASIA

The rocks are cloven, and through the purple night
I see cars drawn by rainbow-wingèd steeds

Which trample the dim winds : in each there stands
A wild-eyed charioteer urging their flight.
Some look behind, as fiends pursued them there,
And yet I see no shapes but the keen stars :
Others, with burning eyes, lean forth, and drink
With eager lips the wind of their own speed,
As if the thing they loved fled on before,
And now, even now, they clasped it.   Their bright locks
Stream like a comet's flashing hair : they all
Sweep onward.

DEMOGORGON

These are the immortal Hours,
Of whom thou didst demand.   One waits for thee.

ASIA

A spirit with a dreadful countenance
Checks its dark chariot by the craggy gulph.
Unlike thy brethren, ghastly charioteer,
Who art thou ?   Whither wouldst thou bear me ?
    Speak !

SPIRIT

I am the shadow of a destiny
More dread than is my aspect : ere yon planet
Has set, the darkness which ascends with me
Shall wrap in lasting night heaven's kingless throne.

ASIA

What meanest thou ?

PANTHEA

That terrible shadow floats
Up from its throne, as may the lurid smoke
Of earthquake-ruined cities o'er the sea.
Lo ! it ascends the car ; the coursers fly
Terrified : watch its path among the stars
Blackening the night !

ASIA

Thus I am answered : strange !

PANTHEA

See, near the verge, another chariot stays ;
An ivory shell inlaid with crimson fire,
Which comes and goes within its sculptured rim
Of delicate strange tracery ; the young spirit
That guides it has the dove-like eyes of hope ;
How its soft smiles attract the soul ! as light
Lures wingèd insects through the lampless air.

SPIRIT

My coursers are fed with the lightning,
    They drink of the whirlwind's stream,
And when the red morning is bright'ning
    They bathe in the fresh sunbeam ;
    They have strength for their swiftness I deem,
Then ascend with me, daughter of Ocean.

I desire : and their speed makes night kindle ;
    I fear : they outstrip the Typhoon ;
Ere the cloud piled on Atlas can dwindle
    We encircle the earth and the moon :
    We shall rest from long labours at noon :
Then ascend with me, daughter of Ocean.

SCENE V. *The Car pauses within a Cloud on the Top
    of a snowy Mountain.* ASIA, PANTHEA, *and the*
    SPIRIT OF THE HOUR

SPIRIT

On the brink of the night and the morning
    My coursers are wont to respire ;
But the Earth has just whispered a warning
    That their flight must be swifter than fire :
    They shall drink the hot speed of desire !

ASIA

Thou breathest on their nostrils, but my breath
Would give them swifter speed.

SPIRIT

Alas ! it could not.

PANTHEA

Oh Spirit ! pause, and tell whence is the light
Which fills the cloud ? the sun is yet unrisen.

SPIRIT

The sun will rise not until noon.   Apollo
Is held in heaven by wonder ; and the light
Which fills this vapour, as the aërial hue
Of fountain-gazing roses fills the water,
Flows from thy mighty sister.

PANTHEA

Yes, I feel—

ASIA

What is it with thee, sister ?   Thou art pale.

PANTHEA

How thou art changed !   I dare not look on thee ;
I feel but see thee not.   I scarce endure
The radiance of thy beauty.   Some good change
Is working in the elements, which suffer
Thy presence thus unveiled.   The Nereids tell
That on the day when the clear hyaline
Was cloven at thy uprise, and thou didst stand
Within a veinèd shell, which floated on
Over the calm floor of the crystal sea,
Among the Ægean isles, and by the shores
Which bear thy name ; love, like the atmosphere
Of the sun's fire filling the living world,
Burst from thee, and illumined earth and heaven
And the deep ocean and the sunless caves

And all that dwells within them ; till grief cast
Eclipse upon the soul from which it came :
Such art thou now ; nor is it I alone,
Thy sister, thy companion, thine own chosen one,
But the whole world which seeks thy sympathy.
Hear'st thou not sounds i' the air which speak the love
Of all articulate beings ?   Feel'st thou not
The inanimate winds enamoured of thee ?   List !

                                                (Music.)

ASIA

Thy words are sweeter than aught else but his
Whose echoes they are : yet all love is sweet,
Given or returned.   Common as light is love,
And its familiar voice wearies not ever.
Like the wide heaven, the all-sustaining air,
It makes the reptile equal to the God :
They who inspire it most are fortunate,
As I am now ; but those who feel it most
Are happier still, after long sufferings,
As I shall soon become.

PANTHEA

List !   Spirits speak.

VOICE *in the Air, singing*

Life of Life ! thy lips enkindle
    With their love the breath between them ;
And thy smiles before they dwindle
    Make the cold air fire ; then screen them
In those looks, where whoso gazes
Faints, entangled in their mazes.

Child of Light ! thy limbs are burning
    Through the vest which seems to hide them ;
As the radiant lines of morning
    Through the clouds ere they divide them ;
And this atmosphere divinest
Shrouds thee wheresoe'er thou shinest.

Fair are others ; none beholds thee,
  But thy voice sounds low and tender
Like the fairest, for it folds thee
  From the sight, that liquid splendour,
And all feel, yet see thee never,
As I feel now, lost for ever !

Lamp of Earth ! where'er thou movest
  Its dim shapes are clad with brightness,
And the souls of whom thou lovest
  Walk upon the winds with lightness,
Till they fail, as I am failing,
Dizzy, lost, yet unbewailing !

ASIA

My soul is an enchanted boat,
  Which, like a sleeping swan, doth float
Upon the silver waves of thy sweet singing ;
  And thine doth like an angel sit
  Beside a helm conducting it,
Whilst all the winds with melody are ringing.
  It seems to float ever, for ever,
  Upon that many-winding river,
  Between mountains, woods, abysses,
  A paradise of wildernesses !
Till, like one in slumber bound,
Borne to the ocean, I float down, around,
Into a sea profound, of ever-spreading sound :

  Meanwhile thy spirit lifts its pinions
  In music's most serene dominions ;
Catching the winds that fan that happy heaven.
  And we sail on, away, afar,
  Without a course, without a star,
But by the instinct of sweet music driven ;
  Till through Elysian garden islets
  By thee, most beautiful of pilots,

Where never mortal pinnace glided,
    The boat of my desire is guided :
Realms where the air we breathe is love,
Which in the winds and on the waves doth move,
Harmonizing this earth with what we feel above.

    We have passed Age's icy caves,
    And Manhood's dark and tossing waves,
And Youth's smooth ocean, smiling to betray :
    Beyond the glassy gulphs we flee
    Of shadow-peopled Infancy,
Through Death and Birth, to a diviner day ;
    A paradise of vaulted bowers,
    Lit by downward-gazing flowers,
    And watery paths that wind between
    Wildernesses calm and green,
Peopled by shapes too bright to see,
And rest, having beheld ; somewhat like thee ;
Which walk upon the sea, and chaunt melodiously !

END OF THE SECOND ACT

ACT III

Scene I. *Heaven.* Jupiter *on his Throne ;* Thetis
and the other Deities assembled

JUPITER

Ye congregated powers of heaven, who share
The glory and the strength of him ye serve,
Rejoice ! henceforth I am omnipotent.
All else had been subdued to me ; alone
The soul of man, like unextinguished fire,
Yet burns towards heaven with fierce reproach and
        doubt,
And lamentation, and reluctant prayer,

Hurling up insurrection, which might make
Our antique empire insecure, though built
On eldest faith, and hell's coeval, fear ;
And though my curses through the pendulous air,
Like snow on herbless peaks, fall flake by flake,
And cling to it ; though under my wrath's might
It climb the crags of life, step after step,
Which wound it, as ice wounds unsandalled feet,
It yet remains supreme o'er misery,
Aspiring, unrepressed, yet soon to fall :
Even now have I begotten a strange wonder,
That fatal child, the terror of the earth,
Who waits but till the destined hour arrive,
Bearing from Demogorgon's vacant throne
The dreadful might of ever-living limbs
Which clothed that awful spirit unbeheld,
To redescend, and trample out the spark.

Pour forth heaven's wine, Idæan Ganymede,
And let it fill the Dædal cups like fire,
And from the flower-inwoven soil divine
Ye all-triumphant harmonies arise,
As dew from earth under the twilight stars :
Drink ! be the nectar circling through your veins
The soul of joy, ye ever-living Gods,
Till exultation burst in one wide voice
Like music from Elysian winds.
                                        And thou
Ascend beside me, veilèd in the light
Of the desire which makes thee one with me,
Thetis, bright image of eternity !
When thou didst cry, " Insufferable might !
God ! Spare me ! I sustain not the quick flames,
The penetrating presence ; all my being,
Like him whom the Numidian seps did thaw
Into a dew with poison, is dissolved,
Sinking through its foundations : " even then
Two mighty spirits, mingling, made a third

Mightier than either, which, unbodied now,
Between us floats, felt, although unbeheld,
Waiting the incarnation, which ascends,
(Hear ye the thunder of the fiery wheels
Griding the winds?) from Demogorgon's throne.
Victory! victory! Feel'st thou not, O world,
The earthquake of his chariot thundering up
Olympus?

> [*The Car of the* HOUR *arrives.* DEMOGORGON
> *descends, and moves towards the Throne of*
> JUPITER.

Awful shape, what art thou? Speak!

DEMOGORGON

Eternity. Demand no direr name.
Descend, and follow me down the abyss.
I am thy child, as thou wert Saturn's child;
Mightier than thee: and we must dwell together
Henceforth in darkness. Lift thy lightnings not.
The tyranny of heaven none may retain,
Or reassume, or hold, succeeding thee:
Yet if thou wilt, as 'tis the destiny
Of trodden worms to writhe till they are dead,
Put forth thy might.

JUPITER

Detested prodigy!
Even thus beneath the deep Titanian prisons
I trample thee! thou lingerest?

Mercy! mercy!
No pity, no release, no respite! Oh,
That thou wouldst make mine enemy my judge,
Even where he hangs, seared by my long revenge,
On Caucasus! he would not doom me thus.
Gentle, and just, and dreadless, is he not
The monarch of the world? What then art thou?
No refuge! no appeal!

Sink with me then,
We two will sink on the wide waves of ruin,

Even as a vulture and a snake outspent
Drop, twisted in inextricable fight,
Into a shoreless sea.   Let hell unlock
Its mounded oceans of tempestuous fire,
And whelm on them into the bottomless void
This desolated world, and thee, and me,
The conqueror and the conquered, and the wreck
Of that for which they combated.

Ai ! Ai !

The elements obey me not.   I sink
Dizzily down, ever, for ever, down.
And, like a cloud, mine enemy above
Darkens my fall with victory !   Ai, Ai !

SCENE II.   *The Mouth of a great River in the Island
    Atlantis.*   OCEAN *is discovered reclining near the
    Shore ;* APOLLO *stands beside him*

OCEAN

He fell, thou sayest, beneath his conqueror's frown ?

APOLLO

Aye, when the strife was ended which made dim
The orb I rule, and shook the solid stars,
The terrors of his eye illumined heaven
With sanguine light, through the thick ragged skirts
Of the victorious darkness, as he fell :
Like the last glare of day's red agony,
Which, from a rent among the fiery clouds,
Burns far along the tempest-wrinkled deep.

OCEAN

He sunk to the abyss ?   To the dark void ?

APOLLO

An eagle so caught in some bursting cloud
On Caucasus, his thunder-baffled wings

Entangled in the whirlwind, and his eyes
Which gazed on the undazzling sun, now blinded
By the white lightning, while the ponderous hail
Beats on his struggling form, which sinks at length
Prone, and the aërial ice clings over it.

OCEAN

Henceforth the fields of Heaven-reflecting sea
Which are my realm will heave, unstained with blood,
Beneath the uplifting winds, like plains of corn
Swayed by the summer air ; my streams will flow
Round many-peopled continents, and round
Fortunate isles ; and from their glassy thrones
Blue Proteus and his humid nymphs shall mark
The shadow of fair ships, as mortals see
The floating bark of the light-laden moon
With that white star, its sightless pilot's crest,
Borne down the rapid sunset's ebbing sea ;
Tracking their path no more by blood and groans,
And desolation, and the mingled voice
Of slavery and command ; but by the light
Of wave-reflected flowers, and floating odours,
And music soft, and mild, free, gentle voices,
And sweetest music, such as spirits love.

APOLLO

And I shall gaze not on the deeds which make
My mind obscure with sorrow, as eclipse
Darkens the sphere I guide ; but list, I hear
The small, clear, silver lute of the young Spirit
That sits i' the morning star.

OCEAN

          Thou must away ;
Thy steeds will pause at even, till when farewell :
The loud deep calls me home even now to feed it
With azure calm out of the emerald urns
Which stand for ever full beside my throne.

Behold the Nereids under the green sea,
Their wavering limbs borne on the wind-like stream,
Their white arms lifted o'er their streaming hair
With garlands pied and starry sea-flower crowns,
Hastening to grace their mighty sister's joy.
                    (*A sound of waves is heard.*)
It is the unpastured sea hungering for calm.
Peace, monster ; I come now.   Farewell.

APOLLO

                                        Farewell.

SCENE III. *Caucasus.* PROMETHEUS, HERCULES, IONE,
    the EARTH, SPIRITS, ASIA, *and* PANTHEA, *borne in
    the Car with the* SPIRIT OF THE HOUR

HERCULES *unbinds* PROMETHEUS, *who descends*

HERCULES

Most glorious among spirits, thus doth strength
To wisdom, courage, and long-suffering love,
And thee, who art the form they animate,
Minister like a slave.

PROMETHEUS

                    Thy gentle words
Are sweeter even than freedom long desired
And long delayed.
                    Asia, thou light of life,
Shadow of beauty unbeheld : and ye,
Fair sister nymphs, who made long years of pain
Sweet to remember, through your love and care :
Henceforth we will not part.   There is a cave,
All overgrown with trailing odorous plants,
Which curtain out the day with leaves and flowers,
And paved with veinèd emerald, and a fountain
Leaps in the midst with an awakening sound.

From its curved roof the mountain's frozen tears
Like snow, or silver, or long diamond spires,
Hang downward, raining forth a doubtful light :
And there is heard the ever-moving air,
Whispering without from tree to tree, and birds,
And bees ; and all around are mossy seats,
And the rough walls are clothed with long soft grass ;
A simple dwelling, which shall be our own ;
Where we will sit and talk of time and change,
As the world ebbs and flows, ourselves unchanged.
What can hide man from mutability ?
And if ye sigh, then I will smile ; and thou,
Ione, shalt chaunt fragments of sea-music,
Until I weep, when ye shall smile away
The tears she brought, which yet were sweet to shed.
We will entangle buds and flowers and beams
Which twinkle on the fountain's brim, and make
Strange combinations out of common things,
Like human babes in their brief innocence ;
And we will search, with looks and words of love,
For hidden thoughts, each lovelier than the last,
Our unexhausted spirits ; and like lutes
Touched by the skill of the enamoured wind,
Weave harmonies divine, yet ever new,
From difference sweet where discord cannot be ;
And hither come, sped on the charmèd winds,
Which meet from all the points of heaven, as bees
From every flower aërial Enna feeds,
At their known island-homes in Himera,
The echoes of the human world, which tell
Of the low voice of love, almost unheard,
And dove-eyed pity's murmured pain, and music,
Itself the echo of the heart, and all
That tempers or improves man's life, now free ;
And lovely apparitions, dim at first,
Then radiant, as the mind, arising bright
From the embrace of beauty, whence the forms
Of which these are the phantoms, casts on them

The gathered rays which are reality,
Shall visit us, the progeny immortal
Of Painting, Sculpture, and rapt Poesy,
And arts, though unimagined, yet to be.
The wandering voices and the shadows these
Of all that man becomes, the mediators
Of that best worship love, by him and us
Given and returned; swift shapes and sounds, which grow
More fair and soft as man grows wise and kind,
And veil by veil, evil and error fall:
Such virtue has the cave and place around.

(Turning to the SPIRIT OF THE HOUR.)

For thee, fair Spirit, one toil remains.   Ione,
Give her that curvèd shell, which Proteus old
Made Asia's nuptial boon, breathing within it
A voice to be accomplished, and which thou
Didst hide in grass under the hollow rock.

IONE

Thou most desired Hour, more loved and lovely
Than all thy sisters, this is the mystic shell;
See the pale azure fading into silver
Lining it with a soft yet glowing light:
Looks it not like lulled music sleeping there?

SPIRIT

It seems in truth the fairest shell of Ocean:
Its sound must be at once both sweet and strange.

PROMETHEUS

Go, borne over the cities of mankind
On whirlwind-footed coursers: once again
Outspeed the sun around the orbèd world;
And as thy chariot cleaves the kindling air,
Thou breathe into the many-folded shell,
Loosening its mighty music; it shall be
As thunder mingled with clear echoes: then
Return; and thou shalt dwell beside our cave.
And thou, O, Mother Earth!——

THE EARTH

                    I hear, I feel ;
Thy lips are on me, and thy touch runs down
Even to the adamantine central gloom
Along these marble nerves ; 'tis life, 'tis joy,
And through my withered, old, and icy frame
The warmth of an immortal youth shoots down
Circling.   Henceforth the many children fair
Folded in my sustaining arms ; all plants,
And creeping forms, and insects rainbow-winged,
And birds, and beasts, and fish, and human shapes,
Which drew disease and pain from my wan bosom,
Draining the poison of despair, shall take
And interchange sweet nutriment ; to me
Shall they become like sister-antelopes
By one fair dam, snow-white and swift as wind,
Nursed among lilies near a brimming stream.
The dew-mists of my sunless sleep shall float
Under the stars like balm : night-folded flowers
Shall suck unwithering hues in their repose :
And men and beasts in happy dreams shall gather
Strength for the coming day, and all its joy :
And death shall be the last embrace of her
Who takes the life she gave, even as a mother
Folding her child, says, " Leave me not again."

ASIA

Oh, mother ! wherefore speak the name of death ?
Cease they to love, and move, and breathe, and speak,
Who die ?

THE EARTH

            It would avail not to reply :
Thou art immortal, and this tongue is known
But to the uncommunicating dead.
Death is the veil which those who live call life :
They sleep, and it is lifted : and meanwhile
In mild variety the seasons mild

With rainbow-skirted showers, and odorous winds,
And long blue meteors cleansing the dull night,
And the life-kindling shafts of the keen sun's
All-piercing bow, and the dew-mingled rain
Of the calm moonbeams, a soft influence mild,
Shall clothe the forests and the fields, aye, even
The crag-built deserts of the barren deep,
With ever-living leaves, and fruits, and flowers.
And thou !   There is a cavern where my spirit
Was panted forth in anguish whilst thy pain
Made my heart mad, and those who did inhale it
Became mad too, and built a temple there,
And spoke, and were oracular, and lured
The erring nations round to mutual war,
And faithless faith, such as Jove kept with thee ;
Which breath now rises, as amongst tall weeds
A violet's exhalation, and it fills
With a serener light and crimson air
Intense, yet soft, the rocks and woods around ;
It feeds the quick growth of the serpent vine,
And the dark linkèd ivy tangling wild,
And budding, blown, or odour-faded blooms
Which star the winds with points of coloured light,
As they rain through them, and bright golden globes
Of fruit, suspended in their own green heaven,
And through their veinèd leaves and amber stems
The flowers whose purple and translucid bowls
Stand ever mantling with aërial dew,
The drink of spirits : and it circles round,
Like the soft waving wings of noonday dreams,
Inspiring calm and happy thoughts, like mine,
Now thou art thus restored.   This cave is thine.
Arise !   Appear !
        (*A Spirit rises in the likeness of a winged child.*)
                This is my torch-bearer ;
Who let his lamp out in old time with gazing
On eyes from which he kindled it anew
With love, which is as fire, sweet daughter mine,

For such is that within thine own.   Run, wayward,
And guide this company beyond the peak
Of Bacchic Nysa, Mænad-haunted mountain,
And beyond Indus and its tribute rivers,
Trampling the torrent streams and glassy lakes
With feet unwet, unwearied, undelaying,
And up the green ravine, across the vale,
Beside the windless and crystàlline pool,
Where ever lies, on unerasing waves,
The image of a temple, built above,
Distinct with column, arch, and architrave,
And palm-like capital, and over-wrought,
And populous most with living imagery,
Praxitelean shapes, whose marble smiles
Fill the hushed air with everlasting love.
It is deserted now, but once it bore
Thy name, Prometheus ; there the emulous youths
Bore to thy honour through the divine gloom
The lamp which was thine emblem ; even as those
Who bear the untransmitted torch of hope
Into the grave, across the night of life,
As thou hast borne it most triumphantly
To this far goal of Time.   Depart, farewell.
Beside that temple is the destined cave.

SCENE IV. *A Forest. In the Background a Cave.*
    PROMETHEUS, ASIA, PANTHEA, IONE, *and the*
    SPIRIT OF THE EARTH.

IONE

Sister, it is not earthly : how it glides
Under the leaves ! how on its head there burns
A light, like a green star, whose emerald beams
Are twined with its fair hair ! how, as it moves,
The splendour drops in flakes upon the grass !
Knowest thou it ?

PANTHEA

It is the delicate spirit
That guides the earth through heaven. From afar
The populous constellations call that light
The loveliest of the planets ; and sometimes
It floats along the spray of the salt sea,
Or makes its chariot of a foggy cloud,
Or walks through fields or cities while men sleep,
Or o'er the mountain tops, or down the rivers,
Or through the green waste wilderness, as now,
Wondering at all it sees. Before Jove reigned
It loved our sister Asia, and it came
Each leisure hour to drink the liquid light
Out of her eyes, for which it said it thirsted
As one bit by a dipsas, and with her
It made its childish confidence, and told her
All it had known or seen, for it saw much,
Yet idly reasoned what it saw ; and called her,—
For whence it sprung it knew not, nor do I,—
" Mother, dear mother."

THE SPIRIT OF THE EARTH (*running to* ASIA)

Mother, dearest mother ;
May I then talk with thee as I was wont ?
May I then hide my eyes in thy soft arms,
After thy looks have made them tired of joy ?
May I then play beside thee the long noons,
When work is none in the bright silent air ?

ASIA

I love thee, gentlest being, and henceforth
Can cherish thee unenvied : speak, I pray :
Thy simple talk once solaced, now delights.

SPIRIT OF THE EARTH

Mother, I am grown wiser, though a child
Cannot be wise like thee, within this day ;

And happier too ; happier and wiser both.
Thou knowest that toads, and snakes, and loathly worms,
And venomous and malicious beasts, and boughs
That bore ill berries in the woods, were ever
An hindrance to my walks o'er the green world :
And that, among the haunts of humankind,
Hard-featured men, or with proud, angry looks,
Or cold, staid gait, or false and hollow smiles,
Or the dull sneer of self-loved ignorance,
Or other such foul masks, with which ill thoughts
Hide that fair being whom we spirits call man ;
And women too, ugliest of all things evil,
(Though fair, even in a world where thou art fair,
When good and kind, free and sincere like thee,)
When false or frowning made me sick at heart
To pass them, though they slept, and I unseen.
Well, my path lately lay through a great city
Into the woody hills surrounding it :
A sentinel was sleeping at the gate :
When there was heard a sound, so loud, it shook
The towers amid the moonlight, yet more sweet
Than any voice but thine, sweetest of all ;
A long, long sound, as it would never end :
And all the inhabitants leapt suddenly
Out of their rest, and gathered in the streets,
Looking in wonder up to Heaven, while yet
The music pealed along. I hid myself
Within a fountain in the public square,
Where I lay like the reflex of the moon
Seen in a wave under green leaves ; and soon
Those ugly human shapes and visages
Of which I spoke as having wrought me pain,
Passed floating through the air, and fading still
Into the winds that scattered them ; and those
From whom they passed seemed mild and lovely forms
After some foul disguise had fallen, and all
Were somewhat changed, and after brief surprise
And greetings of delighted wonder, all

Went to their sleep again : and when the dawn
Came, wouldst thou think that toads, and snakes, and
    efts,
Could e'er be beautiful ? yet so they were,
And that with little change of shape or hue :
All things had put their evil nature off :
I cannot tell my joy, when o'er a lake
Upon a drooping bough with night-shade twined,
I saw two azure halcyons clinging downward
And thinning one bright bunch of amber berries,
With quick long beaks, and in the deep there lay
Those lovely forms imaged as in a sky ;
So with my thoughts full of these happy changes,
We meet again, the happiest change of all.

ASIA

And never will we part, till thy chaste sister
Who guides the frozen and inconstant moon
Will look on thy more warm and equal light
Till her heart thaw like flakes of April snow
And love thee.

SPIRIT OF THE EARTH
    What ; as Asia loves Prometheus ?

ASIA

Peace, wanton, thou art yet not old enough.
Think ye by gazing on each other's eyes
To multiply your lovely selves, and fill
With spherèd fires the interlunar air ?

SPIRIT OF THE EARTH
Nay, mother, while my sister trims her lamp
'Tis hard I should go darkling.

ASIA
                    Listen ; look !

The SPIRIT OF THE HOUR *enters*

PROMETHEUS

We feel what thou hast heard and seen : yet speak.

SPIRIT OF THE HOUR

Soon as the sound had ceased whose thunder filled
The abysses of the sky and the wide earth,
There was a change : the impalpable thin air
And the all-circling sunlight were transformed,
As if the sense of love dissolved in them
Had folded itself round the spherèd world.
My vision then grew clear, and I could see
Into the mysteries of the universe :
Dizzy as with delight I floated down,
Winnowing the lightsome air with languid plumes,
My coursers sought their birth-place in the sun,
Where they henceforth will live exempt from toil
Pasturing flowers of vegetable fire.
And where my moonlike car will stand within
A temple, gazed upon by Phidian forms
Of thee, and Asia, and the Earth, and me,
And you fair nymphs looking the love we feel ;
In memory of the tidings it has borne ;
Beneath a dome fretted with graven flowers,
Poised on twelve columns of resplendent stone,
And open to the bright and liquid sky.
Yoked to it by an amphisbenic snake
The likeness of those wingèd steeds will mock
The flight from which they find repose.   Alas,
Whither has wandered now my partial tongue
When all remains untold which ye would hear ?
As I have said I floated to the earth :
It was, as it is still, the pain of bliss
To move, to breathe, to be ; I wandering went
Among the haunts and dwellings of mankind,
And first was disappointed not to see
Such mighty change as I had felt within
Expressed in outward things ; but soon I looked,
And behold, thrones were kingless, and men walked

One with the other even as spirits do,
None fawned, none trampled ; hate, disdain, or fear,
Self-love or self-contempt, on human brows,
No more inscribed, as o'er the gate of hell,
" All hope abandon ye who enter here ; "
None frowned, none trembled, none with eager fear
Gazed on another's eye of cold command,
Until the subject of the tyrant's will
Became, worse fate, the abject of his own,
Which spurred him, like an outspent horse, to death.
None wrought his lips in truth-entangling lines
Which smiled the lie his tongue disdained to speak ;
None, with firm sneer, trod out in his own heart
The sparks of love and hope till there remained
Those bitter ashes, a soul self-consumed,
And the wretch crept a vampire among men,
Infecting all with his own hideous ill ;
None talked that common, false, cold, hollow talk
Which makes the heart deny the *yes* it breathes,
Yet question that unmeant hypocrisy
With such a self-mistrust as has no name.
And women, too, frank, beautiful, and kind
As the free heaven which rains fresh light and dew
On the wide earth, passed ; gentle radiant forms,
From custom's evil taint exempt and pure ;
Speaking the wisdom once they could not think,
Looking emotions once they feared to feel,
And changed to all which once they dared not be,
Yet being now, made earth like heaven ; nor pride,
Nor jealousy, nor envy, nor ill shame,
The bitterest of those drops of treasured gall,
Spoilt the sweet taste of the nepenthe, love.

Thrones, altars, judgment-seats, and prisons ; wherein,
And beside which, by wretched men were borne
Sceptres, tiaras, swords, and chains, and tomes
Of reasoned wrong, glozed on by ignorance,
Were like those monstrous and barbaric shapes,

The ghosts of a no more remembered fame,
Which, from their unworn obelisks, look forth
In triumph o'er the palaces and tombs
Of those who were their conquerors : mouldering round
Those imaged to the pride of kings and priests,
A dark yet mighty faith, a power as wide
As is the world it wasted, and are now
But an astonishment ; even so the tools
And emblems of its last captivity,
Amid the dwellings of the peopled earth,
Stand, not o'erthrown, but unregarded now.
And those foul shapes, abhorred by god and man,
Which, under many a name and many a form
Strange, savage, ghastly, dark and execrable,
Were Jupiter, the tyrant of the world ;
And which the nations, panic-stricken, served
With blood, and hearts broken by long hope, and love
Dragged to his altars soiled and garlandless,
And slain among men's unreclaiming tears,
Flattering the thing they feared, which fear was hate,
Frown, mouldering fast, o'er their abandoned shrines :
The painted veil, by those who were, called life,
Which mimicked, as with colours idly spread,
All men believed and hoped, is torn aside ;
The loathsome mask has fallen, the man remains
Sceptreless, free, uncircumscribed, but man
Equal, unclassed, tribeless, and nationless,
Exempt from awe, worship, degree, the king
Over himself ; just, gentle, wise : but man
Passionless ; no, yet free from guilt or pain,
Which were, for his will made or suffered them,
Nor yet exempt, though ruling them like slaves,
From chance, and death, and mutability,
The clogs of that which else might oversoar
The loftiest star of unascended heaven,
Pinnacled dim in the intense inane.

END OF THE THIRD ACT

ACT IV

SCENE. *A Part of the Forest near the Cave of* PROME-
    THEUS. PANTHEA *and* IONE *are sleeping : they
    awaken gradually during the first Song.*

VOICE *of unseen Spirits*
The pale stars are gone !
For the sun, their swift shepherd,
To their folds them compelling,
In the depths of the dawn,
Hastes, in meteor-eclipsing array, and they flee
Beyond his blue dwelling,
As fawns flee the leopard.
But where are ye ?

A Train of dark Forms and Shadows passes by confusedly,
                singing
Here, oh, here :
We bear the bier
Of the Father of many a cancelled year !
Spectres we
Of the dead Hours be,
We bear Time to his tomb in eternity.

Strew, oh, strew
Hair, not yew !
Wet the dusty pall with tears, not dew !
Be the faded flowers
Of Death's bare bowers
Spread on the corpse of the King of Hours !

Haste, oh, haste !
As shades are chased,
Trembling, by day, from heaven's blue waste.
We melt away,

Like dissolving spray,
From the children of a diviner day,
With the lullaby
Of winds that die
On the bosom of their own harmony !

IONE

What dark forms were they ?

PANTHEA

The past Hours weak and grey,
With the spoil which their toil
Raked together
From the conquest but One could foil.

IONE

Have they passed ?

PANTHEA

They have passed ;
They outspeeded the blast,—
While 'tis said, they are fled :

IONE

Whither, oh, whither ?

PANTHEA

To the dark, to the past, to the dead.

VOICE *of unseen Spirits*

Bright clouds float in heaven,
Dew-stars gleam on earth,
Waves assemble on ocean,
They are gathered and driven
By the storm of delight, by the panic of glee !
They shake with emotion,
They dance in their mirth.
But where are ye ?

The pine boughs are singing
Old songs with new gladness,
The billows and fountains
Fresh music are flinging,
Like the notes of a spirit from land and from sea ;
The storms mock the mountains
With the thunder of gladness.
But where are ye ?

IONE

What charioteers are these ?

PANTHEA

Where are their chariots ?

SEMICHORUS OF HOURS

The voice of the Spirits of Air and of Earth
Have drawn back the figured curtain of sleep
Which covered our being and darkened our birth
In the deep.

A VOICE

In the deep ?

SEMICHORUS II

Oh, below the deep.

SEMICHORUS I

An hundred ages we had been kept
Cradled in visions of hate and care,
And each one who waked as his brother slept,
Found the truth—

SEMICHORUS II

Worse than his visions were !

SEMICHORUS I

We have heard the lute of Hope in sleep ;
We have known the voice of Love in dreams,
We have felt the wand of Power, and leap—

SEMICHORUS II

As the billows leap in the morning beams !

CHORUS

Weave the dance on the floor of the breeze,
　　Pierce with song heaven's silent light,
Enchant the day that too swiftly flees,
　　To check its flight ere the cave of night.

Once the hungry Hours were hounds
　　Which chased the day like a bleeding deer,
And it limped and stumbled with many wounds
　　Through the nightly dells of the desert year.

But now, oh weave the mystic measure
　　Of music, and dance, and shapes of light,
Let the Hours, and the spirits of might and pleasure,
　　Like the clouds and sunbeams, unite.

A VOICE

　　　　　　　　　　　　　　Unite !

PANTHEA

See, where the Spirits of the human mind
Wrapped in sweet sounds, as in bright veils, approach.

CHORUS OF SPIRITS

We join the throng
Of the dance and the song,
By the whirlwind of gladness borne along ;
As the flying-fish leap
From the Indian deep,
And mix with the sea-birds, half asleep.

CHORUS OF HOURS

Whence come ye, so wild and so fleet,
For sandals of lightning are on your feet,
And your wings are soft and swift as thought,
And your eyes are as love which is veilèd not ?

CHORUS OF SPIRITS

We come from the mind
Of human kind
Which was late so dusk, and obscene, and blind ;
Now 'tis an ocean
Of clear emotion,
A heaven of serene and mighty motion.

From that deep abyss
Of wonder and bliss,
Whose caverns are crystal palaces ;
From those skiey towers
Where Thought's crowned powers
Sit watching your dance, ye happy Hours !

From the dim recesses
Of woven caresses,
Where lovers catch ye by your loose tresses ;
From the azure isles,
Where sweet Wisdom smiles,
Delaying your ships with her syren wiles.

From the temples high
Of Man's ear and eye,
Roofed over Sculpture and Poesy ;
From the murmurings
Of the unsealed springs
Where Science bedews his Dædal wings.

Years after years,
Through blood, and tears,
And a thick hell of hatreds, and hopes, and fears,
We waded and flew,
And the islets were few
Where the bud-blighted flowers of happiness grew.

Our feet now, every palm,
Are sandalled with calm,
And the dew of our wings is a rain of balm ;

> And, beyond our eyes,
> The human love lies
Which makes all it gazes on Paradise.

CHORUS OF SPIRITS AND HOURS

Then weave the web of the mystic measure ;
From the depths of the sky and the ends of the earth,
  Come, swift Spirits of might and of pleasure.
Fill the dance and the music of mirth,
  As the waves of a thousand streams rush by
To an ocean of splendour and harmony !

CHORUS OF SPIRITS

> Our spoil is won,
> Our task is done,
We are free to dive, or soar, or run ;
> Beyond and around,
> Or within the bound
Which clips the world with darkness round.

> We'll pass the eyes
> Of the starry skies
Into the hoar deep to colonize :
> Death, Chaos, and Night,
> From the sound of our flight,
Shall flee, like mist from a tempest's might.

> And Earth, Air, and Light,
> And the Spirit of Might,
Which drives round the stars in their fiery flight ;
> And Love, Thought, and Breath,
> The Powers that quell Death,
Wherever we soar shall assemble beneath.

> And our singing shall build
> In the void's loose field
A world for the Spirit of Wisdom to wield ;
> We will take our plan
> From the new world of man,
And our work shall be called the Promethean.

Chorus of Hours

Break the dance, and scatter the song ;
  Let some depart, and some remain.

Semichorus I

We, beyond heaven, are driven along :

Semichorus II

Us the enchantments of earth retain :

Semichorus I

Ceaseless, and rapid, and fierce, and free,
With the Spirits which build a new earth and sea,
And a heaven where yet heaven could never be.

Semichorus II

Solemn, and slow, and serene, and bright,
Leading the Day and outspeeding the Night,
With the powers of a world of perfect light.

Semichorus I

We whirl, singing loud, round the gathering sphere,
Till the trees, and the beasts, and the clouds appear
From its chaos made calm by love, not fear.

Semichorus II

We encircle the ocean and mountains of earth,
And the happy forms of its death and birth
Change to the music of our sweet mirth.

Chorus of Hours and Spirits

Break the dance, and scatter the song,
  Let some depart, and some remain,
Wherever we fly we lead along
In leashes, like starbeams, soft yet strong,
  The clouds that are heavy with love's sweet rain.

PANTHEA

Ha ! they are gone !

IONE

Yet feel you no delight
From the past sweetness ?

PANTHEA

As the bare green hill
When some soft cloud vanishes into rain,
Laughs with a thousand drops of sunny water
To the unpavilioned sky !

IONE

Even whilst we speak
New notes arise.   What is that awful sound ?

PANTHEA

'Tis the deep music of the rolling world
Kindling within the strings of the waved air,
Æolian modulations.

IONE

Listen too,
How every pause is filled with under-notes,
Clear, silver, icy, keen awakening tones,
Which pierce the sense, and live within the soul,
As the sharp stars pierce winter's crystal air
And gaze upon themselves within the sea.

PANTHEA

But see where through two openings in the forest
Which hanging branches overcanopy,
And where two runnels of a rivulet,
Between the close moss violet-inwoven,
Have made their path of melody, like sisters
Who part with sighs that they may meet in smiles,
Turning their dear disunion to an isle

Of lovely grief, a wood of sweet sad thoughts ;
Two visions of strange radiance float upon
The ocean-like enchantment of strong sound,
Which flows intenser, keener, deeper yet
Under the ground and through the windless air.

Ione

I see a chariot like that thinnest boat,
In which the mother of the months is borne
By ebbing night into her western cave,
When she upsprings from interlunar dreams,
O'er which is curved an orblike canopy
Of gentle darkness, and the hills and woods
Distinctly seen through that dusk airy veil,
Regard like shapes in an enchanter's glass ;
Its wheels are solid clouds, azure and gold,
Such as the genii of the thunder-storm
Pile on the floor of the illumined sea
When the sun rushes under it ; they roll
And move and grow as with an inward wind ;
Within it sits a wingèd infant, white
Its countenance, like the whiteness of bright snow,
Its plumes are as feathers of sunny frost,
Its limbs gleam white, through the wind-flowing folds
Of its white robe, woof of ætherial pearl.
Its hair is white, the brightness of white light
Scattered in strings ; yet its two eyes are heavens
Of liquid darkness, which the Deity
Within seems pouring, as a storm is poured
From jaggèd clouds, out of their arrowy lashes,
Tempering the cold and radiant air around,
With fire that is not brightness ; in its hand
It sways a quivering moonbeam, from whose point
A guiding power directs the chariot's prow
Over its wheelèd clouds, which as they roll
Over the grass, and flowers, and waves, wake sounds,
Sweet as a singing rain of silver dew.

PANTHEA

And from the other opening in the wood
Rushes, with loud and whirlwind harmony,
A sphere, which is as many thousand spheres,
Solid as crystal, yet through all its mass
Flow, as through empty space, music and light :
Ten thousand orbs involving and involved,
Purple and azure, white, and green, and golden,
Sphere within sphere ; and every space between
Peopled with unimaginable shapes,
Such as ghosts dream dwell in the lampless deep,
Yet each inter-transpicuous, and they whirl
Over each other with a thousand motions,
Upon a thousand sightless axles spinning,
And with the force of self-destroying swiftness,
Intensely, slowly, solemnly roll on,
Kindling with mingled sounds, and many tones,
Intelligible words and music wild.
With mighty whirl the multitudinous orb
Grinds the bright brook into an azure mist
Of elemental subtlety, like light ;
And the wild odour of the forest flowers,
The music of the living grass and air,
The emerald light of leaf-entangled beams
Round its intense yet self-conflicting speed,
Seem kneaded into one aërial mass
Which drowns the sense.   Within the orb itself,
Pillowed upon its alabaster arms,
Like to a child o'erwearied with sweet toil,
On its own folded wings, and wavy hair,
The Spirit of the Earth is laid asleep,
And you can see its little lips are moving,
Amid the changing light of their own smiles,
Like one who talks of what he loves in dream.

IONE

'Tis only mocking the orb's harmony.

PANTHEA

And from a star upon its forehead, shoot,
Like swords of azure fire, or golden spears
With tyrant-quelling myrtle overtwined,
Embleming heaven and earth united now,
Vast beams like spokes of some invisible wheel
Which whirl as the orb whirls, swifter than thought,
Filling the abyss with sun-like lightnings,
And perpendicular now, and now transverse,
Pierce the dark soil, and as they pierce and pass,
Make bare the secrets of the earth's deep heart ;
Infinite mine of adamant and gold,
Valueless stones, and unimagined gems,
And caverns on crystàlline columns poised
With vegetable silver overspread ;
Wells of unfathomed fire, and water springs
Whence the great sea, even as a child is fed,
Whose vapours clothe earth's monarch mountain-tops
With kingly, ermine snow.   The beams flash on
And make appear the melancholy ruins
Of cancelled cycles ; anchors, beaks of ships ;
Planks turned to marble ; quivers, helms, and spears,
And gorgon-headed targes, and the wheels
Of scythèd chariots, and the emblazonry
Of trophies, standards, and armorial beasts,
Round which death laughed, sepulchred emblems
Of dead destruction, ruin within ruin !
The wrecks beside of many a city vast,
Whose population which the earth grew over
Was mortal, but not human ; see, they lie,
Their monstrous works, and uncouth skeletons,
Their statues, homes and fanes ; prodigious shapes
Huddled in grey annihilation, split,
Jammed in the hard, black deep ; and over these,
The anatomies of unknown wingèd things,
And fishes which were isles of living scale,
And serpents, bony chains, twisted around

The iron crags, or within heaps of dust
To which the tortuous strength of their last pangs
Had crushed the iron crags ; and over these
The jaggèd alligator, and the might
Of earth-convulsing behemoth, which once
Were monarch beasts, and on the slimy shores,
And weed-overgrown continents of earth,
Increased and multiplied like summer worms
On an abandoned corpse, till the blue globe
Wrapped deluge round it like a cloke, and they
Yelled, gasped, and were abolished ; or some God
Whose throne was in a comet, passed, and cried
Be not ! And like my words they were no more.

THE EARTH

The joy, the triumph, the delight, the madness !
The boundless, overflowing, bursting gladness
The vapourous exultation not to be confined !
Ha ! ha ! the animation of delight
Which wraps me, like an atmosphere of light,
And bears me as a cloud is borne by its own wind.

THE MOON

Brother mine, calm wanderer,
Happy globe of land and air,
Some Spirit is darted like a beam from thee,
Which penetrates my frozen frame,
And passes with the warmth of flame,
With love, and odour, and deep melody
Through me, through me !

THE EARTH

Ha ! ha ! the caverns of my hollow mountains,
My cloven fire-crags, sound-exulting fountains
Laugh with a vast and inextinguishable laughter.
The oceans, and the deserts, and the abysses,
And the deep air's unmeasured wildernesses,
Answer from all their clouds and billows, echoing after.

They cry aloud as I do.　Sceptred curse,
　　Who all our green and azure universe
Threatenedst to muffle round with black destruction,
　　　　sending
　　A solid cloud to rain hot thunder-stones,
　　And splinter and knead down my children's bones,
All I bring forth, to one void mass battering and blending:

　　Until each crag-like tower, and storied column,
　　Palace, and obelisk, and temple solemn,
My imperial mountains crowned with cloud, and snow,
　　　　and fire ;
　　My sea-like forests, every blade and blossom
　　Which finds a grave or cradle in my bosom,
Were stamped by thy strong hate into a lifeless mire.

　　How art thou sunk, withdrawn, covered, drunk up
　　By thirsty nothing, as the brackish cup
Drained by a desert-troop, a little drop for all ;
　　And from beneath, around, within, above,
　　Filling thy void annihilation, love
Burst in like light on caves cloven by the thunder-ball.

The Moon

　　The snow upon my lifeless mountains
　　Is loosened into living fountains,
My solid oceans flow, and sing, and shine :
　　A spirit from my heart bursts forth,
　　It clothes with unexpected birth
My cold bare bosom : Oh ! it must be thine
　　　　On mine, on mine !

　　Gazing on thee I feel, I know
　　Green stalks burst forth, and bright flowers grow,
And living shapes upon my bosom move :
　　Music is in the sea and air,
　　Wingèd clouds soar here and there,
Dark with the rain new buds are dreaming of :
　　　　'Tis love, all love !

The Earth

It interpenetrates my granite mass,
    Through tangled roots and trodden clay doth pass,
Into the utmost leaves and delicatest flowers ;
    Upon the winds, among the clouds 'tis spread,
    It wakes a life in the forgotten dead,
They breathe a spirit up from their obscurest bowers.

    And like a storm bursting its cloudy prison
    With thunder, and with whirlwind, has arisen
Out of the lampless caves of unimagined being :
    With earthquake shock and swiftness making shiver
    Thought's stagnant chaos, unremoved for ever,
Till hate, and fear, and pain, light-vanquished shadows,
      fleeing,

    Leave Man, who was a many-sided mirror,
    Which could distort to many a shape of error,
This true fair world of things, a sea reflecting love ;
    Which over all his kind as the sun's heaven
    Gliding o'er ocean, smooth, serene, and even
Darting from starry depths radiance and life, doth move.

    Leave Man, even as a leprous child is left,
    Who follows a sick beast to some warm cleft
Of rocks, through which the might of healing springs is
      poured ;
    Then when it wanders home with rosy smile,
    Unconscious, and its mother fears awhile
It is a spirit, then, weeps on her child restored.

    Man, oh, not men ! a chain of linkèd thought,
    Of love and might to be divided not,
Compelling the elements with adamantine stress ;
    As the sun rules, even with a tyrant's gaze,
    The unquiet republic of the maze
Of planets, struggling fierce towards heaven's free
      wilderness.

Man, one harmonious soul of many a soul,
Whose nature is its own divine control,
Where all things flow to all, as rivers to the sea ;
Familiar acts are beautiful through love ;
Labour, and pain, and grief, in life's green grove
Sport like tame beasts,—none knew how gentle they
could be !

His will, with all mean passions, bad delights,
And selfish cares, its trembling satellites,
A spirit ill to guide, but mighty to obey,
Is as a tempest-wingèd ship, whose helm
Love rules, through waves which dare not overwhelm,
Forcing life's wildest shores to own its sovereign sway.

All things confess his strength. Through the cold mass
Of marble and of colour his dreams pass ;
Bright threads whence mothers weave the robes their
children wear ;
Language is a perpetual Orphic song,
Which rules with Dædal harmony a throng
Of thoughts and forms, which else senseless and shape-
less were.

The lightning is his slave ; heaven's utmost deep
Gives up her stars, and like a flock of sheep
They pass before his eye, are numbered, and roll on !
The tempest is his steed, he strides the air ;
And the abyss shouts from her depth laid bare,
Heaven, hast thou secrets ? Man unveils me ; I have
none.

THE MOON

The shadow of white death has passed
From my path in heaven at last,
A clinging shroud of solid frost and sleep ;
And through my newly-woven bowers,
Wander happy paramours,
Less mighty, but as mild as those who keep
Thy vales more deep.

THE EARTH

As the dissolving warmth of dawn may fold
A half unfrozen dew-globe, green, and gold,
And crystalline, till it becomes a wingèd mist,
And wanders up the vault of the blue day,
Outlives the noon, and on the sun's last ray
Hangs o'er the sea, a fleece of fire and amethyst.

THE MOON

Thou art folded, thou art lying
In the light which is undying
Of thine own joy, and heaven's smile divine ;
All suns and constellations shower
On thee a light, a life, a power
Which doth array thy sphere ; thou pourest thine
On mine, on mine !

THE EARTH

I spin beneath my pyramid of night,
Which points into the heavens dreaming delight,
Murmuring victorious joy in my enchanted sleep ;
As a youth lulled in love-dreams faintly sighing,
Under the shadow of his beauty lying,
Which round his rest a watch of light and warmth doth
keep.

THE MOON

As in the soft and sweet eclipse,
When soul meets soul on lovers' lips,
High hearts are calm, and brightest eyes are dull ;
So when thy shadow falls on me,
Then am I mute and still, by thee
Covered ; of thy love, Orb most beautiful,
Full, oh, too full !

Thou art speeding round the sun
Brightest world of many a one ;

Green and azure sphere which shinest
With a light which is divinest
Among all the lamps of Heaven
To whom life and light is given ;
I, thy crystal paramour
Borne beside thee by a power
Like the polar Paradise,
Magnet-like of lovers' eyes ;
I, a most enamoured maiden
Whose weak brain is overladen
With the pleasure of her love,
Maniac-like around thee move
Gazing, an insatiate bride,
On thy form from every side
Like a Mænad, round the cup
Which Agave lifted up
In the weird Cadmæan forest.
Brother, wheresoe'er thou soarest
I must hurry, whirl and follow
Through the heavens wide and hollow,
Sheltered by the warm embrace
Of thy soul from hungry space,
Drinking from thy sense and sight
Beauty, majesty, and might,
As a lover or a camelion
Grows like what it looks upon,
As a violet's gentle eye
Gazes on the azure sky
Until its hue grows like what it beholds,
As a grey and watery mist
Glows like solid amethyst
Athwart the western mountain it enfolds,
When the sunset sleeps
Upon its snow.

THE EARTH

And the weak day weeps
That it should be so.

Oh, gentle Moon, the voice of thy delight
Falls on me like thy clear and tender light
Soothing the seaman, borne the summer night,
　　Through isles for ever calm ;
Oh, gentle Moon, thy crystal accents pierce
The caverns of my pride's deep universe,
Charming the tiger joy, whose tramplings fierce
　　Made wounds which need thy balm.

PANTHEA

I rise as from a bath of sparkling water,
A bath of azure light, among dark rocks,
Out of the stream of sound.

IONE

　　　　　　Ah me ! sweet sister,
The stream of sound has ebbed away from us,
And you pretend to rise out of its wave,
Because your words fall like the clear, soft dew
Shaken from a bathing wood-nymph's limbs and hair.

PANTHEA

Peace ! peace ! A mighty Power, which is as darkness,
Is rising out of Earth, and from the sky
Is showered like night, and from within the air
Bursts, like eclipse which had been gathered up
Into the pores of sunlight : the bright visions,
Wherein the singing spirits rode and shone,
Gleam like pale meteors through a watery night.

IONE

There is a sense of words upon mine ear.

PANTHEA

An universal sound like words : Oh, list !

DEMOGORGON

Thou, Earth, calm empire of a happy soul,
　　Sphere of divinest shapes and harmonies,

Beautiful orb ! gathering as thou dost roll
    The love which paves thy path along the skies :

THE EARTH

I hear : I am as a drop of dew that dies.

DEMOGORGON

Thou, Moon, which gazest on the nightly Earth
    With wonder, as it gazes upon thee ;
Whilst each to men, and beasts, and the swift birth
    Of birds, is beauty, love, calm, harmony :

THE MOON

I hear : I am a leaf shaken by thee !

DEMOGORGON

Ye kings of suns and stars, Dæmons and Gods,
    Ætherial Dominations, who possess
Elysian, windless, fortunate abodes
    Beyond Heaven's constellated wilderness :

A VOICE *from above*

Our great Republic hears, we are bless'd, and bless.

DEMOGORGON

Ye happy dead, whom beams of brightest verse
    Are clouds to hide, not colours to portray,
Whether your nature is that universe
    Which once ye saw and suffered—

A VOICE *from beneath*

                    Or as they
Whom we have left, we change and pass away.

DEMOGORGON

Ye elemental Genii, who have homes
    From man's high mind even to the central stone
Of sullen lead ; from Heaven's star-fretted domes
    To the dull weed some sea-worm battens on :

A CONFUSED VOICE

We hear : thy words waken Oblivion.

DEMOGORGON

Spirits, whose homes are flesh : ye beasts and birds,
  Ye worms, and fish ; ye living leaves and buds ;
Lightning and wind ; and ye untameable herds,
  Meteors and mists, which throng air's solitudes :

A VOICE

Thy voice to us is wind among still woods.

DEMOGORGON

Man, who wert once a despot and a slave ;
  A dupe and a deceiver ; a decay ;
A traveller from the cradle to the grave
  Through the dim night of this immortal day :

ALL

Speak : thy strong words may never pass away.

DEMOGORGON

This is the day, which down the void abysm
At the Earth-born's spell yawns for Heaven's despotism,
  And Conquest is dragged captive through the deep :
Love, from its awful throne of patient power
In the wise heart, from the last giddy hour
  Of dead endurance, from the slippery, steep,
And narrow verge of crag-like agony, springs
And folds over the world its healing wings.

Gentleness, Virtue, Wisdom, and Endurance,
These are the seals of that most firm assurance
  Which bars the pit over Destruction's strength ;
And if, with infirm hand, Eternity,
Mother of many acts and hours, should free

The serpent that would clasp her with his length ;
These are the spells by which to re-assume
An empire o'er the disentangled doom.

To suffer woes which Hope thinks infinite ;
To forgive wrongs darker than death or night ;
 To defy Power, which seems omnipotent ;
To love, and bear ; to hope till Hope creates
From its own wreck the thing it contemplates ;
 Neither to change, nor falter, nor repent ;
This, like thy glory, Titan, is to be
Good, great and joyous, beautiful and free ;
This is alone Life, Joy, Empire, and Victory.

ADONAIS

AN ELEGY ON THE DEATH OF JOHN KEATS

PREFACE

Φάρμακον ἦλθε, Βίων, ποτὶ σὸν στόμα, φάρμακον εἶδες·
Πῶς τευ τοῖς χείλεσσι ποτέδραμε, κοὺκ ἐγλυκάνθη ;
Τίς δὲ βροτὸς τοσσοῦτον ἀνάμερος ἢ κεράσαι τοι,
Ἢ δοῦναι λαλέοντι τὸ φάρμακον ; ἔκφυγεν ῷδάν.

MOSCHUS, *Epitaph. Bion.*

IT is my intention to subjoin to the London edition of
this poem a criticism upon the claims of its lamented
object to be classed among the writers of the highest
genius who have adorned our age. My known repug-
nance to the narrow principles of taste on which several
of his earlier compositions were modelled proves at
least that I am an impartial judge. I consider the
fragment of *Hyperion* as second to nothing that was
ever produced by a writer of the same years.

John Keats died at Rome of a consumption, in his
twenty-fourth year, on the —— of —— 1821 ; and was
buried in the romantic and lonely cemetery of the Pro-
testants in that city, under the pyramid which is the
tomb of Cestius, and the massy walls and towers, now
mouldering and desolate, which formed the circuit of
ancient Rome. The cemetery is an open space among
the ruins covered in winter with violets and daisies.
It might make one in love with death, to think that
one should be buried in so sweet a place.

The genius of the lamented person to whose memory
I have dedicated these unworthy verses was not less
delicate and fragile than it was beautiful ; and, where
cankerworms abound, what wonder if its young flower
was blighted in the bud ? The savage criticism on his
Endymion, which appeared in *The Quarterly Review,*
produced the most violent effect on his susceptible

mind; the agitation thus originated ended in the rupture of a blood-vessel in the lungs; a rapid consumption ensued, and the succeeding acknowledgments from more candid critics, of the true greatness of his powers, were ineffectual to heal the wound thus wantonly inflicted.

It may be well said that these wretched men know not what they do. They scatter their insults and their slanders without heed as to whether the poisoned shaft lights on a heart made callous by many blows, or one like Keats's, composed of more penetrable stuff. One of their associates is, to my knowledge, a most base and unprincipled calumniator. As to *Endymion*,—was it a poem, whatever might be its defects, to be treated contemptuously by those who had celebrated, with various degrees of complacency and panegyric, *Paris*, and *Woman*, and *A Syrian Tale*, and Mrs. Lefanu, and Mr. Barrett, and Mr. Howard Payne, and a long list of the illustrious obscure? Are these the men who, in their venal good nature, presumed to draw a parallel between the Rev. Mr. Milman and Lord Byron? What gnat did they strain at here, after having swallowed all those camels? Against what woman taken in adultery dares the foremost of these literary prostitutes to cast his opprobrious stone? Miserable man! you, one of the meanest, have wantonly defaced one of the noblest specimens of the workmanship of God. Nor shall it be your excuse that, murderer as you are, you have spoken daggers, but used none.

The circumstances of the closing scene of poor Keats's life were not made known to me until the Elegy was ready for the press. I am given to understand that the wound which his sensitive spirit had received from the criticism of *Endymion* was exasperated by the bitter sense of unrequited benefits; the poor fellow seems to have been hooted from the stage of life, no less by those on whom he had wasted the promise of his genius, than those on whom he had lavished his fortune and his care. He was accompanied to Rome, and attended in his last illness, by Mr. Severn, a young artist of the highest promise, who, I have been informed, " almost risked his own life, and sacrificed every prospect to unwearied attendance upon his dying friend." Had I known these circumstances before the completion of my poem, I should have been tempted to add my feeble tribute of applause to the more solid recompense which the virtuous man finds in the recollection of his own motives. Mr. Severn can dispense with a reward from " such stuff as dreams are made of." His conduct is a golden augury of the success of his future career—may the unextinguished Spirit of his illustrious friend animate the creations of his pencil, and plead against Oblivion for his name !

ADONAIS

Ἀστὴρ πρὶν μὲν ἔλαμπες ἐνὶ ζώοισιν ἑῷος.
Νῦν δὲ θανὼν λάμπεις ἔσπερος ἐν φθιμένοις.

PLATO.

I

I WEEP for Adonais—he is dead!
O, weep for Adonais! though our tears
Thaw not the frost which binds so dear a head!
And thou, sad Hour, selected from all years
To mourn our loss, rouse thy obscure compeers,
And teach them thine own sorrow, say: with me
Died Adonais; till the Future dares
Forget the Past, his fate and fame shall be
An echo and a light unto eternity.

II

Where wert thou, mighty Mother, when he lay,
When thy Son lay, pierced by the shaft which flies
In darkness? where was lorn Urania
When Adonais died?   With veilèd eyes,
'Mid listening Echoes, in her Paradise
She sate, while one, with soft enamoured breath,
Rekindled all the fading melodies,
With which, like flowers that mock the corse beneath,
He had adorned and hid the coming bulk of death. ·

III

O, weep for Adonais—he is dead!
Wake, melancholy Mother, wake and weep!
Yet wherefore?   Quench within their burning bed

Thy fiery tears, and let thy loud heart keep,
Like his, a mute and uncomplaining sleep ;
For he is gone, where all things wise and fair
Descend ;—oh, dream not that the amorous Deep
Will yet restore him to the vital air ;
Death feeds on his mute voice, and laughs at our despair.

IV

Most musical of mourners, weep again !
Lament anew, Urania !—He died,
Who was the Sire of an immortal strain,
Blind, old, and lonely, when his country's pride,
The priest, the slave, and the liberticide,
Trampled and mocked with many a loathèd rite
Of lust and blood ; he went, unterrified,
Into the gulph of death ; but his clear Sprite
Yet reigns o'er earth ; the third among the sons of light.

V

Most musical of mourners, weep anew !
Not all to that bright station dared to climb ;
And happier they their happiness who knew,
Whose tapers yet burn through that night of time
In which suns perished ; others more sublime,
Struck by the envious wrath of man or God,
Have sunk, extinct in their refulgent prime ;
And some yet live, treading the thorny road,
Which leads, through toil and hate, to Fame's serene
        abode.

VI

But now, thy youngest, dearest one has perished,
The nursling of thy widowhood, who grew,
Like a pale flower by some sad maiden cherished,
And fed with true love tears, instead of dew ;
Most musical of mourners, weep anew !
Thy extreme hope, the loveliest and the last,
The bloom, whose petals, nipped before they blew,
Died on the promise of the fruit, is waste ;
The broken lily lies—the storm is overpast.

VII

To that high Capital, where kingly Death
Keeps his pale court in beauty and decay,
He came ; and bought, with price of purest breath,
A grave among the eternal.—Come away !
Haste, while the vault of blue Italian day
Is yet his fitting charnel-roof ! while still
He lies, as if in dewy sleep he lay ;
Awake him not ! surely he takes his fill
Of deep and liquid rest, forgetful of all ill.

VIII

He will awake no more, oh, never more !—
Within the twilight chamber spreads apace,
The shadow of white Death, and at the door
Invisible Corruption waits to trace
His extreme way to her dim dwelling-place ;
The eternal Hunger sits, but pity and awe
Soothe her pale rage, nor dares she to deface
So fair a prey, till darkness, and the law
Of change, shall o'er his sleep the mortal curtain draw.

IX

O, weep for Adonais !—The quick Dreams,
The passion-wingèd Ministers of thought,
Who were his flocks, whom near the living streams
Of his young spirit he fed, and whom he taught
The love which was its music, wander not,—
Wander no more, from kindling brain to brain,
But droop there, whence they sprung ; and mourn
      their lot
Round the cold heart, where, after their sweet pain,
They ne'er will gather strength, or find a home again.

X

And one with trembling hands clasps his cold head,
And fans him with her moonlight wings, and cries ;

" Our love, our hope, our sorrow, is not dead ;
See, on the silken fringe of his faint eyes,
Like dew upon a sleeping flower, there lies
A tear some Dream has loosened from his brain."
Lost Angel of a ruined Paradise !
She knew not 'twas her own ; as with no stain
She faded, like a cloud which had outwept its rain.

XI

One from a lucid urn of starry dew
Washed his light limbs as if embalming them ;
Another clipped her profuse locks, and threw
The wreath upon him, like an anadem,
Which frozen tears instead of pearls begem ;
Another in her wilful grief would break
Her bow and wingèd reeds, as if to stem
A greater loss with one which was more weak ;
And dull the barbèd fire against his frozen cheek.

XII

Another Splendour on his mouth alit,
That mouth, whence it was wont to draw the breath
Which gave it strength to pierce the guarded wit,
And pass into the panting heart beneath
With lightning and with music : the damp death
Quenched its caress upon his icy lips ;
And, as a dying meteor stains a wreath
Of moonlight vapour, which the cold night clips,
It flushed through his pale limbs, and passed to its
    eclipse.

XIII

And others came . . . Desires and Adorations,
Wingèd Persuasions and veiled Destinies,
Splendours, and Glooms, and glimmering Incarnations
Of hopes and fears, and twilight Phantasies ;
And Sorrow, with her family of Sighs,
And Pleasure, blind with tears, led by the gleam
Of her own dying smile instead of eyes,

Came in slow pomp ;—the moving pomp might seem
Like pageantry of mist on an autumnal stream.

XIV

All he had loved, and moulded into thought,
From shape, and hue, and odour, and sweet sound,
Lamented Adonais.   Morning sought
Her eastern watch-tower, and her hair unbound,
Wet with the tears which should adorn the ground,
Dimmed the aërial eyes that kindle day ;
Afar the melancholy thunder moaned,
Pale Ocean in unquiet slumber lay,
And the wild winds flew round, sobbing in their dismay.

XV

Lost Echo sits amid the voiceless mountains,
And feeds her grief with his remembered lay,
And will no more reply to winds or fountains,
Or amorous birds perched on the young green spray,
Or herdsman's horn, or bell at closing day ;
Since she can mimic not his lips, more dear
Than those for whose disdain she pined away
Into a shadow of all sounds :—a drear
Murmur, between their songs, is all the woodmen hear.

XVI

Grief made the young Spring wild, and she threw down
Her kindling buds, as if she Autumn were,
Or they dead leaves ; since her delight is flown
For whom should she have waked the sullen year ?
To Phœbus was not Hyacinth so dear
Nor to himself Narcissus, as to both
Thou, Adonais : wan they stand and sere
Amid the faint companions of their youth,
With dew all turned to tears ; odour, to sighing ruth.

XVII

Thy spirit's sister, the lorn nightingale,
Mourns not her mate with such melodious pain ;

Not so the eagle, who like thee could scale
Heaven, and could nourish in the sun's domain
Her mighty youth with morning, doth complain,
Soaring and screaming round her empty nest,
As Albion wails for thee : the curse of Cain
Light on his head who pierced thy innocent breast,
And scared the angel soul that was its earthly guest !

XVIII

Ah woe is me ! Winter is come and gone,
But grief returns with the revolving year ;
The airs and streams renew their joyous tone ;
The ants, the bees, the swallows reappear ;
Fresh leaves and flowers deck the dead Seasons' bier ;
The amorous birds now pair in every brake,
And build their mossy homes in field and brere ;
And the green lizard, and the golden snake,
Like unimprisoned flames, out of their trance awake.

XIX

Through wood and stream and field and hill and Ocean
A quickening life from the Earth's heart has burst
As it has ever done, with change and motion
From the great morning of the world when first
God dawned on Chaos ; in its stream immersed
The lamps of Heaven flash with a softer light ;
All baser things pant with life's sacred thirst ;
Diffuse themselves ; and spend in love's delight
The beauty and the joy of their renewèd might.

XX

The leprous corpse touched by this spirit tender
Exhales itself in flowers of gentle breath ;
Like incarnations of the stars, when splendour
Is changed to fragrance, they illumine death
And mock the merry worm that wakes beneath ;
Naught we know, dies. Shall that alone which knows
Be as a sword consumed before the sheath

By sightless lightning ?—th' intense atom glows
A moment, then is quenched in a most cold repose.

XXI

Alas ! that all we loved of him should be,
But for our grief, as if it had not been,
And grief itself be mortal ! Woe is me !
Whence are we, and why are we ? of what scene
The actors or spectators ? Great and mean
Meet massed in death, who lends what life must
　　　borrow.
As long as skies are blue, and fields are green,
Evening must usher night, night urge the morrow,
Month follow month with woe, and year wake year to
　　　sorrow.

XXII

He will awake no more, oh, never more !
" Wake thou," cried Misery, " childless Mother,
　　　rise
Out of thy sleep, and slake, in thy heart's core,
A wound more fierce than his with tears and sighs."
And all the Dreams that watched Urania's eyes,
And all the Echoes whom their sister's song
Had held in holy silence, cried : " Arise ! "
Swift as a Thought by the snake Memory stung,
From her ambrosial rest the fading Splendour sprung.

XXIII

She rose like an autumnal Night, that springs
Out of the East, and follows wild and drear
The golden Day, which, on eternal wings,
Even as a ghost abandoning a bier,
Had left the Earth a corpse. Sorrow and fear
So struck, so roused, so rapt Urania ;
So saddened round her like an atmosphere
Of stormy mist ; so swept her on her way
Even to the mournful place where Adonais lay.

XXIV

Out of her secret Paradise she sped,
Through camps and cities rough with stone, and steel,
And human hearts, which to her aëry tread
Yielding not, wounded the invisible
Palms of her tender feet where'er they fell :
And barbèd tongues, and thoughts more sharp than
        they,
Rent the soft Form they never could repel,
Whose sacred blood, like the young tears of May,
Paved with eternal flowers that undeserving way.

XXV

In the death chamber for a moment Death,
Shamed by the presence of that living Might,
Blushed to annihilation, and the breath
Revisited those lips, and life's pale light
Flashed through those limbs, so late her dear delight.
" Leave me not wild and drear and comfortless,
As silent lightning leaves the starless night !
Leave me not ! " cried Urania : her distress
Roused Death : Death rose and smiled, and met her
        vain caress.

XXVI

" Stay yet awhile ! speak to me once again ;
Kiss me, so long but as a kiss may live ;
And in my heartless breast and burning brain
That word, that kiss shall all thoughts else survive,
With food of saddest memory kept alive,
Now thou art dead, as if it were a part
Of thee, my Adonais ! I would give
All that I am to be as thou now art !
But I am chained to Time, and cannot thence depart !

XXVII

" Oh gentle child, beautiful as thou wert,
Why didst thou leave the trodden paths of men

Too soon, and with weak hands though mighty heart
Dare the unpastured dragon in his den ?
Defenceless as thou wert, oh where was then
Wisdom the mirrored shield, or scorn the spear ?
Or hadst thou waited the full cycle, when
Thy spirit should have filled its crescent sphere,
The monsters of life's waste had fled from thee like deer.

XXVIII

" The herded wolves, bold only to pursue ;
The obscene ravens, clamorous o'er the dead ;
The vultures to the conqueror's banner true,
Who feed where Desolation first has fed,
And whose wings rain contagion ;—how they fled,
When like Apollo, from his golden bow,
The Pythian of the age one arrow sped
And smiled !—The spoilers tempt no second blow ;
They fawn on the proud feet that spurn them lying low.

XXIX

" The sun comes forth, and many reptiles spawn ;
He sets, and each ephemeral insect then
Is gathered into death without a dawn,
And the immortal stars awake again ;
So is it in the world of living men :
A godlike mind soars forth, in its delight
Making earth bare and veiling heaven, and when
It sinks, the swarms that dimmed or shared its light
Leave to its kindred lamps the spirit's awful night."

XXX

Thus ceased she : and the mountain shepherds came,
Their garlands sere, their magic mantles rent ;
The Pilgrim of Eternity, whose fame
Over his living head like Heaven is bent,
An early but enduring monument,
Came, veiling all the lightnings of his song

In sorrow ; from her wilds Ierne sent
The sweetest lyrist of her saddest wrong,
And love taught grief to fall like music from his tongue.

XXXI

Midst others of less note, came one frail Form,
A phantom among men, companionless
As the last cloud of an expiring storm
Whose thunder is its knell ; he, as I guess,
Had gazed on Nature's naked loveliness,
Actæon-like, and now he fled astray
With feeble steps o'er the world's wilderness,
And his own thoughts, along that rugged way,
Pursued, like raging hounds, their father and their prey.

XXXII

A pardlike Spirit beautiful and swift—
A Love in desolation masked ;—a Power
Girt round with weakness ;—it can scarce uplift
The weight of the superincumbent hour ;
It is a dying lamp, a falling shower,
A breaking billow ;—even whilst we speak
Is it not broken ?   On the withering flower
The killing sun smiles brightly ; on a cheek
The life can burn in blood, even while the heart may
      break.

XXXIII

His head was bound with pansies overblown,
And faded violets, white, and pied, and blue ;
And a light spear topped with a cypress cone,
Round whose rude shaft dark ivy tresses grew
Yet dripping with the forest's noonday dew,
Vibrated, as the ever-beating heart
Shook the weak hand that grasped it ; of that
      crew
He came the last, neglected and apart ;
A herd-abandoned deer struck by the hunter's dart.

XXXIV

All stood aloof, and at his partial moan
Smiled through their tears ; well knew that gentle band
Who in another's fate now wept his own ;
As, in the accents of an unknown land,
He sung new sorrow ; sad Urania scanned
The Stranger's mien, and murmured : "Who art thou?"
He answered not, but with a sudden hand
Made bare his branded and ensanguined brow,
Which was like Cain's or Christ's—Oh ! that it should
    be so !

XXXV

What softer voice is hushed over the dead ?
Athwart what brow is that dark mantle thrown ?
What form leans sadly o'er the white death-bed,
In mockery of monumental stone,
The heavy heart heaving without a moan ?
If it be He, who, gentlest of the wise,
Taught, soothed, loved, honoured the departed one,
Let me not vex with inharmonious sighs
The silence of that heart's accepted sacrifice.

XXXVI

Our Adonais has drunk poison—oh !
What deaf and viperous murderer could crown
Life's early cup with such a draught of woe ?
The nameless worm would now itself disown :
It felt, yet could escape the magic tone
Whose prelude held all envy, hate, and wrong,
But what was howling in one breast alone,
Silent with expectation of the song,
Whose master's hand is cold, whose silver lyre unstrung.

XXXVII

Live thou, whose infamy is not thy fame !
Live ! fear no heavier chastisement from me,
Thou noteless blot on a remembered name !

But be thyself, and know thyself to be !
And ever at thy season be thou free
To spill the venom when thy fangs o'erflow :
Remorse and Self-contempt shall cling to thee ;
Hot Shame shall burn upon thy secret brow,
And like a beaten hound, tremble thou shalt—as now.

XXXVIII

Nor let us weep that our delight is fled
Far from these carrion kites that scream below ;
He wakes or sleeps with the enduring dead ;
Thou canst not soar where he is sitting now.—
Dust to the dust ! but the pure spirit shall flow
Back to the burning fountain whence it came,
A portion of the Eternal, which must glow
Through time and change, unquenchably the same,
Whilst thy cold embers choke the sordid hearth of shame.

XXXIX

Peace, peace ! he is not dead, he doth not sleep—
He hath awakened from the dream of life—
'Tis we who, lost in stormy visions, keep
With phantoms an unprofitable strife,
And in mad trance strike with our spirit's knife
Invulnerable nothings.—*We* decay
Like corpses in a charnel ; fear and grief
Convulse us and consume us day by day,
And cold hopes swarm like worms within our living clay.

XL

He has outsoared the shadow of our night ;
Envy and calumny and hate and pain,
And that unrest which men miscall delight,
Can touch him not and torture not again ;
From the contagion of the world's slow stain
He is secure, and now can never mourn
A heart grown cold, a head grown grey in vain ;
Nor, when the spirit's self has ceased to burn,
With sparkless ashes load an unlamented urn.

XLI

He lives, he wakes—'tis Death is dead, not he ;
Mourn not for Adonais.—Thou young Dawn
Turn all thy dew to splendour, for from thee
The spirit thou lamentest is not gone ;
Ye caverns and ye forests, cease to moan !
Cease ye faint flowers and fountains, and thou Air
Which like a mourning veil thy scarf hadst thrown
O'er the abandoned Earth, now leave it bare
Even to the joyous stars which smile on its despair !

XLII

He is made one with Nature : there is heard
His voice in all her music, from the moan
Of thunder, to the song of night's sweet bird ;
He is a presence to be felt and known
In darkness and in light, from herb and stone,
Spreading itself where'er that Power may move
Which has withdrawn his being to its own :
Which wields the world with never wearied love,
Sustains it from beneath, and kindles it above.

XLIII

He is a portion of the loveliness
Which once he made more lovely : he doth bear
His part, while the one Spirit's plastic stress
Sweeps through the dull dense world, compelling there
All new successions to the forms they wear ;
Torturing th' unwilling dross that checks its flight
To its own likeness, as each mass may bear ;
And bursting in its beauty and its might
From trees and beasts and men into the Heaven's light.

XLIV

The splendours of the firmament of time
May be eclipsed, but are extinguished not ;
Like stars to their appointed height they climb

And death is a low mist which cannot blot
The brightness it may veil.   When lofty thought
Lifts a young heart above its mortal lair,
And love and life contend in it, for what
Shall be its earthly doom, the dead live there
And move like winds of light on dark and stormy air.

XLV

The inheritors of unfulfilled renown
Rose from their thrones, built beyond mortal thought
Far in the Unapparent.   Chatterton
Rose pale, his solemn agony had not
Yet faded from him ; Sidney, as he fought
And as he fell and as he lived and loved
Sublimely mild, a Spirit without spot,
Arose ; and Lucan, by his death approved :
Oblivion as they rose shrank like a thing reproved.

XLVI

And many more, whose names on Earth are dark
But whose transmitted effluence cannot die
So long as fire outlives the parent spark,
Rose, robed in dazzling immortality.
" Thou art become as one of us," they cry,
" It was for thee yon kingless sphere has long
Swung blind in unascended majesty,
Silent alone amid an Heaven of Song.
Assume thy wingèd throne, thou Vesper of our throng ! "

XLVII

Who mourns for Adonais ? oh come forth
Fond wretch ! and know thyself and him aright.
Clasp with thy panting soul the pendulous Earth ;
As from a centre, dart thy spirit's light
Beyond all worlds, until its spacious might
Satiate the void circumference : then shrink
Even to a point within our day and night ;
And keep thy heart light lest it make thee sink
When hope has kindled hope, and lured thee to the brink

XLVIII

Or go to Rome, which is the sepulchre,
O, not of him, but of our joy : 'tis naught
That ages, empires, and religions there
Lie buried in the ravage they have wrought :
For such as he can lend,—they borrow not
Glory from those who made the world their prey ;
And he is gathered to the kings of thought
Who waged contention with their time's decay,
And of the past are all that cannot pass away.

XLIX

Go thou to Rome,—at once the Paradise,
The grave, the city, and the wilderness ;
And where its wrecks like shattered mountains rise,
And flowering weeds and fragrant copses dress
The bones of Desolation's nakedness
Pass, till the Spirit of the spot shall lead
Thy footsteps to a slope of green access
Where, like an infant's smile, over the dead,
A light of laughing flowers along the grass is spread.

L

And grey walls moulder round, on which dull Time
Feeds, like slow fire upon a hoary brand ;
And one keen pyramid with wedge sublime,
Pavilioning the dust of him who planned
This refuge for his memory, doth stand
Like flame transformed to marble ; and beneath,
A field is spread, on which a newer band
Have pitched in Heaven's smile their camp of death
Welcoming him we lose with scarce extinguished breath.

LI

Here pause : these graves are all too young as yet
To have outgrown the sorrow which consigned
Its charge to each ; and if the seal is set,
Here, on one fountain of a mourning mind,

Break it not thou ! too surely shalt thou find
Thine own well full, if thou returnest home,
Of tears and gall.   From the world's bitter wind
Seek shelter in the shadow of the tomb.
What Adonais is, why fear we to become ?

LII

The One remains, the many change and pass ;
Heaven's light forever shines, Earth's shadows fly;
Life, like a dome of many-coloured glass,
Stains the white radiance of Eternity,
Until Death tramples it to fragments.—Die,
If thou wouldst be with that which thou dost seek !
Follow where all is fled !—Rome's azure sky,
Flowers, ruins, statues, music, words, are weak
The glory they transfuse with fitting truth to speak.

LIII

Why linger, why turn back, why shrink, my Heart ?
Thy hopes are gone before : from all things here
They have departed ; thou shouldst now depart !
A light is past from the revolving year,
And man, and woman ; and what still is dear
Attracts to crush, repels to make thee wither.
The soft sky smiles,—the low wind whispers near ;
'Tis Adonais calls ! oh, hasten thither,
No more let Life divide what Death can join together.

LIV

That Light whose smile kindles the Universe,
That Beauty in which all things work and move,
That Benediction which the eclipsing Curse
Of birth can quench not, that sustaining Love
Which, through the web of being blindly wove
By man and beast and earth and air and sea,
Burns bright or dim, as each are mirrors of
The fire for which all thirst, now beams on me,
Consuming the last clouds of cold mortality.

LV

The breath whose might I have invoked in song
Descends on me ; my spirit's bark is driven,
Far from the shore, far from the trembling throng
Whose sails were never to the tempest given ;
The massy earth and sphered skies are riven !
I am borne darkly, fearfully, afar :
Whilst burning through the inmost veil of Heaven,
The soul of Adonais, like a star,
Beacons from the abode where the Eternal are

THE SENSITIVE PLANT

THE SENSITIVE PLANT

PART FIRST

A SENSITIVE Plant in a garden grew,
And the young winds fed it with silver dew,
And it opened its fan-like leaves to the light,
And closed them beneath the kisses of night.

And the Spring arose on the garden fair,
Like the Spirit of Love felt every where ;
And each flower and herb on Earth's dark breast
Rose from the dreams of its wintry rest.

But none ever trembled and panted with bliss
In the garden, the field, or the wilderness,
Like a doe in the noontide with love's sweet want,
As the companionless Sensitive Plant.

The snow-drop, and then the violet,
Arose from the ground with warm rain wet,
And their breath was mixed with fresh odour, sent
From the turf, like the voice and the instrument.

Then the pied wind-flowers and the tulip tall,
And narcissi, the fairest among them all,
Who gaze on their eyes in the stream's recess,
Till they die of their own dear loveliness ;

And the Naiad-like lily of the vale,
Whom youth makes so fair and passion so pale,
That the light of its tremulous bells is seen
Through their pavilions of tender green ;

And the hyacinth purple, and white, and blue,
Which flung from its bells a sweet peal anew
Of music so delicate, soft, and intense,
It was felt like an odour within the sense ;

And the rose like a nymph to the bath addressed,
Which unveiled the depth of her glowing breast,
Till, fold after fold, to the fainting air
The soul of her beauty and love lay bare :

And the wand-like lily, which lifted up,
As a Mænad, its moonlight-coloured cup,
Till the fiery star, which is its eye,
Gazed through clear dew on the tender sky ;

And the jessamine faint, and the sweet tuberose,
The sweetest flower for scent that blows ;
And all rare blossoms from every clime
Grew in that garden in perfect prime.

And on the stream whose inconstant bosom
Was prankt under boughs of embowering blossom,
With golden and green light, slanting through
Their heaven of many a tangled hue,

Broad water lilies lay tremulously,
And starry river-buds glimmered by,
And around them the soft stream did glide and dance
With a motion of sweet sound and radiance.

And the sinuous paths of lawn and of moss,
Which led through the garden along and across,
Some open at once to the sun and the breeze,
Some lost among bowers of blossoming trees,

Were all paved with daisies and delicate bells
As fair as the fabulous asphodels,
And flowrets which drooping as day drooped too
Fell into pavilions, white, purple, and blue,
To roof the glow-worm from the evening dew.

And from this undefiled Paradise
The flowers (as an infant's awakening eyes
Smile on its mother, whose singing sweet
Can first lull, and at last must awaken it),

When Heaven's blithe winds had unfolded them,
As mine-lamps enkindle a hidden gem,
Shone smiling to Heaven, and every one
Shared joy in the light of the gentle sun ;

For each one was interpenetrated
With the light and the odour its neighbour shed,
Like young lovers whom youth and love make dear
Wrapped and filled by their mutual atmosphere.

But the Sensitive Plant, which could give small fruit
Of the love which it felt from the leaf to the root,
Received more than all,—it loved more than ever
(Where none wanted but it) could belong to the giver :

For the Sensitive Plant has no bright flower ;
Radiance and odour are not its dower ;
It loves, even like Love ; its deep heart is full ;
It desires what it has not, the beautiful !

The light winds which from unsustaining wings
Shed the music of many murmurings ;
The beams which dart from many a star
Of the flowers whose hues they bear afar ;

The plumèd insects swift and free,
Like golden boats on a sunny sea,
Laden with light and odour, which pass
Over the gleam of the living grass ;

The unseen clouds of the dew, which lie
Like fire in the flowers till the sun rides high,
Then wander like spirits among the spheres,
Each cloud faint with the fragrance it bears ;

The quivering vapours of dim noontide,
Which like a sea o'er the warm earth glide,
In which every sound, and odour, and beam,
Move, as reeds in a single stream ;

Each and all like ministering angels were
For the Sensitive Plant sweet joy to bear,
Whilst the lagging hours of the day went by
Like windless clouds o'er a tender sky.

And when evening descended from heaven above,
And the Earth was all rest, and the air was all love,
And delight, though less bright, was far more deep,
And the day's veil fell from the world of sleep,

And the beasts, and the birds, and the insects were
      drowned
In an ocean of dreams without a sound ;
Whose waves never mark, though they ever impress
The light sand which paves it, consciousness ;

(Only over head the sweet nightingale
Ever sang more sweet as the day might fail,
And snatches of its Elysian chant
Were mixed with the dreams of the Sensitive Plant.)

The Sensitive Plant was the earliest
Up-gathered into the bosom of rest ;
A sweet child weary of its delight,
The feeblest and yet the favourite,
Cradled within the embrace of night.

PART SECOND

There was a Power in this sweet place,
An Eve in this Eden ; a ruling grace
Which to the flowers, did they waken or dream,
Was as God is to the starry scheme.

A Lady, the wonder of her kind,
Whose form was upborne by a lovely mind
Which, dilating, had moulded her mien and motion
Like a sea-flower unfolded beneath the ocean,

Tended the garden from morn to even :
And the meteors of that sublunar heaven,
Like the lamps of the air when night walks forth,
Laughed round her footsteps up from the Earth !

She had no companion of mortal race,
But her tremulous breath and her flushing face
Told, whilst the morn kissed the sleep from her eyes,
That her dreams were less slumber than Paradise :

As if some bright Spirit for her sweet sake
Had deserted heaven while the stars were awake,
As if yet around her he lingering were,
Though the veil of daylight concealed him from her.

Her step seemed to pity the grass it pressed ;
You might hear by the heaving of her breast,
That the coming and going of the wind
Brought pleasure there and left passion behind.

And wherever her airy footstep trod,
Her trailing hair from the grassy sod
Erased its light vestige, with shadowy sweep,
Like a sunny storm o'er the dark green deep.

I doubt not the flowers of that garden sweet
Rejoiced in the sound of her gentle feet ;
I doubt not they felt the spirit that came
From her glowing fingers through all their frame.

She sprinkled bright water from the stream
On those that were faint with the sunny beam ;
And out of the cups of the heavy flowers
She emptied the rain of the thunder showers.

She lifted their heads with her tender hands,
And sustained them with rods and ozier bands ;
If the flowers had been her own infants she
Could never have nursed them more tenderly.

And all killing insects and gnawing worms,
And things of obscene and unlovely forms,
She bore in a basket of Indian woof,
Into the rough woods far aloof,

In a basket, of grasses and wild flowers full,
The freshest her gentle hands could pull
For the poor banished insects, whose intent,
Although they did ill, was innocent.

But the bee and the beamlike ephemeris
Whose path is the lightning's, and soft moths that kiss
The sweet lips of the flowers, and harm not, did she
Make her attendant angels be.

And many an antenatal tomb,
Where butterflies dream of the life to come,
She left clinging round the smooth and dark
Edge of the odorous cedar bark.

This fairest creature from earliest spring
Thus moved through the garden ministering
All the sweet season of summer tide,
And ere the first leaf looked brown—she died !

PART THIRD

Three days the flowers of the garden fair
Like stars when the moon is awakened were,
Or the waves of Baiæ, ere luminous
She floats up through the smoke of Vesuvius.

And on the fourth, the Sensitive Plant
Felt the sound of the funeral chaunt,
And the steps of the bearers, heavy and slow,
And the sobs of the mourners deep and low ;

The weary sound and the heavy breath,
And the silent motions of passing death,
And the smell, cold, oppressive, and dank,
Sent through the pores of the coffin plank ;

The dark grass, and the flowers among the grass,
Were bright with tears as the crowd did pass ;
From their sighs the wind caught a mournful tone,
And sate in the pines, and gave groan for groan.

The garden, once fair, became cold and foul,
Like the corpse of her who had been its soul,
Which at first was lovely as if in sleep,
Then slowly changed, till it grew a heap
To make men tremble who never weep.

Swift summer into the autumn flowed,
And frost in the mist of morning rode,
Though the noonday sun looked clear and bright,
Mocking the spoil of the secret night.

The rose leaves, like flakes of crimson snow,
Paved the turf and the moss below,
The lilies were drooping, and white, and wan,
Like the head and the skin of a dying man.

And Indian plants, of scent and hue
The sweetest that ever were fed on dew,
Leaf by leaf, day after day,
Were massed into the common clay.

And the leaves, brown, yellow, and grey, and red,
And white with the whiteness of what is dead,
Like troops of ghosts on the dry wind passed ;
Their whistling noise made the birds aghast.

And the gusty winds waked the wingèd seeds,
Out of their birthplace of ugly weeds,
Till they clung round many a sweet flower's stem,
Which rotted into the earth with them.

The water-blooms under the rivulet
Fell from the stalks on which they were set ;
And the eddies drove them here and there,
As the winds did those of the upper air.

Then the rain came down, and the broken stalks,
Were bent and tangled across the walks ;
And the leafless net-work of parasite bowers
Massed into ruin ; and all sweet flowers.

Between the time of the wind and the snow,
All loathliest weeds began to grow,
Whose coarse leaves were splashed with many a speck,
Like the water-snake's belly and the toad's back.

And thistles, and nettles, and darnels rank,
And the dock, and henbane, and hemlock dank,
Stretched out its long and hollow shank,
And stifled the air till the dead wind stank.

And plants, at whose names the verse feels loath,
Filled the place with a monstrous undergrowth,
Prickly, and pulpous, and blistering, and blue,
Livid, and starred with a lurid dew.

And agarics, and fungi, with mildew and mould
Started like mist from the wet ground cold ;
Pale, fleshy, as if the decaying dead
With a spirit of growth had been animated !

Spawn, weeds, and filth, a leprous scum,
Made the running rivulet thick and dumb,
And at its outlet flags huge as stakes
Dammed it up with roots knotted like water snakes.

And hour by hour, when the air was still,
The vapours arose which have strength to kill :
At morn they were seen, at noon they were felt,
At night they were darkness no star could melt.

And unctuous meteors from spray to spray
Crept and flitted in broad noon-day
Unseen ; every branch on which they alit
By a venomous blight was burned and bit.

The Sensitive Plant like one forbid
Wept, and the tears within each lid
Of its folded leaves which together grew
Were changed to a blight of frozen glue.

For the leaves soon fell, and the branches soon
By the heavy axe of the blast were hewn ;
The sap shrank to the root through every pore
As blood to a heart that will beat no more.

For Winter came : the wind was his whip :
One choppy finger was on his lip :
He had torn the cataracts from the hills
And they clanked at his girdle like manacles ;

His breath was a chain which without a sound
The earth, and the air, and the water bound ;
He came, fiercely driven, in his chariot-throne,
By the tenfold blasts of the arctic zone.

Then the weeds which were forms of living death
Fled from the frost to the earth beneath.
Their decay and sudden flight from frost
Was but like the vanishing of a ghost !

And under the roots of the Sensitive Plant
The moles and the dormice died for want :
The birds dropped stiff from the frozen air
And were caught in the branches naked and bare.

First there came down a thawing rain
And its dull drops froze on tne boughs again ;
Then there steamed up a freezing dew
Which to the drops of the thaw-rain grew ;

And a northern whirlwind, wandering about
Like a wolf that had smelt a dead child out,
Shook the boughs thus laden, and heavy and stiff,
And snapped them off with his rigid griff.

When winter had gone and spring came back
The Sensitive Plant was a leafless wreck ;
But the mandrakes, and toadstools, and docks and
    darnels,
Rose like the dead from their ruined charnels.

CONCLUSION

Whether the Sensitive Plant, or that
Which within its boughs like a spirit sat
Ere its outward form had known decay,
Now felt this change, I cannot say.

Whether that Lady's gentle mind,
No longer with the form combined
Which scattered love, as stars do light,
Found sadness, where it left delight,

I dare not guess ; but in this life
Of error, ignorance, and strife,
Where nothing is, but all things seem,
And we the shadows of the dream,

It is a modest creed, and yet
Pleasant if one considers it,
To own that death itself must be,
Like all the rest, a mockery.

That garden sweet, that Lady fair,
And all sweet shapes and odours there,
In truth have never passed away :
'Tis we, 'tis ours, are changed ; not they.

For love, and beauty, and delight,
There is no death nor change : their might
Exceeds our organs, which endure
No light, being themselves obscure.

SHORTER POEMS

SHORTER POEMS

MUTABILITY

WE are as clouds that veil the midnight moon ;
  How restlessly they speed, and gleam, and quiver,
Streaking the darkness radiantly !—yet soon
  Night closes round, and they are lost for ever :

Or like forgotten lyres, whose dissonant strings
  Give various response to each varying blast,
To whose frail frame no second motion brings
  One mood or modulation like the last.

We rest.—A dream has power to poison sleep ;
  We rise.—One wandering thought pollutes the day ;
We feel, conceive or reason, laugh or weep ;
  Embrace fond woe, or cast our cares away :

It is the same !—For, be it joy or sorrow,
  The path of its departure still is free :
Man's yesterday may ne'er be like his morrow ;
  Naught may endure but Mutability.

A SUMMER-EVENING CHURCH-YARD,
LECHLADE, GLOUCESTERSHIRE

THE wind has swept from the wide atmosphere
    Each vapour that obscured the sunset's ray ;
And pallid evening twines its beaming hair
    In duskier braids around the languid eyes of day :
Silence and twilight, unbeloved of men,
Creep hand in hand from yon obscurest glen.

They breathe their spells towards the departing day,
    Encompassing the earth, air, stars, and sea ;
Light, sound, and motion own the potent sway,
    Responding to the charm with its own mystery.
The winds are still, or the dry church-tower grass
Knows not their gentle motions as they pass.

Thou too, aërial Pile ! whose pinnacles
    Point from one shrine like pyramids of fire,
Obeyest in silence their sweet solemn spells,
    Clothing in hues of heaven thy dim and distant spire,
Around whose lessening and invisible height
Gather among the stars the clouds of night.

The dead are sleeping in their sepulchres :
    And, mouldering as they sleep, a thrilling sound
Half sense, half thought, among the darkness stirs,
    Breathed from their wormy beds all living things around,
And mingling with the still night and mute sky
Its awful hush is felt inaudibly.

Thus solemnized and softened, death is mild
    And terrorless as this serenest night :
Here could I hope, like some enquiring child
    Sporting on graves, that death did hide from human sight
Sweet secrets, or beside its breathless sleep
That loveliest dreams perpetual watch did keep.

TO WORDSWORTH

Poet of Nature, thou hast wept to know
    That things depart which never may return:
Childhood and youth, friendship and love's first glow,
    Have fled like sweet dreams, leaving thee to mourn.
These common woes I feel. One loss is mine
    Which thou too feel'st, yet I alone deplore.
Thou wert as a lone star, whose light did shine
    On some frail bark in winter's midnight roar:
Thou hast like to a rock-built refuge stood
Above the blind and battling multitude:
In honoured poverty thy voice did weave
    Songs consecrate to truth and liberty,—
Deserting these, thou leavest me to grieve,
    Thus having been, that thou shouldst cease to be.

MONT BLANC

LINES WRITTEN IN THE VALE OF CHAMOUNI

I

The everlasting universe of things
Flows through the mind, and rolls its rapid waves,
Now dark—now glittering—now reflecting gloom—
Now lending splendour, where from secret springs
The source of human thought its tribute brings
Of waters,—with a sound but half its own,
Such as a feeble brook will oft assume
In the wild woods, among the mountains lone,
Where waterfalls around it leap for ever,
Where woods and winds contend, and a vast river
Over its rocks ceaselessly bursts and raves.

II

Thus thou, Ravine of Arve—dark, deep Ravine—
Thou many-coloured, many-voicèd vale,
Over whose pines, and crags, and caverns sail
Fast cloud-shadows and sunbeams : awful scene,
Where Power in likeness of the Arve comes down
From the ice gulphs that gird his secret throne,
Bursting through these dark mountains like the flame
Of lightning through the tempest ;—thou dost lie,
Thy giant brood of pines around thee clinging,
Children of elder time, in whose devotion
The chainless winds still come and ever came
To drink their odours, and their mighty swinging
To hear—an old and solemn harmony ;
Thine earthly rainbows stretched across the sweep
Of the ætherial waterfall, whose veil
Robes some unsculptured image ; the strange sleep
Which when the voices of the desert fail
Wraps all in its own deep eternity ;—
Thy caverns echoing to the Arve's commotion,
A loud, lone sound no other sound can tame ;
Thou art pervaded with that ceaseless motion,
Thou art the path of that unresting sound—
Dizzy Ravine ! and when I gaze on thee
I seem as in a trance sublime and strange
To muse on my own separate phantasy,
My own, my human mind, which passively
Now renders and receives fast influencings,
Holding an unremitting interchange
With the clear universe of things around ;
One legion of wild thoughts, whose wandering wings
Now float above thy darkness, and now rest
Where that or thou art no unbidden guest,
In the still cave of the witch Poesy,
Seeking among the shadows that pass by
Ghosts of all things that are, some shade of thee,

Some phantom, some faint image ; till the breast
From which they fled recalls them, thou art there !

III

Some say that gleams of a remoter world
Visit the soul in sleep,—that death is slumber,
And that its shapes the busy thoughts outnumber
Of those who wake and live.—I look on high ;
Has some unknown omnipotence unfurled
The veil of life and death ? or do I lie
In dream, and does the mightier world of sleep
Spread far around and inaccessibly
Its circles ? For the very spirit fails,
Driven like a homeless cloud from steep to steep
That vanishes among the viewless gales !
Far, far above, piercing the infinite sky,
Mont Blanc appears,—still, snowy, and serene—
Its subject mountains their unearthly forms
Pile around it, ice and rock ; broad vales between
Of frozen floods, unfathomable deeps,
Blue as the overhanging heaven, that spread
And wind among the accumulated steeps ;
A desert peopled by the storms alone,
Save when the eagle brings some hunter's bone,
And the wolf tracks her there—how hideously
Its shapes are heaped around ! rude, bare, and high,
Ghastly, and scarred, and riven.—Is this the scene
Where the old Earthquake-dæmon taught her young
Ruin ? Were these their toys ? or did a sea
Of fire envelope once this silent snow ?
None can reply—all seems eternal now.
The wilderness has a mysterious tongue
Which teaches awful doubt, or faith so mild,
So solemn, so serene, that man may be
But for such faith with nature reconciled ;
Thou hast a voice, great Mountain, to repeal
Large codes of fraud and woe ; not understood

By all, but which the wise, and great, and good
Interpret, or make felt, or deeply feel.

IV

The fields, the lakes, the forests, and the streams,
Ocean, and all the living things that dwell
Within the dædal earth ; lightning, and rain,
Earthquake, and fiery flood, and hurricane,
The torpor of the year when feeble dreams
Visit the hidden buds, or dreamless sleep
Holds every future leaf and flower ;—the bound
With which from that detested trance they leap ;
The works and ways of man, their death and birth,
And that of him and all that his may be ;
All things that move and breathe with toil and sound
Are born and die ; revolve, subside and swell.
Power dwells apart in its tranquillity
Remote, serene, and inaccessible :
And *this*, the naked countenance of earth,
On which I gaze, even these primeval mountains
Teach the adverting mind.   The glaciers creep
Like snakes that watch their prey, from their far
        fountains,
Slow rolling on ; there, many a precipice,
Frost and the Sun in scorn of mortal power
Have piled : dome, pyramid, and pinnacle,
A city of death, distinct with many a tower
And wall impregnable of beaming ice.
Yet not a city, but a flood of ruin
Is there, that from the boundaries of the sky
Rolls its perpetual stream ; vast pines are strewing
Its destined path, or in the mangled soil
Branchless and shattered stand ; the rocks, drawn down
From yon remotest waste, have overthrown
The limits of the dead and living world,
Never to be reclaimed.   The dwelling-place
Of insects, beasts, and birds, becomes its spoil ;

Their food and their retreat for ever gone,
So much of life and joy is lost.   The race
Of man, flies far in dread ; his work and dwelling
Vanish, like smoke before the tempest's stream,
And their place is not known.   Below, vast caves
Shine in the rushing torrent's restless gleam,
Which from those secret chasms in tumult welling
Meet in the vale, and one majestic River,
The breath and blood of distant lands, for ever
Rolls its loud waters to the ocean waves,
Breathes its swift vapours to the circling air.

V

Mont Blanc yet gleams on high :—the power is there,
The still and solemn power of many sights,
And many sounds, and much of life and death.
In the calm darkness of the moonless nights,
In the lone glare of day, the snows descend
Upon that Mountain ; none beholds them there,
Nor when the flakes burn in the sinking sun,
Or the star-beams dart through them :—Winds contend
Silently there, and heap the snow with breath
Rapid and strong, but silently !   Its home
The voiceless lightning in these solitudes
Keeps innocently, and like vapour broods
Over the snow.   The secret strength of things
Which governs thought, and to the infinite dome
Of heaven is as a law, inhabits thee !
And what were thou, and earth, and stars, and sea,
If to the human mind's imaginings
Silence and solitude were vacancy ?

July 23, 1816.

FEELINGS OF A REPUBLICAN ON THE FALL
OF BONAPARTE

I HATED thee, fallen tyrant ! I did groan
    To think that a most unambitious slave,
    Like thou, shouldst dance and revel on the grave
Of Liberty. Thou mightst have built thy throne
Where it had stood even now : thou didst prefer
    A frail and bloody pomp which time has swept
In fragments towards oblivion. Massacre,
    For this I prayed, would on thy sleep have crept,
Treason and Slavery, Rapine, Fear, and Lust,
    And stifled thee, their minister. I know
Too late, since thou and France are in the dust,
    That virtue owns a more eternal foe
Than force or fraud : old Custom, legal Crime,
And bloody Faith the foulest birth of time.

LINES WRITTEN AMONG THE EUGANEAN
HILLS

OCTOBER, 1818

MANY a green isle needs must be
In the deep wide sea of misery,
Or the mariner, worn and wan,
Never thus could voyage on
Day and night, and night and day,
Drifting on his dreary way,
With the solid darkness black
Closing round his vessel's track ;
Whilst above the sunless sky,
Big with clouds, hangs heavily,
And behind the tempest fleet

Hurries on with lightning feet,
Riving sail, and cord, and plank,
Till the ship has almost drank
Death from the o'er-brimming deep;
And sinks down, down, like that sleep
When the dreamer seems to be
Weltering through eternity;
And the dim low line before
Of a dark and distant shore
Still recedes, as ever still
Longing with divided will,
But no power to seek or shun,
He is ever drifted on
O'er the unreposing wave
To the haven of the grave.
What if there no friends will greet;
What if there no heart will meet
His with love's impatient beat;
Wander wheresoe'er he may,
Can he dream before that day
To find refuge from distress
In friendship's smile, in love's caress?
Then 'twill wreak him little woe
Whether such there be or no:
Senseless is the breast, and cold,
Which relenting love would fold;
Bloodless are the veins and chill
Which the pulse of pain did fill;
Every little living nerve
That from bitter words did swerve
Round the tortured lips and brow,
Are like sapless leaflets now
Frozen upon December's bough.
On the beach of a northern sea
Which tempests shake eternally,
As once the wretch there lay to sleep,
Lies a solitary heap,
One white skull and seven dry bones,

On the margin of the stones,
Where a few grey rushes stand,
Boundaries of the sea and land :
Nor is heard one voice of wail
But the sea-mews', as they sail
O'er the billows of the gale ;
Or the whirlwind up and down
Howling, like a slaughtered town,
When a king in glory rides
Through the pomp of fratricides :
Those unburied bones around
There is many a mournful sound ;
There is no lament for him,
Like a sunless vapour, dim,
Who once clothed with life and thought
What now moves nor murmurs not.

Aye, many flowering islands lie
In the waters of wide Agony :
To such a one this morn was led,
My bark by soft winds piloted :
'Mid the mountains Euganean
I stood listening to the pæan,
With which the legioned rooks did hail
The sun's uprise majestical ;
Gathering round with wings all hoar,
Through the dewy mist they soar
Like grey shades, till the eastern heaven
Bursts, and then, as clouds of even,
Flecked with fire and azure, lie
In the unfathomable sky,
So their plumes of purple grain,
Starred with drops of golden rain,
Gleam above the sunlight woods,
As in silent multitudes
On the morning's fitful gale
Through the broken mist they sail,
And the vapours cloven and gleaming

Follow down the dark steep streaming,
Till all is bright, and clear, and still,
Round the solitary hill.

Beneath is spread like a green sea
The waveless plain of Lombardy,
Bounded by the vaporous air,
Islanded by cities fair ;
Underneath day's azure eyes,
Ocean's nursling, Venice lies,
A peopled labyrinth of walls,
Amphitrite's destined halls,
Which her hoary sire now paves
With his blue and beaming waves.
Lo ! the sun upsprings behind,
Broad, red, radiant, half reclined
On the level quivering line
Of the waters crystalline ;
And before that chasm of light,
As within a furnace bright,
Column, tower, and dome, and spire,
Shine like obelisks of fire,
Pointing with inconstant motion
From the altar of dark ocean
To the sapphire-tinted skies ;
As the flames of sacrifice
From the marble shrines did rise,
As to pierce the dome of gold
Where Apollo spoke of old.

Sun-girt City, thou hast been
Ocean's child, and then his queen ;
Now is come a darker day,
And thou soon must be his prey,
If the power that raised thee here
Hallow so thy watery bier.
A less drear ruin then than now,
With thy conquest-branded brow

Stooping to the slave of slaves
From thy throne, among the waves
Wilt thou be, when the sea-mew
Flies, as once before it flew,
O'er thine isles depopulate,
And all is in its ancient state,
Save where many a palace gate
With green sea-flowers overgrown
Like a rock of ocean's own,
Topples o'er the abandoned sea
As the tides change sullenly.
The fisher on his watery way,
Wandering at the close of day,
Will spread his sail and seize his oar
Till he pass the gloomy shore,
Lest thy dead should, from their sleep
Bursting o'er the starlight deep,
Lead a rapid mask of death
O'er the waters of his path.

Those who alone thy towers behold
Quivering through aërial gold,
As I now behold them here,
Would imagine not they were
Sepulchres, where human forms,
Like pollution-nourished worms
To the corpse of greatness cling,
Murdered, and now mouldering:
But if Freedom should awake
In her omnipotence, and shake
From the Celtic Anarch's hold
All the keys of dungeons cold,
Where a hundred cities lie
Chained like thee, ingloriously,
Thou and all thy sister band
Might adorn this sunny land,
Twining memories of old time
With new virtues more sublime;

If not, perish thou and they,
Clouds which stain truth's rising day
By her sun consumed away,
Earth can spare ye : while like flowers,
In the waste of years and hours,
From your dust new nations spring
With more kindly blossoming.
Perish—let there only be
Floating o'er thy heartless sea
As the garment of thy sky
Clothes the world immortally,
One remembrance, more sublime
Than the tattered pall of time,
Which scarce hides thy visage wan ;—
That a tempest-cleaving Swan
Of the songs of Albion,
Driven from his ancestral streams
By the might of evil dreams,
Found a nest in thee ; and Ocean
Welcomed him with such emotion
That its joy grew his, and sprung
From his lips like music flung
O'er a mighty thunder-fit
Chastening terror :—what though yet
Poesy's unfailing River,
Which through Albion winds for ever
Lashing with melodious wave
Many a sacred Poet's grave,
Mourn its latest nursling fled ?
What though thou with all thy dead
Scarce can for this fame repay
Aught thine own ? oh, rather say
Though thy sins and slaveries foul
Overcloud a sunlike soul ?
As the ghost of Homer clings
Round Scamander's wasting springs ;
As divinest Shakespeare's might
Fills Avon and the world with light

Like omniscient power which he
Imaged 'mid mortality ;
As the love from Petrarch's urn,
Yet amid yon hills doth burn,
A quenchless lamp by which the heart
Sees things unearthly ;—so thou art,
Mighty spirit—so shall be
The City that did refuge thee.

Lo, the sun floats up the sky
Like thought-wingèd Liberty,
Till the universal light
Seems to level plain and height ;
From the sea a mist has spread,
And the beams of morn lie dead
On the towers of Venice now,
Like its glory long ago.
By the skirts of that grey cloud
Many-domèd Padua proud
Stands, a peopled solitude,
'Mid the harvest-shining plain,
Where the peasant heaps his grain
In the garner of his foe,
And the milk-white oxen slow
With the purple vintage strain,
Heaped upon the creaking wain,
That the brutal Celt may swill
Drunken sleep with savage will ;
And the sickle to the sword
Lies unchanged, though many a lord,
Like a weed whose shade is poison,
Overgrows this region's foison,
Sheaves of whom are ripe to come
To destruction's harvest home :
Men must reap the things they sow,
Force from force must ever flow,
Or worse ; but 'tis a bitter woe

That love or reason cannot change
The despot's rage, the slave's revenge.

Padua, thou within whose walls
Those mute guests at festivals,
Son and Mother, Death and Sin,
Played at dice for Ezzelin,
Till Death cried, " I win, I win ! "
And Sin cursed to lose the wager,
But Death promised, to assuage her,
That he would petition for
Her to be made Vice-Emperor,
When the destined years were o'er
Over all between the Po
And the eastern Alpine snow,
Under the mighty Austrian.
Sin smiled so as Sin only can,
And since that time, aye, long before,
Both have ruled from shore to shore,
That incestuous pair, who follow
Tyrants as the sun the swallow,
As Repentance follows Crime,
And as changes follow Time.

In thine halls the lamp of learning,
Padua, now no more is burning ;
Like a meteor, whose wild way
Is lost over the grave of day,
It gleams betrayed and to betray :
Once remotest nations came
To adore that sacred flame,
When it lit not many a hearth
On this cold and gloomy earth :
Now new fires from antique light
Spring beneath the wide world's might ;
But their spark lies dead in thee,
Trampled out by tyranny.
As the Norway woodman quells,

In the depth of piny dells,
One light flame among the brakes,
While the boundless forest shakes,
And its mighty trunks are torn
By the fire thus lowly born :
The spark beneath his feet is dead,
He starts to see the flames it fed
Howling through the darkened sky
With a myriad tongues victoriously,
And sinks down in fear : so thou,
O Tyranny, beholdest now
Light around thee, and thou hearest
The loud flames ascend, and fearest :
Grovel on the earth : aye, hide
In the dust thy purple pride !

Noon descends around me now :
'Tis the noon of autumn's glow,
When a soft and purple mist
Like a vaporous amethyst,
Or an air-dissolvèd star
Mingling light and fragrance, far
From the curved horizon's bound
To the point of heaven's profound,
Fills the overflowing sky ;
And the plains that silent lie
Underneath, the leaves unsodden
Where the infant frost has trodden
With his morning-wingèd feet,
Whose bright print is gleaming yet ;
And the red and golden vines,
Piercing with their trellised lines
The rough, dark-skirted wilderness ;
The dun and bladed grass no less,
Pointing from this hoary tower
In the windless air ; the flower
Glimmering at my feet ; the line
Of the olive-sandalled Apennine

In the south dimly islanded ;
And the Alps, whose snows are spread
High between the clouds and sun ;
And of living things each one ;
And my spirit which so long
Darkened this swift stream of song,
Interpenetrated lie
By the glory of the sky :
Be it love, light, harmony,
Odour, or the soul of all
Which from heaven like dew doth fall,
Or the mind which feeds this verse
Peopling the lone universe.

Noon descends, and after noon
Autumn's evening meets me soon,
Leading the infantine moon,
And that one star, which to her
Almost seems to minister
Half the crimson light she brings
From the sunset's radiant springs :
And the soft dreams of the morn,
(Which like wingèd winds had borne
To that silent isle, which lies
'Mid remembered agonies,
The frail bark of this lone being,)
Pass, to other sufferers fleeing,
And its ancient pilot, Pain,
Sits beside the helm again.

Other flowering isles must be
In the sea of life and agony :
Other spirits float and flee
O'er that gulph : even now, perhaps,
On some rock the wild wave wraps,
With folded wings they waiting sit
For my bark, to pilot it
To some calm and blooming cove,

Where for me, and those I love,
May a windless bower be built,
Far from passion, pain, and guilt,
In a dell 'mid lawny hills,
Which the wild sea-murmur fills,
And soft sunshine, and the sound
Of old forests echoing round,
And the light and smell divine
Of all flowers that breathe and shine :
We may live so happy there,
That the spirits of the air,
Envying us, may even entice
To our healing paradise
The polluting multitude ;
But their rage would be subdued
By that clime divine and calm,
And the winds whose wings rain balm
On the uplifted soul, and leaves
Under which the bright sea heaves ;
While each breathless interval
In their whisperings musical
The inspired soul supplies
With its own deep melodies,
And the love which heals all strife
Circling, like the breath of life,
All things in that sweet abode
With its own mild brotherhood :
They, not it, would change ; and soon
Every sprite beneath the moon
Would repent its envy vain,
And the earth grow young again.

HYMN TO INTELLECTUAL BEAUTY

1

THE awful shadow of some unseen Power
  Floats though unseen amongst us,—visiting
  This various world with as inconstant wing
As summer winds that creep from flower to flower,—
Like moonbeams that behind some piny mountain
      shower,
    It visits with inconstant glance
    Each human heart and countenance ;
Like hues and harmonies of evening,—
    Like clouds in starlight widely spread,—
    Like memory of music fled,—
    Like aught that for its grace may be
Dear, and yet dearer for its mystery.

2

Spirit of BEAUTY, that dost consecrate
  With thine own hues all thou dost shine upon
  Of human thought or form,—where art thou gone ?
Why dost thou pass away and leave our state,
This dim vast vale of tears, vacant and desolate ?
    Ask why the sunlight not for ever
    Weaves rainbows o'er yon mountain river,
Why aught should fail and fade that once is shown,
    Why fear and dream and death and birth
    Cast on the daylight of this earth
    Such gloom,—why man has such a scope
For love and hate, despondency and hope ?

3

No voice from some sublimer world hath ever
  To sage or poet these responses given—

Therefore the names of Dæmon, Ghost, and Heaven,
Remain the records of their vain endeavour,
Frail spells—whose uttered charm might not avail to
    sever,
    From all we hear and all we see,
    Doubt, chance, and mutability.
Thy light alone—like mist o'er mountains driven,
    Or music by the night wind sent,
    Through strings of some still instrument,
    Or moonlight on a midnight stream,
Gives grace and truth to life's unquiet dream.

4

Love, Hope, and Self-esteem, like clouds depart
    And come, for some uncertain moments lent,
    Man were immortal, and omnipotent,
Didst thou, unknown and awful as thou art,
Keep with thy glorious train firm state within his heart.
    Thou messenger of sympathies,
    That wax and wane in lovers' eyes—
Thou—that to human thought art nourishment,
    Like darkness to a dying flame !
    Depart not as thy shadow càme,
    Depart not—lest the grave should be,
Like life and fear, a dark reality.

5

While yet a boy I sought for ghosts, and sped
    Through many a listening chamber, cave and ruin,
    And starlight wood, with fearful steps pursuing
Hopes of high talk with the departed dead,
I called on poisonous names with which our youth is fed,
    I was not heard—I saw them not—
    When musing deeply on the lot
Of life, at the sweet time when winds are wooing
    All vital things that wake to bring

News of birds and blossoming,—
    Sudden, thy shadow fell on me ;
I shrieked, and clasped my hands in ecstasy !

6

I vowed that I would dedicate my powers
    To thee and thine—have I not kept the vow ?
    With beating heart and streaming eyes, even now
I call the phantoms of a thousand hours
Each from his voiceless grave : they have in visioned
        bowers
    Of studious zeal or love's delight
    Outwatched with me the envious night—
They know that never joy illumed my brow
    Unlinked with hope that thou wouldst free
    This world from its dark slavery,
    That thou—O awful LOVELINESS,
Wouldst give whate'er these words cannot express.

7

The day becomes more solemn and serene
    When noon is past—there is a harmony
    In autumn, and a lustre in its sky,
Which through the summer is not heard or seen,
As if it could not be, as if it had not been !
    Thus let thy power, which like the truth
    Of nature on my passive youth
Descended, to my onward life supply
    Its calm—to one who worships thee,
    And every form containing thee,
    Whom, SPIRIT fair, thy spells did bind
To fear himself, and love all human kind.

ODE TO THE WEST WIND [1]

I

O, WILD West Wind, thou breath of Autumn's being,
Thou, from whose unseen presence the leaves dead
Are driven, like ghosts from an enchanter fleeing,

Yellow, and black, and pale, and hectic red,
Pestilence-stricken multitudes : O, thou,
Who chariotest to their dark wintry bed

The wingèd seeds, where they lie cold and low,
Each like a corpse within its grave, until
Thine azure sister of the spring shall blow

Her clarion o'er the dreaming earth, and fill
(Driving sweet buds like flocks to feed in air)
With living hues and odours plain and hill :

Wild Spirit, which art moving every where ;
Destroyer and preserver ; hear, O, hear !

II

Thou on whose stream, 'mid the steep sky's commotion
Loose clouds like earth's decaying leaves are shed,
Shook from the tangled boughs of Heaven and Ocean,

[1] This poem was conceived and chiefly written in a wood that skirts the Arno, near Florence, and on a day when that tempestuous wind, whose temperature is at once mild and animating, was collecting the vapours which pour down the autumnal rains. They began, as I foresaw, at sunset with a violent tempest of hail and rain, attended by that magnificent thunder and lightning peculiar to the Cisalpine regions.

The phenomenon alluded to at the conclusion of the third stanza is well known to naturalists. The vegetation at the bottom of the sea, of rivers, and of lakes, sympathizes with that of the land in the change of seasons, and is consequently influenced by the winds which announce it.

Angels of rain and lightning : there are spread
On the blue surface of thine airy surge,
Like the bright hair uplifted from the head

Of some fierce Mænad, even from the dim verge
Of the horizon to the zenith's height
The locks of the approaching storm. Thou dirge

Of the dying year, to which this closing night
Will be the dome of a vast sepulchre,
Vaulted with all thy congregated might

Of vapours, from whose solid atmosphere
Black rain, and fire, and hail will burst : O, hear !

III

Thou who didst waken from his summer dreams
The blue Mediterranean, where he lay,
Lulled by the coil of his crystàlline streams,

Beside a pumice isle in Baiæ's bay,
And saw in sleep old palaces and towers
Quivering within the wave's intenser day,

All overgrown with azure moss and flowers
So sweet, the sense faints picturing them ! Thou
For whose path the Atlantic's level powers

Cleave themselves into chasms, while far below
The sea-blooms and the oozy woods which wear
The sapless foliage of the ocean, know

Thy voice, and suddenly grow grey with fear,
And tremble and despoil themselves : O, hear !

IV

If I were a dead leaf thou mightest bear ;
If I were a swift cloud to fly with thee ;
A wave to pant beneath thy power, and share

The impulse of thy strength, only less free
Than thou, O, uncontrollable ! If even
I were as in my boyhood, and could be

The comrade of thy wanderings over heaven,
As then, when to outstrip thy skiey speed
Scarce seemed a vision ; I would ne'er have striven

As thus with thee in prayer in my sore need,
Oh ! lift me as a wave, a leaf, a cloud !
I fall upon the thorns of life ! I bleed !

A heavy weight of hours has chained and bowed
One too like thee : tameless, and swift, and proud.

v

Make me thy lyre, even as the forest is :
What if my leaves are falling like its own !
The tumult of thy mighty harmonies

Will take from both a deep, autumnal tone,
Sweet though in sadness. Be thou, spirit fierce,
My spirit ! Be thou me, impetuous one !

Drive my dead thoughts over the universe
Like withered leaves to quicken a new birth !
And, by the incantation of this verse,

Scatter, as from an unextinguished hearth
Ashes and sparks, my words among mankind !
Be through my lips to unawakened earth

The trumpet of a prophecy ! O, wind,
If Winter comes, can Spring be far behind ?

ODE TO LIBERTY

Yet, Freedom, yet thy banner torn but flying,
Streams like a thunder-storm against the wind.
BYRON.

I

A GLORIOUS people vibrated again
  The lightning of the nations : Liberty
From heart to heart, from tower to tower, o'er Spain,
  Scattering contagious fire into the sky,
Gleamed. My soul spurned the chains of its dismay,
      And, in the rapid plumes of song,
      Clothed itself, sublime and strong ;
As a young eagle soars the morning clouds among,
    Hovering in verse o'er its accustomed prey ;
      Till from its station in the heaven of fame
    The Spirit's whirlwind rapt it, and the ray
      Of the remotest sphere of living flame
Which paves the void was from behind it flung,
  As foam from a ship's swiftness, when there came
A voice out of the deep : I will record the same.

II

The Sun and the serenest Moon sprang forth :
  The burning stars of the abyss were hurled
Into the depths of heaven. The Dædal earth,
  That island in the ocean of the world,
Hung in its cloud of all-sustaining air :
      But this divinest universe
      Was yet a chaos and a curse,
For thou wert not : but power from worst producing
          worse,
    The spirit of the beasts was kindled there,
      And of the birds, and of the watery forms,
    And there was war among them, and despair

Within them, raging without truce or terms :
The bosom of their violated nurse
    Groaned, for beasts warred on beasts, and worms on
        worms,
    And men on men ; each heart was as a hell of storms.

III

Man, the imperial shape, then multiplied
    His generations under the pavilion
Of the Sun's throne : palace and pyramid,
    Temple and prison, to many a swarming million,
Were, as to mountain-wolves their ragged caves.
        This human living multitude
        Was savage, cunning, blind, and rude,
For thou wert not ; but o'er the populous solitude,
    Like one fierce cloud over a waste of waves
        Hung Tyranny ; beneath, sate deified
    The sister-pest, congregator of slaves ;
        Into the shadow of her pinions wide
Anarchs and priests who feed on gold and blood,
    Till with the stain their inmost souls are dyed,
    Drove the astonished herds of men from every side.

IV

The nodding promontories, and blue isles,
    And cloud-like mountains, and dividuous waves
Of Greece, basked glorious in the open smiles
    Of favouring heaven ; from their enchanted caves
Prophetic echoes flung dim melody.
        On the unapprehensive wild
        The vine, the corn, the olive mild,
Grew savage yet, to human use unreconciled ;
    And, like unfolded flowers beneath the sea,
        Like the man's thought dark in the infant's brain,
    Like aught that is which wraps what is to be,
        Art's deathless dreams lay veiled by many a vein

Of Parian stone ; and, yet a speechless child,
  Verse murmured, and Philosophy did strain
  Her lidless eyes for thee ; when o'er the Ægean main

V

Athens arose : a city such as vision
  Builds from the purple crags and silver towers
Of battlemented cloud, as in derision
  Of kingliest masonry : the ocean-floors
Pave it ; the evening sky pavilions it ;
      Its portals are inhabited
      By thunder-zonèd winds, each head
Within its cloudy wings with sunfire garlanded,
  A divine work ! Athens diviner yet
    Gleamed with its crest of columns, on the will
Of man, as on a mount of diamond, set ;
  For thou wert, and thine all-creative skill
Peopled with forms that mock the eternal dead
  In marble immortality, that hill
  Which was thine earliest throne and latest oracle.

VI

Within the surface of Time's fleeting river
  Its wrinkled image lies, as then it lay
Immovably unquiet, and for ever
  It trembles, but it cannot pass away !
The voices of thy bards and sages thunder
      With an earth-awakening blast
      Through the caverns of the past ;
Religion veils her eyes ; Oppression shrinks aghast :
  A wingèd sound of joy, and love, and wonder,
    Which soars where Expectation never flew,
Rending the veil of space and time asunder !
  One ocean feeds the clouds, and streams, and dew ;
One sun illumines heaven ; one spirit vast
  With life and love makes chaos ever new,
  As Athens doth the world with thy delight renew.

13

VII

Then Rome was, and from thy deep bosom fairest,
  Like a wolf-cub from a Cadmæan Mænad,
She drew the milk of greatness, though thy dearest
  From that Elysian food was yet unweanèd ;
And many a deed of terrible uprightness
    By thy sweet love was sanctified ;
    And in thy smile, and by thy side,
Saintly Camillus lived, and firm Atilius died.
  But when tears stained thy robe of vestal whiteness,
    And gold profaned thy capitolian throne,
  Thou didst desert, with spirit-wingèd lightness,
    The senate of the tyrants : they sunk prone
Slaves of one tyrant : Palatinus sighed
    Faint echoes of Ionian song ; that tone
Thou didst delay to hear, lamenting to disown.

VIII

From what Hyrcanian glen or frozen hill,
  Or piny promontory of the Arctic main,
Or utmost islet inaccessible,
  Didst thou lament the ruin of thy reign,
Teaching the woods and waves, and desert rocks,
    And every Naiad's ice-cold urn,
    To talk in echoes sad and stern,
Of that sublimest lore which man had dared unlearn ?
  For neither didst thou watch the wizard flocks
    Of the Scald's dreams, nor haunt the Druid's sleep.
  What if the tears rained through thy shattered locks
    Were quickly dried ? for thou didst groan, not weep,
When from its sea of death to kill and burn,
    The Galilean serpent forth did creep,
And made thy world an undistinguishable heap.

IX

A thousand years the Earth cried, Where art thou ?
  And then the shadow of thy coming fell

On Saxon Alfred's olive-cinctured brow :
  And many a warrior-peopled citadel,
Like rocks which fire lifts out of the flat deep,
      Arose in sacred Italy,
      Frowning o'er the tempestuous sea
Of kings, and priests, and slaves, in tower-crowned
        majesty ;
  That multitudinous anarchy did sweep,
    And burst around their walls, like idle foam,
  Whilst from the human spirit's deepest deep
    Strange melody with love and awe struck dumb
Dissonant arms ; and Art, which cannot die,
  With divine wand traced on our earthly home
  Fit imagery to pave heaven's everlasting dome.

X

Thou huntress swifter than the Moon ! thou terror
  Of the world's wolves ! thou bearer of the quiver,
Whose sunlike shafts pierce tempest-wingèd Error,
  As light may pierce the clouds when they dissever
In the calm regions of the orient day !
      Luther caught thy wakening glance ;
      Like lightning, from his leaden lance
Reflected, it dissolved the visions of the trance
  In which, as in a tomb, the nations lay ;
    And England's prophets hailed thee as their queen,
  In songs whose music cannot pass away,
    Though it must flow for ever : not unseen
Before the spirit-sighted countenance
  Of Milton didst thou pass, from the sad scene
  Beyond whose night he saw, with a dejected mien.

XI

The eager hours and unreluctant years
  As on a dawn-illumined mountain stood,
Trampling to silence their loud hopes and fears,
  Darkening each other with their multitude,

And cried aloud, Liberty ! Indignation
        Answered Pity from her cave ;
        Death grew pale within the grave,
And Desolation howled to the destroyer, Save !
    When like heaven's sun girt by the exhalation
        Of its own glorious light, thou didst arise,
    Chasing thy foes from nation unto nation
        Like shadows : as if day had cloven the skies
At dreaming midnight o'er the western wave,
    Men started, staggering with a glad surprise,
    Under the lightnings of thine unfamiliar eyes.

XII

Thou heaven of earth ! what spells could pall thee then,
    In ominous eclipse ? a thousand years
Bred from the slime of deep oppression's den
    Dyed all thy liquid light with blood and tears,
Till thy sweet stars could weep the stain away ;
            How like Bacchanals of blood
            Round France, the ghastly vintage, stood
Destruction's sceptred slaves, and Folly's mitred brood !
    When one, like them, but mightier far than they,
        The Anarch of thine own bewildered powers
    Rose : armies mingled in obscure array,
        Like clouds with clouds, darkening the sacred bowers
Of serene heaven. He, by the past pursued,
    Rests with those dead, but unforgotten hours,
    Whose ghosts scare victor kings in their ancestral
            towers.

XIII

England yet sleeps : was she not called of old ?
    Spain calls her now, as with its thrilling thunder
Vesuvius wakens Ætna, and the cold
    Snow-crags by its reply are cloven in sunder :
O'er the lit waves every Æolian isle
            From Pithecusa to Pelorus
            Howls, and leaps, and glares in chorus :

They cry, Be dim, ye lamps of heaven suspended o'er us.
Her chains are threads of gold, she need but smile
And they dissolve ; but Spain's were links of steel,
Till bit to dust by virtue's keenest file.
Twins of a single destiny ! appeal
To the eternal years enthroned before us,
In the dim West ; impress us from a seal,
All ye have thought and done ! Time cannot dare
conceal.

XIV

Tomb of Arminius ! render up thy dead,
Till, like a standard from a watch-tower's staff,
His soul may stream over the tyrant's head ;
Thy victory shall be his epitaph,
Wild Bacchanal of truth's mysterious wine,
King-deluded Germany,
His dead spirit lives in thee.
Why do we fear or hope ? thou art already free !
And thou, lost Paradise of this divine
And glorious world ! thou flowery wilderness !
Thou island of eternity ! thou shrine
Where desolation clothed with loveliness,
Worships the thing thou wert ! O Italy,
Gather thy blood into thy heart ; repress
The beasts who make their dens thy sacred palaces.

XV

O, that the free would stamp the impious name
Of KING into the dust ! or write it there,
So that this blot upon the page of fame
Were as a serpent's path, which the light air
Erases, and the flat sands close behind !
Ye the oracle have heard :
Lift the victory-flashing sword,
And cut the snaky knots of this foul gordian word,
Which weak itself as stubble, yet can bind
Into a mass, irrefragably firm,

The axes and the rods which awe mankind ;
  The sound has poison in it, 'tis the sperm
Of what makes life foul, cankerous, and abhorred ;
  Disdain not thou, at thine appointed term,
  To set thine armèd heel on this reluctant worm.

XVI

O, that the wise from their bright minds would kindle
  Such lamps within the dome of this dim world,
That the pale name of PRIEST might shrink and dwindle
  Into the hell from which it first was hurled,
A scoff of impious pride from fiends impure ;
      Till human thoughts might kneel alone
      Each before the judgment-throne
Of its own aweless soul, or of the power unknown !
  O, that the words which make the thoughts obscure
    From which they spring, as clouds of glimmering dew
From a white lake blot heaven's blue portraiture,
    Were stripped of their thin masks and various hue
And frowns and smiles and splendours not their own,
  Till in the nakedness of false and true
  They stand before their Lord, each to receive its due.

XVII

He who taught man to vanquish whatsoever
  Can be between the cradle and the grave
Crowned him the King of Life.   O vain endeavour !
  If on his own high will, a willing slave,
He has enthroned the oppression and the oppressor.
      What if earth can clothe and feed
      Amplest millions at their need,
And power in thought be as the tree within the seed ?
  O, what if Art, an ardent intercessor,
    Driving on fiery wings to Nature's throne,
Checks the great mother stooping to caress her,
    And cries : Give me, thy child, dominion

Over all height and depth ? if Life can breed
  New wants, and wealth from those who toil and groan
  Rend of thy gifts and hers a thousand fold for one.

XVIII

Come Thou, but lead out of the inmost cave
  Of man's deep spirit, as the morning-star
Beckons the Sun from the Eoan wave,
  Wisdom.   I hear the pennons of her car
Self-moving, like cloud charioted by flame ;
      Comes she not, and come ye not,
       Rulers of eternal thought,
To judge, with solemn truth, life's ill-apportioned lot ?
  Blind Love, and equal Justice, and the Fame
    Of what has been, the Hope of what will be ?
  O, Liberty ! if such could be thy name
    Wert thou disjoined from these, or they from thee :
If thine or theirs were treasures to be bought
  By blood or tears, have not the wise and free
  Wept tears, and blood like tears ?   The solemn
      harmony

XIX

Paused, and the spirit of that mighty singing
  To its abyss was suddenly withdrawn ;
Then, as a wild swan, when sublimely winging
  Its path athwart the thunder-smoke of dawn,
Sinks headlong through the aërial golden light
      On the heavy sounding plain,
      When the bolt has pierced its brain ;
As summer clouds dissolve, unburthened of their rain ;
  As a far taper fades with fading night,
    As a brief insect dies with dying day,
  My song, its pinions disarrayed of might,
    Drooped ; o'er it closed the echoes far away
Of the great voice which did its flight sustain,
    As waves which lately paved his watery way
    Hiss round a drowner's head in their tempestuous play.

TO A SKYLARK

HAIL to thee, blithe spirit !
　　Bird thou never wert,
That from heaven, or near it,
　　Pourest thy full heart
In profuse strains of unpremeditated art.

　　Higher still and higher
　　From the earth thou springest
Like a cloud of fire ;
　　The blue deep thou wingest,
And singing still dost soar, and soaring ever singest.

　　In the golden lightning
　　Of the sunken sun,
O'er which clouds are bright'ning,
　　Thou dost float and run ;
Like an unbodied joy whose race is just begun.

　　The pale purple even
　　Melts around thy flight ;
Like a star of heaven
　　In the broad daylight
Thou art unseen, but yet I hear thy shrill delight,

　　Keen as are the arrows
　　Of that silver sphere,
Whose intense lamp narrows
　　In the white dawn clear,
Until we hardly see, we feel that it is there.

　　All the earth and air
　　With thy voice is loud,
As, when night is bare,
　　From one lonely cloud
The moon rains out her beams, and heaven is over-
　　　flowed.

What thou art we know not
    What is most like thee ?
From rainbow clouds there flow not
    Drops so bright to see
As from thy presence showers a rain of melody.

Like a poet hidden
    In the light of thought,
Singing hymns unbidden,
    Till the world is wrought
To sympathy with hopes and fears it heeded not—

Like a high-born maiden
    In a palace tower,
Soothing her love-laden
    Soul in secret hour
With music sweet as love, which overflows her bower—

Like a glow-worm golden
    In a dell of dew,
Scattering unbeholden
    Its aërial hue
Among the flowers and grass which screen it from the
        view—

Like a rose embowered
    In its own green leaves,
By warm winds deflowered,
    Till the scent it gives
Makes faint with too much sweet these heavy-wingèd
        thieves.

Sound of vernal showers
    On the twinkling grass,
Rain-awakened flowers,
    All that ever was
Joyous, and clear, and fresh, thy music doth surpass.

Teach us, sprite or bird,
    What sweet thoughts are thine ;
I have never heard
    Praise of love or wine
That panted forth a flood of rapture so divine :

Chorus Hymenæal,
    Or triumphal chaunt,
Matched with thine, would be all
    But an empty vaunt,
A thing wherein we feel there is some hidden want.

What objects are the fountains
    Of thy happy strain ?
What fields, or waves, or mountains ?
    What shapes of sky or plain ?
What love of thine own kind ? what ignorance of
        pain ?

With thy clear keen joyance
    Languor cannot be—
Shadow of annoyance
    Never came near thee :
Thou lovest—but ne'er knew love's sad satiety.

Waking or asleep,
    Thou of death must deem
Things more true and deep
    Than we mortals dream,
Or how could thy notes flow in such a crystal stream ?

We look before and after
    And pine for what is not :
Our sincerest laughter
    With some pain is fraught ;
Our sweetest songs are those that tell of saddest
        thought.

Yet if we could scorn
    Hate, and pride, and fear ;
If we were things born
    Not to shed a tear,
I know not how thy joy we ever should come near.

Better than all measures
    Of delightful sound—
Better than all treasures
    That in books are found—
Thy skill to poet were, thou scorner of the ground !

Teach me half the gladness
    That thy brain must know,
Such harmonious madness
    From my lips would flow,
The world should listen then—as I am listening now.

THE CLOUD

I BRING fresh showers for the thirsting flowers
    From the seas and the streams ;
I bear light shade for the leaves when laid
    In their noonday dreams.
From my wings are shaken the dews that waken
    The sweet buds every one,
When rocked to rest on their mother's breast,
    As she dances about the sun.
I wield the flail of the lashing hail,
    And whiten the green plains under,
And then again I dissolve it in rain,
    And laugh as I pass in thunder.

I sift the snow on the mountains below,
    And their great pines groan aghast ;

And all the night 'tis my pillow white,
  While I sleep in the arms of the blast.
Sublime on the towers of my skiey bowers,
  Lightning my pilot sits ;
In a cavern under is fettered the thunder,—
  It struggles and howls at fits ;
Over earth and ocean, with gentle motion,
  This pilot is guiding me,
Lured by the love of the genii that move
  In the depths of the purple sea ;
Over the rills, and the crags, and the hills,
  Over the lakes and the plains,
Wherever he dream, under mountain or stream,
  The Spirit he loves remains ;
And I all the while bask in heaven's blue smile,
  Whilst he is dissolving in rains.

The sanguine sunrise, with his meteor eyes,
  And his burning plumes outspread,
Leaps on the back of my sailing rack,
  When the morning star shines dead,
As on the jag of a mountain crag,
  Which an earthquake rocks and swings,
An eagle alit one moment may sit
  In the light of its golden wings.
And when sunset may breathe, from the lit sea beneath
  Its ardours of rest and of love,
And the crimson pall of eve may fall
  From the depth of heaven above,
With wings folded I rest, on mine airy nest,
  As still as a brooding dove.

That orbèd maiden with white fire laden,
  Whom mortals call the moon,
Glides glimmering o'er my fleece-like floor,
  By the midnight breezes strewn ;
And wherever the beat of her unseen feet,
  Which only the angels hear,

May have broken the woof of my tent's thin roof,
    The stars peep behind her and peer ;
And I laugh to see them whirl and flee,
    Like a swarm of golden bees,
When I widen the rent in my wind-built tent,
    Till the calm rivers, lakes, and seas,
Like strips of the sky fallen through me on high,
    Are each paved with the moon and these.

I bind the sun's throne with a burning zone,
    And the moon's with a girdle of pearl ;
The volcanoes are dim, and the stars reel and swim,
    When the whirlwinds my banner unfurl.
From cape to cape, with a bridge-like shape,
    Over a torrent sea,
Sunbeam-proof, I hang like a roof,
    The mountains its columns be.
The triumphal arch through which I march
    With hurricane, fire, and snow,
When the powers of the air are chained to my chair,
    Is the million-coloured bow ;
The sphere-fire above its soft colours wove,
    While the moist earth was laughing below.

I am the daughter of earth and water,
    And the nursling of the sky ;
I pass through the pores of the ocean and shores ;
    I change, but I cannot die.
For after the rain when, with never a stain,
    The pavilion of heaven is bare,
And the winds and sunbeams with their convex gleams
    Build up the blue dome of air,
I silently laugh at my own cenotaph,
    And out of the caverns of rain,
Like a child from the womb, like a ghost from the tomb,
    I arise and unbuild it again.

THE MASK OF ANARCHY

WRITTEN ON THE OCCASION OF THE MASSACRE AT MANCHESTER

1819

As I lay asleep in Italy
There came a voice from over the Sea,
And with great power it forth led me
To walk in the visions of Poesy.

I met Murder on the way—
He had a mask like Castlereagh—
Very smooth he looked, yet grim ;
Seven bloodhounds followed him :

All were fat ; and well they might
Be in admirable plight,
For one by one, and two by two,
He tossed them human hearts to chew
Which from his wide cloke he drew.

Next came Fraud, and he had on,
Like Eldon, an ermined gown ;
His big tears, for he wept well,
Turned to millstones as they fell.

And the little children, who
Round his feet played to and fro,
Thinking every tear a gem,
Had their brains knocked out by them.

Clothed with the Bible, as with light,
And the shadows of the night,
Like Sidmouth, next, Hypocrisy
On a crocodile rode by.

And many more Destructions played
In this ghastly masquerade,
All disguised, even to the eyes,
Like Bishops, lawyers, peers or spies.

Last came Anarchy : he rode
On a white horse, splashed with blood ;
He was pale even to the lips,
Like Death in the Apocalypse.

And he wore a kingly crown ;
And in his grasp a sceptre shone ;
On his brow this mark I saw—
" I AM GOD, AND KING, AND LAW ! "

With a pace stately and fast,
Over English land he passed,
Trampling to a mire of blood
The adoring multitude.

And a mighty troop around
With their trampling shook the ground,
Waving each a bloody sword
For the service of their Lord.

And with glorious triumph they
Rode through England proud and gay,
Drunk as with intoxication
Of the wine of desolation.

O'er fields and towns, from sea to sea,
Passed that Pageant swift and free,
Tearing up, and trampling down,
Till they came to London town.

And each dweller, panic-stricken,
Felt his heart with terror sicken,
Hearing the tempestuous cry
Of the triumph of Anarchy.

For with pomp to meet him came,
Clothed in arms like blood and flame,
The hired murderers, who did sing
" Thou art God, and Law, and King.

" We have waited, weak and lone,
For thy coming, Mighty One !
Our purses are empty, our swords are cold,
Give us glory, and blood, and gold."

Lawyers and priests, a motley crowd,
To the earth their pale brows bowed ;
Like a bad prayer not over loud,
Whispering—" Thou art Law and God."—

Then all cried with one accord,
" Thou art King, and God, and Lord ;
Anarchy, to thee we bow,
Be thy name made holy now ! "

And Anarchy, the Skeleton,
Bowed and grinned to every one,
As well as if his education
Had cost ten millions to the nation.

For he knew the Palaces
Of our Kings were rightly his ;
His the sceptre, crown, and globe,
And the gold-inwoven robe.

So he sent his slaves before
To seize upon the Bank and Tower,
And was proceeding with intent
To meet his pensioned Parliament,

When one fled past, a maniac maid,
And her name was Hope, she said :
But she looked more like Despair,
And she cried out in the air :

" My father Time is weak and grey
With waiting for a better day ;
See how idiot-like he stands,
Fumbling with his palsied hands !

" He has had child after child,
And the dust of death is piled
Over every one but me—
Misery, oh, Misery ! "

Then she lay down in the street,
Right before the horses' feet,
Expecting, with a patient eye,
Murder, Fraud and Anarchy.

When between her and her foes
A mist, a light, an image rose,
Small at first, and weak, and frail
Like the vapour of a vale :

Till as clouds grow on the blast,
Like tower-crowned giants striding fast,
And glare with lightnings as they fly,
And speak in thunder to the sky,

It grew—a Shape arrayed in mail
Brighter than the viper's scale,
And upborne on wings whose grain
Was as the light of sunny rain.

On its helm, seen far away,
A planet, like the Morning's, lay ;
And those plumes its light rained through
Like a shower of crimson dew.

With step as soft as wind it passed
O'er the heads of men—so fast
That they knew the presence there,
And looked,—but all was empty air.

As flowers beneath May's footstep waken,
As stars from Night's loose hair are shaken,
As waves arise when loud winds call,
Thoughts sprung where'er that step did fall.

And the prostrate multitude
Looked—and ankle-deep in blood,
Hope, that maiden most serene,
Was walking with a quiet mien :

And Anarchy, the ghastly birth,
Lay dead earth upon the earth ;
The Horse of Death tameless as wind
Fled, and with his hoofs did grind
To dust the murderers thronged behind.

A rushing light of clouds and splendour,
A sense awakening and yet tender,
Was heard and felt—and at its close
These words of joy and fear arose,

As if their own indignant Earth
Which gave the sons of England birth
Had felt their blood upon her brow,
And, shuddering with a mother's throe,

Had turnèd every drop of blood
By which her face had been bedewed
To an accent unwithstood,—
As if her heart had cried aloud :

" Men of England, heirs of Glory,
Heroes of unwritten story,
Nurslings of one mighty Mother,
Hopes of her, and one another ;

" Rise like Lions after slumber
In unvanquishable number,
Shake your chains to earth like dew
Which in sleep had fallen on you—
Ye are many—they are few.

" What is Freedom ?—ye can tell
That which slavery is, too well—
For its very name has grown
To an echo of your own.

" 'Tis to work and have such pay
As just keeps life from day to day
In your limbs, as in a cell
For the tyrants' use to dwell :

" So that ye for them are made
Loom, and plough, and sword, and spade,
With or without your own will bent
To their defence and nourishment.

" 'Tis to see your children weak
With their mothers pine and peak,
When the winter winds are bleak,—
They are dying whilst I speak.

" 'Tis to hunger for such diet
As the rich man in his riot
Casts to the fat dogs that lie
Surfeiting beneath his eye ;

" 'Tis to let the Ghost of Gold
Take from Toil a thousandfold
More than e'er its substance could
In the tyrannies of old.

Paper coin—that forgery
Of the title-deeds which ye
Hold to something of the worth
Of the inheritance of Earth.

" 'Tis to be a slave in soul
And to hold no strong control
Over your own will, but be
All that others make of ye.

" And at length when ye complain
With a murmur weak and vain,
'Tis to see the Tyrant's crew
Ride over your wives and you—
Blood is on the grass like dew.

" Then it is to feel revenge
Fiercely thirsting to exchange
Blood for blood—and wrong for wrong—
Do not thus when ye are strong.

" Birds find rest in narrow nest
When weary of their wingèd quest ;
Beasts find fare in woody lair
When storm and snow are in the air.

" Asses, swine, have litter spread
And with fitting food are fed ;
All things have a home but one—
Thou, Oh, Englishman, hast none !

" This is Slavery—savage men,
Or wild beasts within a den
Would endure not as ye do—
But such ills they never knew.

" What art thou, Freedom ?   O ! could slaves
Answer from their living graves
This demand—tyrants would flee
Like a dream's dim imagery :

" Thou art not, as impostors say,
A shadow soon to pass away,
A superstition, and a name
Echoing from the cave of Fame.

" For the labourer thou art bread,
And a comely table spread,
From his daily labour come,
In a neat and happy home.

" Thou art clothes, and fire, and food
For the trampled multitude—
No—in countries that are free
Such starvation cannot be
As in England now we see.

" To the rich thou art a check,
When his foot is on the neck
Of his victim, thou dost make
That he treads upon a snake.

" Thou art Justice—ne'er for gold
May thy righteous laws be sold
As laws are in England—thou
Shield'st alike the high and low.

" Thou art Wisdom—Freemen never
Dream that God will damn for ever
All who think those things untrue
Of which Priests make such ado.

" Thou art Peace—never by thee
Would blood and treasure wasted be
As tyrants wasted them, when all
Leagued to quench thy flame in Gaul.

" What if English toil and blood
Was poured forth, even as a flood ?
It availed, Oh, Liberty !
To dim, but not extinguish thee.

" Thou art Love—the rich have kissed
Thy feet, and like him following Christ
Give their substance to the free
And through the rough world follow thee,

" Or turn their wealth to arms, and make
War for thy belovèd sake
On wealth, and war, and fraud—whence they
Drew the power which is their prey.

" Science, Poetry and Thought
Are thy lamps ; they make the lot
Of the dwellers in a cot
So serene, they curse it not.

" Spirit, Patience, Gentleness.
All that can adorn and bless
Art thou—let deeds, not words, express
Thine exceeding loveliness.

" Let a great Assembly be
Of the fearless and the free
On some spot of English ground
Where the plains stretch wide around.

" Let the blue sky overhead,
The green earth on which ye tread,
All that must eternal be,
Witness the solemnity.

" From the corners uttermost
Of the bounds of English coast ;
From every hut, village and town
Where those who live and suffer moan
For others' misery or their own,

" From the workhouse and the prison
Where, pale as corpses newly risen,
Women, children, young and old
Groan for pain, and weep for cold—

" From the haunts of daily life
Where is waged the daily strife
With common wants and common cares
Which sows the human heart with tares—

" Lastly from the palaces
Where the murmur of distress
Echoes, like the distant sound
Of a wind alive around

" Those prison halls of wealth and fashion
Where some few feel such compassion
For those who groan, and toil, and wail
As must make their brethren pale—

" Ye who suffer woes untold,
Or to feel, or to behold
Your lost country bought and sold
With a price of blood and gold—

" Let a vast assembly be,
And with great solemnity
Declare with measured words that ye
Are, as God has made ye, free—

" Be your strong and simple words
Keen to wound as sharpened swords,
And wide as targes let them be,
With their shade to cover ye.

" Let the tyrants pour around
With a quick and startling sound,
Like the loosening of a sea,
Troops of armed emblazonry.

" Let the charged artillery drive
Till the dead air seems alive
With the clash of clanging wheels,
And the tramp of horses' heels.

" Let the fixèd bayonet
Gleam with sharp desire to wet
Its bright point in English blood
Looking keen as one for food.

" Let the horsemen's scymitars
Wheel and flash, like sphereless stars
Thirsting to eclipse their burning
In a sea of death and mourning.

" Stand ye calm and resolute,
Like a forest close and mute,
With folded arms and looks which are
Weapons of unvanquished war ;

" And let Panic, who outspeeds
The career of armèd steeds,
Pass, a disregarded shade,
Through your phalanx undismayed.

" Let the laws of your own land,
Good or ill, between ye stand
Hand to hand, and foot to foot,
Arbiters of the dispute,

" The old laws of England—they
Whose reverend heads with age are grey,
Children of a wiser day ;
And whose solemn voice must be
Thine own echo—Liberty !

" On those who first should violate
Such sacred heralds in their state
Rest the blood that must ensue . . .
And it will not rest on you.

" And if then the tyrants dare,
Let them ride among you there,
Slash, and stab, and maim, and hew,—
What they like, that let them do.

" With folded arms and steady eyes,
And little fear, and less surprise,
Look upon them as they slay
Till their rage has died away.

" Then they will return with shame
To the place from which they came,
And the blood thus shed will speak
In hot blushes on their cheek.

" Every woman in the land
Will point at them as they stand—
They will hardly dare to greet
Their acquaintance in the street.

" And the bold, true warriors
Who have hugged Danger in wars
Will turn to those who would be free
Ashamed of such base company.

" And that slaughter to the Nation
Shall steam up like inspiration,
Eloquent, oracular ;
A volcano heard afar.

" And these words shall then become
Like oppression's thundered doom
Ringing through each heart and brain,
Heard again—again—again—

" Rise like Lions after slumber
In unvanquishable number—
Shake your chains to earth like dew
Which in sleep had fallen on you—
Ye are many—they are few."

LINES

I

THE cold earth slept below,
    Above the cold sky shone ;
And all around, with a chilling sound,
    From caves of ice and fields of snow,
    The breath of night like death did flow
        Beneath the sinking moon.

II

The wintry hedge was black,
    The green grass was not seen,
The birds did rest on the bare thorn's breast,
    Whose roots, beside the pathway track,
    Had bound their folds o'er many a crack,
        Which the frost had made between.

III

Thine eyes glowed in the glare
　　Of the moon's dying light ;
As a fenfire's beam on a sluggish stream
　Gleams dimly, so the moon shone there,
　And it yellowed the strings of thy raven hair,
　　That shook in the wind of night.

IV

The moon made thy lips pale, beloved——
　　The wind made thy bosom chill——
The night did shed on thy dear head
　Its frozen dew, and thou didst lie
　Where the bitter breath of the naked sky
　　Might visit thee at will.

A WIDOW BIRD

A widow bird sate mourning for her love
　　Upon a wintry bough ;
The frozen wind crept on above,
　　The freezing stream below.

There was no leaf upon the forest bare,
　　No flower upon the ground,
And little motion in the air
　　Except the mill-wheel's sound.

SONG

I

RARELY, rarely, comest thou,
  Spirit of Delight !
Wherefore hast thou left me now
  Many a day and night ?
Many a weary night and day
'Tis since thou art fled away.

II

How shall ever one like me
  Win thee back again ?
With the joyous and the free
  Thou wilt scoff at pain.
Spirit false ! thou hast forgot
All but those who need thee not.

III

As a lizard with the shade
  Of a trembling leaf,
Thou with sorrow art dismayed ;
  Even the sighs of grief
Reproach thee, that thou art not near,
And reproach thou wilt not hear.

IV

Let me set my mournful ditty
  To a merry measure,
Thou wilt never come for pity,
  Thou wilt come for pleasure.
Pity then will cut away
Those cruel wings, and thou wilt stay.

V

I love all that thou lovest,
    Spirit of Delight !
The fresh Earth in new leaves dressed,
    And the starry night ;
Autumn evening, and the morn
When the golden mists are born.

VI

I love snow, and all the forms
    Of the radiant frost ;
I love waves, and winds, and storms,
    Every thing almost
Which is Nature's, and may be
Untainted by man's misery.

VII

I love tranquil solitude,
    And such society
As is quiet, wise and good ;
    Between thee and me
What difference ? but thou dost possess
The things I seek, not love them less.

VIII

I love Love—though he has wings,
    And like light can flee,
But above all other things,
    Spirit, I love thee—
Thou art love and life ! O come,
Make once more my heart thy home.

THE FUGITIVES

I

THE waters are flashing,
The white hail is dashing,
The lightnings are glancing,
The hoar spray is dancing—
    Away !

The whirlwind is rolling,
The thunder is tolling,
The forest is swinging,
The minster bells ringing—
    Come away !

The Earth is like Ocean,
Wreck-strewn and in motion :
Bird, beast, man and worm
Have crept out of the storm—
    Come away !

II

" Our boat has one sail,
And the helmsman is pale ;—
A bold pilot I trow,
Who should follow us now,"—
    Shouted He—

And she cried : " Ply the oar !
Put off gaily from shore ! "—
As she spoke, bolts of death
Mixed with hail, specked their path
    O'er the sea.

And from isle, tower and rock,
The blue beacon cloud broke,
And though dumb in the blast,
The red cannon flashed fast
    From the lee.

III

" And fear'st thou, and fear'st thou ?
And seest thou, and hear'st thou ?
And drive we not free
O'er the terrible sea,
    I and thou ? "

One boat-cloke did cover
The loved and the lover—
Their blood beats one measure,
They murmur proud pleasure
    Soft and low ;—

While around the lashed Ocean,
Like mountains in motion,
Is withdrawn and uplifted,
Sunk, shattered and shifted
    To and fro.

IV

In the court of the fortress
Beside the pale portress,
Like a bloodhound well beaten,
The bridegroom stands, eaten
    By shame ;

On the topmost watch-turret,
As a death-boding spirit,
Stands the grey tyrant father,—
To his voice the mad weather
    Seems tame ;

And with curses as wild
As e'er clung to child,
He devotes to the blast
The best, loveliest and last
    Of his name !

REMEMBRANCE

I

SWIFTER far than summer's flight—
Swifter far than youth's delight—
Swifter far than happy night,
    Art thou come and gone—
As the wood when leaves are shed,
As the night when sleep is fled,
As the heart when joy is dead,
    I am left lone, alone.

II

The swallow summer comes again—
The owlet night resumes his reign—
But the wild-swan youth is fain
    To fly with thee, false as thou.
My heart each day desires the morrow ;
Sleep itself is turned to sorrow ;
Vainly would my winter borrow
    Sunny leaves from any bough.

III

Lilies for a bridal bed—
Roses for a matron's head—
Violets for a maiden dead—
    Pansies let *my* flowers be :
On the living grave I bear
Scatter them without a tear—
Let no friend, however dear,
    Waste one hope, one fear for me.

A LAMENT

I

Oh, world ! oh, life ! oh, time !
On whose last steps I climb
  Trembling at that where I had stood before ;
When will return the glory of your prime ?
    No more—O, never more !

II

Out of the day and night
A joy has taken flight ;
  Fresh spring, and summer, and winter hoar,
Move my faint heart with grief, but with delight
    No more—O, never more !

TO JANE—THE INVITATION

Best and brightest, come away !
Fairer far than this fair Day,
Which, like thee to those in sorrow,
Comes to bid a sweet good-morrow
To the rough Year just awake
In its cradle on the brake.
The brightest hour of unborn Spring,
Through the winter wandering,
Found, it seems, the halcyon Morn
To hoar February born ;
Bending from Heaven, in azure mirth,
It kissed the forehead of the Earth,
And smiled upon the silent sea,
And bade the frozen streams be free,
And waked to music all their fountains,

And breathed upon the frozen mountains,
And like a prophetess of May
Strewed flowers upon the barren way,
Making the wintry world appear
Like one on whom thou smilest, dear.

Away, away, from men and towns,
To the wild wood and the downs—
To the silent wilderness
Where the soul need not repress
Its music lest it should not find
An echo in another's mind,
While the touch of Nature's art
Harmonizes heart to heart.
I leave this notice on my door
For each accustomed visitor :—
" I am gone into the fields
To take what this sweet hour yields ;—
Reflexion, you may come to-morrow,
Sit by the fireside with Sorrow.—
You with the unpaid bill, Despair,—
You tiresome verse-reciter, Care,—
I will pay you in the grave,—
Death will listen to your stave.
Expectation too, be off !
To-day is for itself enough ;
Hope, in pity mock not Woe
With smiles, nor follow where I go ;
Long having lived on thy sweet food,
At length I find one moment's good
After long pain—with all your love,
This you never told me of."

Radiant Sister of the Day,
Awake ! arise ! and come away !
To the wild woods and the plains,
And the pools where winter rains
Image all their roof of leaves,

Where the pine its garland weaves
Of sapless green and ivy dun
Round stems that never kiss the sun;
Where the lawns and pastures be,
And the sand-hills of the sea;—
Where the melting hoar-frost wets
The daisy-star that never sets,
And wind-flowers, and violets,
Which yet join not scent to hue,
Crown the pale year weak and new;
When the night is left behind
In the deep east, dun and blind,
And the blue noon is over us,
And the multitudinous
Billows murmur at our feet,
Where the earth and ocean meet,
And all things seem only one
In the universal sun.

TO NIGHT

I

SWIFTLY walk o'er the western wave,
      Spirit of Night!
Out of the misty eastern cave,
Where all the long and lone daylight,
Thou wovest dreams of joy and fear,
Which make thee terrible and dear,—
      Swift be thy flight!

II

Wrap thy form in a mantle grey,
      Star-inwrought!
Blind with thine hair the eyes of Day;

Kiss her until she be wearied out,
Then wander o'er city, and sea, and land,
Touching all with thine opiate wand—
    Come, long sought !

III

When I arose and saw the dawn,
    I sighed for thee ;
When light rode high, and the dew was gone,
And noon lay heavy on flower and tree,
And the weary Day turned to his rest,
Lingering like an unloved guest,
    I sighed for thee.

IV

Thy brother Death came, and cried,
    Wouldst thou me ?
Thy sweet child Sleep, the filmy-eyed,
Murmured like a noon-tide bee,
Shall I nestle near thy side ?
Wouldst thou me ?—And I replied,
    No, not thee !

V

Death will come when thou art dead,
    Soon, too soon—
Sleep will come when thou art fled ;
Of neither would I ask the boon
I ask of thee, belovèd Night—
Swift be thine approaching flight,
    Come soon, soon !

EVENING: PONTE A MARE, PISA

I

THE sun is set; the swallows are asleep;
  The bats are flitting fast in the grey air;
The slow soft toads out of damp corners creep,
  And evening's breath, wandering here and there
Over the quivering surface of the stream,
Wakes not one ripple from its summer dream.

II

There is no dew on the dry grass to-night,
  Nor damp within the shadow of the trees;
The wind is intermitting, dry, and light;
  And in the inconstant motion of the breeze
The dust and straws are driven up and down,
And whirled about the pavement of the town.

III

Within the surface of the fleeting river
  The wrinkled image of the city lay,
Immovably unquiet, and for ever
  It trembles, but it never fades away;
Go to the . . .
You, being changed, will find it then as now.

IV

The chasm in which the sun has sunk is shut
  By darkest barriers of cinereous cloud, .
Like mountain over mountain huddled—but
  Growing and moving upwards in a crowd,
And over it a space of watery blue,
Which the keen evening star is shining through.

LOVE'S PHILOSOPHY

I

THE Fountains mingle with the River
　　And the Rivers with the Ocean,
The winds of Heaven mix for ever
　　With a sweet emotion ;
Nothing in the world is single ;
　　All things by a law divine
In one spirit meet and mingle.
　　Why not I with thine ?——

II

See the mountains kiss high Heaven
　　And the waves clasp one another ;
No sister-flower would be forgiven
　　If it disdained its brother,
And the sunlight clasps the earth
　　And the moonbeams kiss the sea :
What is all this sweet work worth
　　If thou kiss not me ?

TO ——

I

I FEAR thy kisses, gentle maiden,
　　Thou needest not fear mine ;
My spirit is too deeply laden
　　Ever to burthen thine.

II

I fear thy mien, thy tones, thy motion.
　　Thou needest not fear mine ;
Innocent is the heart's devotion
　　With which I worship thine.

LINES

I

WHEN the lamp is shattered
The light in the dust lies dead—
　When the cloud is scattered
The rainbow's glory is shed.
　When the lute is broken,
Sweet tones are remembered not ;
　When the lips have spoken,
Loved accents are soon forgot.

II

As music and splendour
Survive not the lamp and the lute,
　The heart's echoes render
No song when the spirit is mute,—
　No song but sad dirges,
Like the wind through a ruined cell,
　Or the mournful surges
That ring the dead seaman's knell.

III

When hearts have once mingled
Love first leaves the well-built nest,—
　The weak one is singled
To endure what it once possessed.
　O, Love ! who bewailest
The frailty of all things here,
　Why choose you the frailest
For your cradle, your home and your bier ?

IV

Its passions will rock thee
As the storms rock the ravens on high :
 Bright reason will mock thee,
Like the sun from a wintry sky.
 From thy nest every rafter
Will rot, and thine eagle home
 Leave thee naked to laughter,
When leaves fall and cold winds come.

MUTABILITY

I

The flower that smiles to-day
 To-morrow dies ;
All that we wish to stay
 Tempts and then flies.
What is this world's delight ?
Lightning that mocks the night,
 Brief even as bright.

II

Virtue, how frail it is !
 Friendship how rare !
Love, how it sells poor bliss
 For proud despair !
But we, though soon they fall,
Survive their joy, and all
 Which ours we call.

III

Whilst skies are blue and bright,
 Whilst flowers are gay,
Whilst eyes that change ere night
 Make glad the day ;
Whilst yet the calm hours creep,
Dream thou—and from thy sleep
 Then wake to weep.

TO ———

I

ONE word is too often profaned
    For me to profane it,
One feeling too falsely disdained
    For thee to disdain it.
One hope is too like despair
    For prudence to smother,
And pity from thee more dear
    Than that from another.

II

I can give not what men call love,
    But wilt thou accept not
The worship the heart lifts above
    And the Heavens reject not,—
The desire of the moth for the star,
    Of the night for the morrow,
The devotion to something afar
    From the sphere of our sorrow?

DIRGE FOR THE YEAR

I

ORPHAN hours, the year is dead,—
    Come and sigh, come and weep!
Merry hours, smile instead,
    For the year is but asleep.
See, it smiles as it is sleeping,
Mocking your untimely weeping.

II

As an earthquake rocks a corse
  In its coffin in the clay,
So White Winter, that rough nurse,
  Rocks the death-cold year to-day ;
Solemn hours ! wail aloud
For your mother in her shroud.

III

As the wild air stirs and sways
  The tree-swung cradle of a child,
So the breath of these rude days
  Rocks the year :—be calm and mild,
Trembling hours,—she will arise
With new love within her eyes.

IV

January grey is here,
  Like a sexton by her grave ;
February bears the bier,
  March with grief doth howl and rave,
And April weeps—but, O, ye hours,
Follow with May's fairest flowers.

AUTUMN

A DIRGE

I

THE warm sun is failing, the bleak wind is wailing,
The bare boughs are sighing, the pale flowers are dying,
      And the year
On the earth her death-bed, in a shroud of leaves dead,
      Is lying.

Come, months, come away,
From November to May,
In your saddest array ;
Follow the bier
Of the dead cold year,
And like dim shadows watch by her sepulchre.

II

The chill rain is falling, the nipped worm is crawling,
The rivers are swelling, the thunder is knelling
      For the year ;
The blithe swallows are flown, and the lizards each gone
        To his dwelling ;
    Come, months, come away ;
    Put on white, black, and grey ;
    Let your light sisters play—
    Ye, follow the bier
    Of the dead cold year,
And make her grave green with tear on tear.

ARETHUSA

I

ARETHUSA arose
    From her couch of snows
In the Acroceraunian mountains,—
    From cloud and from crag,
    With many a jag,
Shepherding her bright fountains.
    She leapt down the rocks,
    With her rainbow locks
Streaming among the streams ;—
    Her steps paved with green
    The downward ravine
Which slopes to the western gleams :

And gliding and springing
She went, ever singing,
In murmurs as soft as sleep ;
The Earth seemed to love her,
And Heaven smiled above her,
As she lingered towards the deep.

II

Then Alpheus bold,
On his glacier cold,
With his trident the mountains strook
And opened a chasm
In the rocks ;—with the spasm
All Erymanthus shook
And the black south wind
It concealed behind
The urns of the silent snow,
And earthquake and thunder
Did rend in sunder
The bars of the springs below :
The beard and the hair
Of the River-god were
Seen through the torrent's sweep,
As he followed the light
Of the fleet nymph's flight
To the brink of the Dorian deep.

III

" Oh, save me ! Oh, guide me !
And bid the deep hide me,
For he grasps me now by the hair ! "
The loud Ocean heard,
To its blue depth stirred,
And divided at her prayer ;
And under the water
The Earth's white daughter
Fled like a sunny beam ;

Behind her descended
Her billows, unblended
With the brackish Dorian stream :—
    Like a gloomy stain
    On the emerald main
Alpheus rushed behind,—
    As an eagle pursuing
    A dove to its ruin
Down the streams of the cloudy wind.

IV

    Under the bowers
    Where the Ocean Powers
Sit on their pearlèd thrones,
    Through the coral woods
    Of the weltering floods,
Over heaps of unvalued stones ;
    Through the dim beams
    Which amid the streams
Weave a net-work of coloured light ;
    And under the caves,
    Where the shadowy waves
Are as green as the forest's night :—
    Outspeeding the shark
    And the sword-fish dark,
Under the ocean foam,
    And up through the rifts
    Of the mountain clifts
They passed to their Dorian home.

V

    And now from their fountains
    In Enna's mountains,
Down one vale where the morning basks,
    Like friends once parted
    Grown single-hearted,
They ply their watery tasks.

At sunrise they leap
From their cradles steep
In the cave of the shelving hill ;
At noontide they flow
Through the woods below
And the meadows of Asphodel ;
And at night they sleep
In the rocking deep
Beneath the Ortygian shore ;—
Like spirits that lie
In the azure sky
When they love but live no more.

THE QUESTION

I

I DREAMED that, as I wandered by the way,
    Bare winter suddenly was changed to spring,
And gentle odours led my steps astray,
    Mixed with a sound of waters murmuring
Along a shelving bank of turf, which lay
    Under a copse, and hardly dared to fling
Its green arms round the bosom of the stream,
But kissed it and then fled, as thou mightest in dream.

II

There grew pied wind-flowers and violets,
    Daisies, those pearled Arcturi of the earth,
The constellated flower that never sets ;
    Faint oxlips ; tender bluebells, at whose birth
The sod scarce heaved ; and that tall flower that wets
    (Like a child, half in tenderness and mirth)
Its mother's face with heaven-collected tears,
When the low wind, its playmate's voice, it hears.

III

And in the warm hedge grew lush eglantine,
   Green cowbind and the moonlight-coloured May,
And cherry-blossoms, and white cups, whose wine
   Was the bright dew, yet drained not by the day ;
And wild roses, and ivy serpentine,
   With its dark buds and leaves, wandering astray ;
And flowers azure, black, and streaked with gold,
Fairer than any wakened eyes behold.

IV

And nearer to the river's trembling edge
   There grew broad flag-flowers, purple prankt with
      white,
And starry river-buds among the sedge,
   And floating water-lilies, broad and bright,
Which lit the oak that overhung the hedge
   With moonlight beams of their own watery light ;
And bulrushes and reeds of such deep green
As soothed the dazzled eye with sober sheen.

V

Methought that of these visionary flowers
   I made a nosegay, bound in such a way
That the same hues, which in their natural bowers
   Were mingled or opposed, the like array
Kept these imprisoned children of the Hours
   Within my hand,—and then, elate and gay,
I hastened to the spot whence I had come,
That I might there present it !—oh ! to whom ?

HYMN OF APOLLO

I

THE sleepless Hours who watch me as I lie,
   Curtained with star-inwoven tapestries,

From the broad moonlight of the sky,
    Fanning the busy dreams from my dim eyes,—
Waken me when their Mother, the grey Dawn,
Tells them that dreams and that the moon is gone.

II

Then I arise, and climbing Heaven's blue dome,
    I walk over the mountains and the waves,
Leaving my robe upon the ocean foam ;
    My footsteps pave the clouds with fire ; the caves
Are filled with my bright presence, and the air
Leaves the green earth to my embraces bare.

III

The sunbeams are my shafts, with which I kill
    Deceit, that loves the night and fears the day ;
All men who do or even imagine ill
    Fly me, and from the glory of my ray
Good minds and open actions take new might,
Until diminished by the reign of night.

IV

I feed the clouds, the rainbows and the flowers
    With their ætherial colours ; the Moon's globe
And the pure stars in their eternal bowers
    Are cinctured with my power as with a robe ;
Whatever lamps on Earth or Heaven may shine,
Are portions of one power, which is mine.

V

I stand at noon upon the peak of Heaven,
    Then with unwilling steps I wander down
Into the clouds of the Atlantic even ;
    For grief that I depart they weep and frown :
What look is more delightful than the smile
With which I soothe them from the western isle ?

VI

I am the eye with which the Universe
   Beholds itself and knows itself divine ;
All harmony of instrument or verse,
   All prophecy, all medicine are mine,
All light of art or nature ;—to my song,
Victory and praise in their own right belong.

HYMN OF PAN

I

FROM the forests and highlands
    We come, we come ;
From the river-girt islands,
     Where loud waves are dumb
       Listening to my sweet pipings.
The wind in the reeds and the rushes,
   The bees on the bells of thyme,
The birds on the myrtle bushes,
The cicale above in the lime,
And the lizards below in the grass,
Were as silent as ever old Tmolus was,
       Listening to my sweet pipings.

II

Liquid Peneus was flowing,
    And all dark Tempe lay
In Pelion's shadow, outgrowing
    The light of the dying day,
      Speeded by my sweet pipings.
The Sileni, and Sylvans, and Fauns,
    And the Nymphs of the woods and waves,
To the edge of the moist river-lawns,
    And the brink of the dewy caves,
And all that did then attend and follow
Were silent with love, as you now, Apollo,
      With envy of my sweet pipings.

III

I sang of the dancing stars,
  I sang of the dædal Earth,
And of Heaven—and the giant wars,
  And Love, and Death, and Birth,—
    And then I changed my pipings,—
Singing how down the vale of Menalus
  I pursued a maiden and clasped a reed :
Gods and men, we are all deluded thus !
  It breaks in our bosom and then we bleed :
All wept, as I think both ye now would,
If envy or age had not frozen your blood,
    At the sorrow of my sweet pipings.

TO THE MOON

I

ART thou pale for weariness
Of climbing heaven and gazing on the earth,
  Wandering companionless
Among the stars that have a different birth,—
And ever changing, like a joyless eye
That finds no object worth its constancy ?

II

Thou chosen sister of the spirit,
That gazes on thee till in thee it pities . . .

SONG OF PROSERPINE,

WHILE GATHERING FLOWERS ON THE PLAIN OF ENNA

I

SACRED Goddess, Mother Earth,
  Thou from whose immortal bosom

Gods and men and beasts have birth,
    Leaf and blade and bud and blossom,
Breathe thine influence most divine
On thine own child, Proserpine.

II

If with mists of evening dew
    Thou dost nourish these young flowers
Till they grow, in scent and hue,
    Fairest children of the hours,
Breathe thine influence most divine
On thine own child, Proserpine.

SONNETS

POLITICAL GREATNESS

Nor happiness, nor majesty, nor fame,
Nor peace, nor strength, nor skill in arms or arts,
Shepherd those herds whom tyranny makes tame ;
Verse echoes not one beating of their hearts,
History is but the shadow of their shame,
Art veils her glass, or from the pageant starts
As to oblivion their blind millions fleet,
Staining that Heaven with obscene imagery
Of their own likeness.   What are numbers knit
By force or custom ?   Man who man would be,
Must rule the empire of himself ; in it
Must be supreme, establishing his throne
On vanquished will, quelling the anarchy
Of hopes and fears, being himself alone.

LINES TO A REVIEWER

ALAS, good friend, what profit can you see
In hating such a hateless thing as me ?
There is no sport in hate when all the rage
Is on one side : in vain would you assuage
Your frowns upon an unresisting smile,
In which not even contempt lurks to beguile
Your heart, by some faint sympathy of hate.
O, conquer what you cannot satiate ;
For to your passion I am far more coy
Than ever yet was coldest maid or boy
In winter noon.   Of your antipathy,
If I am the Narcissus, you are free
To pine into a sound with hating me.

TO BYRON

[I AM afraid these verses will not please you, but]
If I esteemed you less, Envy would kill
Pleasure, and leave to Wonder and Despair
The ministration of the thoughts that fill
The mind which, like a worm whose life may share
A portion of the unapproachable,
Marks your creations rise as fast and fair
As perfect worlds at the Creator's will.
But such is my regard that nor your power
To soar above the heights where others [climb],
Nor fame, that shadow of the unborn hour
Cast from the envious future on the time,
Move one regret for his unhonoured name
Who dares these words :—the worm beneath the sod
May lift itself in homage of the God.

OZYMANDIAS

I MET a traveller from an antique land
Who said : Two vast and trunkless legs of stone
Stand in the desert.   Near them, on the sand,
Half sunk, a shattered visage lies, whose frown,
And wrinkled lip, and sneer of cold command,
Tell that its sculptor well those passions read
Which yet survive, (stamped on these lifeless things,)
The hand that mocked them and the heart that fed :
And on the pedestal these words appear :
" My name is Ozymandias, king of kings :
Look on my works, ye Mighty, and despair ! "
Nothing beside remains.   Round the decay
Of that colossal wreck, boundless and bare
The lone and level sands stretch far away.

THE END

**PRINTED IN GREAT BRITAIN AT
THE PRESS OF THE PUBLISHERS**

Nelson Classics

Cloth gilt.   1s. 6d. *net.*

This famous series is now more attractive than ever, for it is being re-issued in striking new wrappers, with new bindings —Sundour cloths, fadeless and washable, in ten attractive colours—tinted tops, and modern title pages. At the same time it is being extended to include novels by famous modern authors, and books for the more studious reader—Dean Inge's *Protestantism*, for example, Sir Robert Rait's *British History*, and J. B. Priestley's *The English Novel*.

The latest additions include : SEA STORIES, selected by John Hampden. Good yarns of the sea in many moods by H. G. Wells, John Buchan, John Masefield, W. W. Jacobs, Jack London, etc.—PROTESTANTISM. W. R. Inge. A new revised edition of this challenging book.—AGNES GREY. Anne Brontë. With the *Poems* of Charlotte, Emily, and Anne Brontë, portraits, and a ninety-page introduction by Flora Masson.—A PRIMER OF ENGLISH LITERATURE. A. Compton-Rickett. From the beginnings to the present day. 56 illustrations and index. An attractive survey.—TRENT'S LAST CASE. E. C. Bentley. Perhaps the best detective story in our language.—PROSE OF OUR TIME, by the foremost writers of to-day. Edited by A. J. J. Ratcliff.—MONEY. Hartley Withers. A masterly book on a vital subject.—THE ATOM. Professor E. N. da C. Andrade. Lucid, authoritative, right up to date.—OLD PETER'S RUSSIAN TALES. Arthur Ransome. Illustrated. A delightful modern classic for children.

Please send for complete list : Nelsons, 35–36 Paternoster Row, London, E.C.4 ; Parkside Works, Edinburgh ; 25 rue Denfert-Rochereau, Paris ; 91–93 Wellington Street West, Toronto ; 381–385 Fourth Avenue, New York ; 312 Flinders Street, Melbourne.

NELSON'S POETS

Cloth, 1s. 6d. net

POEMS OF	INTRODUCTION BY
*ARNOLD	John Buchan
*BROWNING	John Buchan
COLERIDGE	Sir Henry Newbolt
COWPER	John Bailey
DRYDEN	John St. Loe Strachey
GOLDSMITH	Professor Garrod
HERRICK	J. C. Squire
*KEATS	Sir Henry Newbolt
MILTON	Sir Henry Newbolt
MORRIS	John Buchan
POPE	John Bailey
ROSSETTI	John Buchan
SHAKESPEARE (6 vols.)	
*SHELLEY	Sir Henry Newbolt
*WORDSWORTH	Viscount Grey
17TH-CENTURY DEVOTIONAL POETRY	
	Sir Henry Newbolt

* Also bound in limp rexine gilt, gilt top, at 2s. 6d. net.

THOMAS NELSON AND SONS, LTD.
London, Edinburgh, New York, Toronto, and Paris